Benjamin C. Leslie

Trinitarian Hermeneutics

The Hermeneutical Significance of Karl Barth's Doctrine of the Trinity

PETER LANG
New York · San Francisco · Bern
Frankfurt am Main · Paris · London

Library of Congress Cataloging-in-Publication Data

Leslie, Benjamin C.
    Trinitarian hermeneutics : the hermeneutical
significance of Karl Barth's doctrine of the Trinity /
Benjamin C. Leslie.
        p. cm. — (American university studies. Series VII,
Theology and religion ; vol. 66)
        Revisions of the author's thesis (Ph.D.) — Universität
Zürich, 1989.
        Includes bibliographical references.
        1. Barth, Karl, 1886-1968 — Contributions in doctrine
of the Trinity.   2. Trinity — History of doctrines — 20th
century.   3. Hermeneutics — Religious aspects
— Christianity — History of doctrines — 20th century.
        I. Title.   II. Series.
BT109.L47   1991   231'.044'092 — dc20   91-17450
ISBN 0-8204-1461-1   CIP
ISSN 0740-0446

Die Deutsche Bibliothek-CIP-Einheitsaufnahme

Leslie, Benjamin C.:
Trinitarian hermeneutics : the hermeneutical significance
of Karl Barth's doctrine of the trinity / Benjamin C. Leslie.
— New York; Berlin; Bern; Frankfurt/M.; Paris; Wien:
Lang, 1991
    (American university studies : Ser. 7, Theology and
religion ; Vol. 66)
    ISBN 0-8204-1461-1
NE: American university studies / 07

The paper in this book meets the guidelines for permanence and durability
of the Committee on Production Guidelines for Book Longevity of the
Council on Library Resources.

$$\infty$$

© Peter Lang Publishing, Inc., New York 1991

Printed in the United States of America.

Trinitarian Hermeneutics

American University Studies

Series VII
Theology and Religion

Vol. 66

PETER LANG
New York · San Francisco · Bern
Frankfurt am Main · Paris · London

To my parents
For love and encouragement along the way

ACKNOWLEDGMENTS

Quotations from the following works of Karl Barth appear here through the kind permission of the °Theologischer Verlag Zürich: *Die christliche Dogmatik im Entwurf* (1982), *Dogmatik im Grundriss* (1987), *Einführung in die evangelische Theologie* (1985), *Fides Quaerens Intellectum* (1986), *Die Kirchliche Dogmatik*, I/1 (1989), I/2 (1983), II/1 (1982), II/2 (1986), III/1 (1988), III/2 (1979), IV/1 (1986), IV/2 (1985), *Die protestantische Theologie im 19. Jahrhundert* (1985), *Der Römerbrief*, 1919 (1985), *Der Römerbrief*, 1922 (1989), *Theologische Fragen und Antworten* (1986), *Briefe*, 1961-1968 (1979), *Karl Barth—Eduard Thurneysen, Briefwechsel*, II, 1921-1930 (1979), *Karl Barth—Rudolf Bultmann, Briefwechsel*, 1922-1966 (1971). Grateful appreciation is also extended to my "doctor-father," Professor Dr. Hans Geisser of the University of Zurich. His constant encouragement and guidance were necessary for bringing this work to fruition. His willingness to take time from a sabbatical leave from the University in order to assist with the final stages of production of this project is the expression of a kindness which extends above and beyond the call of duty. I would also like to express appreciation to a number of others who have offered assistance in different ways: to Dr. Dixon Sutherland of the Baptist Theological Seminary, Rüschlikon, Switzerland, for stimulating discussions which offered helpful perspectives on a number of the issues dealt with in this work; to Dorothy Moore and Marie Walker, the Librarians of the Baptist Theological Seminary, for assistance in obtaining materials not locally available; to the Baptist Theological Seminary itself for its community support during the period of doctoral research; to Dr. Stanley Crabb, Director of the European Baptist Press Service, for the use of the technical facilities which produced the original version of the text; and to my teaching assistant Howard Hart for editing and indexing the text. My greatest debt in the production of this work is to my family, particularly to my wife, for love and support throughout the process, whithout which this book would not have come to completion.

Sioux Falls, May, 1991.

TABLE OF CONTENTS

ABBREVIATIONS

I. Works by Karl Barth

CD	*Die christliche Dogmatik im Entwurf.* 1927.
DG	*Dogmatik im Grundriss.* 1947.
Einführung	*Einführung in die evangelische Theologie.* 1962.
"Feuerbach"	"Ludwig Feuerbach," *Die Theologie und die Kirche.* 1928.
FQI	*Fides Quaerens Intellectum.* 1931.
"Die Kirche"	"Die Kirche—die lebendige Gemeinde des lebendigen Herrn Jesus Christus," *Die Schrift und die Kirche*, ThStn 22 (1947).
KD	*Die Kirchliche Dogmatik.* 1932-1968.
ProtTh	*Die Protestantische Theologie im 19. Jahrhundert.* 1947.
^{1}Römerbrief	*Der Römerbrief.* 1919.
^{2}Römerbrief	*Der Römerbrief.* ^{2}1922.
TFA	*Theologische Fragen und Antworten.* 1957.
TT	*Karl Barth's Table Talk.* Ed. J. Godsey. 1962.
"Wort Gottes"	"Das Wort Gottes als Aufgabe der Theologie," *Das Wort Gottes und die Theologie.* 1924.

II. Periodicals and Reference Works

Dia	Dialog
EvTh	Evangelische Theologie
JThSt	Journal of Theological Studies
NZThR	Neue Zeitschrift für systematische Theologie und Religionsphilosophie
PRSt	Perspectives in Religious Studies
^{3}RGG	Religion in Geschichte und Gegenwart. 3rd ed.
SJTh	Scottish Journal of Theology
StTh	Studia Theologica
ThS	Theological Studies
ThStn	Theologische Studien
ThT	Theology Today
TR	Theologische Rundschau
TRE	Theologische Realenzyclopedia
TZ	Theologische Zeitschrift
USQR	Union Seminary Quarterly Review
ZKTh	Zeitschrift für katholische Theologie
ZThK	Zeitschrift für Theologie und Kirche

Italicized text in quotations represents the emphasis of the author cited except where indicated otherwise. The page numbers enclosed within brackets in the text refer to pages of the *Kirchliche Dogmatik.* Where the volume number is not shown, page numbers refer to the volume previously cited.

INTRODUCTION
The Problem of Method
in Contemporary Barth Research

The aim of this study is a critical analysis of the hermeneutical significance exercised by Karl Barth's doctrine of the Trinity within the *Kirchliche Dogmatik*. The term "hermeneutics" is employed here to signify reflection upon the process of human interpretation. This process includes the interpretation and subsequent understanding of texts, but is by no means restricted to it. Also included is reflection upon those structures which are attendant to and which aid human understanding and upon the essence of understanding itself. By inquiring after the hermeneutical significance of Barth's Trinity doctrine our concern is with the functional aspect of the doctrine which *directs* the subsequent interpretation of Scripture, the formulation of language about God, and an understanding of the human self. Equally relevant is the concept of human understanding operative in the Barthian doctrine and how this concept exercises an influence on the shape of the theological task.

The question of method is particularly significant for the present moment of Barth research. Since his death in 1968, posthumously published lectures and letters of Barth have continued to appear along with new editions of older works. A stream of secondary literature on Barth and his theology is in constant production in spite of a waning popularity of Barthian themes. And yet, the rapid changes in the theological climate throughout the Christian world within the last twenty years press the question of whether Barth research belongs now more to the sphere of the history of dogma than to that of systematic theology. Indeed much of the Barth literature appearing within the last decade has been less interested in an engagement with the themes and subject-matter of Barth's work than with an attempt to interpret Barth against the background of his own biography and the historical forces which shaped his thought.[1] This is not the path, however, which we undertake here.

The rationale behind the method employed here will become more visible if viewed in light of the three publications which have already treated our theme to a significant degree. The book of Friedrich Schmid, *Verkündigung und Dogmatik in der Theologie Karl Barths*,[2] whose subtitle "Hermeneutik und Ontologie in einer Theologie des Wortes Gottes" is a far better indication of the theme of the book than the title itself, marks the first attempt to develop the hermeneutical significance of Barth's Trinity doctrine at any length. The study undertakes to follow the logical relationship of hermeneutics to theological ontology as it develops in Barth's thought from the first edition of the *Römerbrief* to the end of the third volume of the *Kirchliche Dogmatik*. In a methodological reflection at the beginning of the study Schmid identifies three models of Barth-research which have strong precedent and then proposes a fourth which is intended as a description of his own course.

One may, first of all, interpret Barth from the perspective of the historical influences which led to the development of his thought.[3] While such influences are clearly there to be found, this form of inquiry suffers from a perennial failure to arrive at the actual questions with which Barth's theology wants to deal. Here Schmid reflects a loyalty to Barth's recurrent call for a focus upon the content and object of theological reflection over and against the distraction of secondary concerns. This principle finds justification in the simple fact that the complex development of Barth's thought defies interpretation from any single historical form or line of thought, since none remains dominant for very long.[4]

G. C. Berkouwer's book, *The Triumph of Grace in the Theology of Karl Barth*,[5] represents for Schmid the model of a second approach, namely one which seeks to understand Barth by organizing the principal elements of his thought into a coherent whole by means of theological motifs.[6] This represents an advance on the historical alternative in its focus upon material concerns. At risk, however, is a neglect of theology's fundamental questions regarding the problem of the possibility of theological thought and speech at all and the structures which best bring that possibility to fruition.

The third alternative, which functions as a correction to the second, finds its representative model in Hans Urs von Balthasar's study, *Karl Barth: Darstellung und Deutung seiner Theologie*.[7] Von Balthasar moves directly to the principal methodological questions. He focuses upon the formal elements of Barth's thought, and yet does so without abstracting these from the material concerns and without sacrificing faithfulness to Barth's basic aims.

Schmid intends to build on the formidable results the latter two methods by proposing a fourth alternative which takes up the crucial question of *function*, a concern which remains on the periphery of the works of von Balthasar and Berkouwer.[8] Preeminently, Schmid wants to understand the function of Barth's theology from the perspective of his declared intention to bring theology into the service of proclamation. Proclamation as the "place" of theological reflection raises the question of the appropriate hermeneutic which is itself inseparable from the question of ontology. When the functional analysis is applied to the *Kirchliche Dogmatik* in the final chapter of the work, it is the doctrine of the Trinity which is identified as the critical hermeneutical device.

> Im Aufbau der Barthschen Dogmatik zeigt sich: Der herme-
> neutische Versuch, den Barth in seiner KD unternimmt, ist von
> den ontologischen Voraussetzungen her, die das Anselmbuch
> erarbeitet hat, nicht anders zu verstehen und anzugreifen denn in
> Form einer *Interpretation der Trinitätslehre. Hermeneutik als Vollzug
> der Trinitätslehre*, darin wird sich der umfassende Charakter seiner
> theologischen Hermeneutik ausweisen. Vollzug der Trinitätslehre
> heisst nichts anderes als Anerkennung der *kyriotēs* Jesu Christi, der
> das Wort Gottes an uns ist, der selbst jenes letzte Geschehen ist
> als das der junge Barth unter verschiedenen Chiffren die
> Offenbarung bezeichnet hatte.[9]

The relation between ontology and the hermeneutical function of the Trinity doctrine is neither arbitrary nor external. On the contrary it is the immanent

Trinity which grounds the hermeneutic which the doctrine of the Trinity brings to expression.[10]

Schmid's investigation of Barth's reinterpretation of the doctrine of the Trinity is without question a profound contribution to Barth studies which offers clear insight to the functional value of the doctrine for the *Kirchliche Dogmatik* as a whole. It is questionable, however, whether Schmid is really successful in escaping the abstraction which he so ardently sets himself apart from in his methodological reflection. The doctrine of the Trinity is never considered apart from its function as a structural device, so that the material aspects of the doctrine which determine that function are pressed far into the background.

The year following the publication of Schmid's book saw the appearance of a short work by Eberhard Jüngel entitled, *Gottes Sein ist im Werden*.[11] Jüngel's book is virtually a commentary on Barth's doctrine of the Trinity. While Jüngel was by no means the first to note the hermeneutical significance of Barth's Trinity doctrine, it is his investigation which has won the widespread recognition of this aspect of the doctrine. Jüngel's method claims no specialization other than a desire to take seriously Barth's own theological language within the context in which it wants to be understood. Questions of historical background play no significant role in Jüngel's study. Nor is there any attempt to uncover the methodological sub-structures in the Barthian doctrine. Jüngel, rather, allows himself to enter into a conversation with Barth, offering a subtle of paraphrase of particular moments of Barth discussion which allow hidden or little noticed aspects to come into the foreground. It is the process of careful concept analysis in a material engagement with the content of Barth's doctrine which allows Jüngel to glean insights which would inform the problem of meaningful language about God which is the chief concern of the book.

The hermeneutical significance of Barth's doctrine of the Trinity is developed primarily in two directions: first, by noting the critical-polemical function of the doctrine with regard to responsible talk of God, and secondly, by noting the doctrine's ontological function in providing a ground for responsible talk of God and the crucial and necessary link which relates talk of God to human existence. In developing the critical-polemical function of the doctrine, Jüngel hopes thereby to establish a common ground between Barth's theological aims and those of "hermeneutical theology." The critical-polemic of Barth's Trinity parallels the critical-polemic of Bultmann's program of demythologization.[12] While the definition of myth varies between the theologians, the intention to disallow mythical and irresponsible talk of God is shared in common. What Bultmann does with his demythologizing, Barth does with the concept of revelation as the root of all talk of God.

The ontological aspect of Barth's trinitarian hermeneutic is developed on the basis of Barth's understanding of the relationship between God's temporal revelation and God's eternal being. Jüngel demonstrates that the "becoming" in which God enters human history, taking human being and historical objectivity upon Himself is the reiteration of a possibility eternally present in the eternal, triune history of God. Specifically, the possibility of God entering into relationship with concrete human beings is a possibility grounded in the eternal relationality of the triune Modes of Being.[13] This historical repetition or reiteration in history of what God is antecedently and eternally in Himself is carried out on the basis of a particular conception of revelation which for Barth is axiomatic. Jüngel expresses this principle in terms of analogical correspondence: "God corresponds to Himself."[14] "God's being *ad extra* corresponds essentially to his being *ad intra* in which it has its basis and prototype."[15] Jüngel extends the discussion beyond the groundwork laid by Barth by seeking to develop the implications of the death of the Son on the cross for the eternal divine being on the basis of the correspondence schema. In the death on the cross the being of God confronts non-being, exposes itself to it, and prevails, albeit as suffering being.[16] In the death on the cross, not only does the Son suffer, but the Father is moved and likewise suffers. The Son gives Himself over to the contradiction of human existence thereby making human existence the object of divine concern. The doctrine of the Trinity becomes for Jüngel a hermeneutic of decisive significance for interpreting the being of God in relationship to human existence.

Jüngel's insights are indispensable for an understanding of the hermeneutical function exercised by the doctrine of the Trinity within the *Kirchliche Dogmatik*. They represent to a large degree the groundwork from which our own critical analysis will proceed. Jüngel's insights, however, derive from the limited focus of his own theological aims and require supplementation if a deeper penetration into the function of the doctrine for Barth is to be attained. While the function of the doctrine is indeed emphasized within its own material context, the limited focus blocks from view both the historical context out of which Barth developed the doctrine, as well as the structural elements which compose and influence it.[17]

A recently published doctoral dissertation from the University of Bonn by Ernstpeter Maurer, entitled *Sprachphilosophische Aspekte in Karl Barths "Prolegomena zur Kirchlichen Dogmatik"*,[18] offers a critical interpretation of Barth's dogmatic prolegomena from the perspective of linguistic philosophy of the recent analytic tradition, drawing especially upon the later work of Ludwig Wittgenstein.[19] Maurer is, like Schmid and Jüngel before him, interested in the functional structures which shape Barth's thought. Maurer undertakes to expose the inner semantic logic at work in Barth's methodological program by means of careful and detailed analysis of the semantic structures. While Maurer does not wish to minimize the significance of historical influences upon the development of Barth's peculiar method, he does allow these to slip into the background in order to allow the sharpest focus possible upon an articulation of the method itself.[20] The internal connection which justifies the interpretation of Barth in Wittgensteinian terms is what Maurer describes as the "anhypostatic" conception of theological language. Maurer's "anhypostatic semantic" corresponds to Wittgenstein's theory of a plurality of indissoluble language-reality relations which, because of their characteristic dependence upon rules, are termed "language games."[21] Language thereby finds its authenticity in the set of life-relations which bring it into being and to which its meaningfulness is bound. A corresponding pattern is Barth's form-content relation whereby the content of theological concepts may not be dissolved from their linguistic forms.[22] In the case of the doctrine of the Trinity, the relation of the doctrine to the divine truth which is its content becomes the focal point of semantic interest.[23]

Maurer's study highlights the decisive significance of the doctrine of the Trinity for Barth's theological "language game" insofar as it represents the "grammar of the name of the Lord."[24] The doctrine itself represents an instance of an "anhypostatic semantic" according to which the human form of the doctrine forms an indissoluble unity with the divine content.[25] Barth's development of the "root of the Trinity" on the basis of an analysis of the statement, "God reveals Himself as Lord," represents an analytical "extension" of the "name" which in this case is God. The extension is necessary as the axiomatic formulation of the basic "rules" to which talk of God must conform.[26] Barth's ontological grounding of theological truth in the internal relations of the immanent Trinity corresponds in semantic terms to the rejection of external criteria for the determination of the "grammar" of a given "language game." The trinitarian grammar represents an *Urphänomen* which grounds the execution of the theological "language game."[27]

This articulation in semantic terms allows a surprising interpretation which Maurer hopes will show a line of compatibility between Barth's theological method and the demands of the post-modern era.[28] Maurer also hopes to blaze a path which will lead Barthian thought beyond the impasse of revelational positivism, which, proclaims Maurer, must remain the final verdict upon Barth unless a reinterpretation such as the one he has offered is taken up.[29] Barth's theory for the possibility of "talk of God" is interpreted as an instance of a Wittgensteinian "language game," which is rooted in a particular "life relation." Thus the "non-distantiated" talk of God which is the ideal of theological hermeneutics finds a convergence with Barth's method which would not be possible outside of the semantic interpretation.[30]

Maurer's interpretation of Barth's doctrine of the Trinity represents a convergence with our study in its recognition of the determinative function of the doctrine for all theological language. The grammatical function of the doctrine articulated by Maurer corresponds to the interpretive and ordering functions of the doctrine recognized here. Maurer is thus able to bring the central hermeneutical function of the doctrine into sharp relief while remaining faithful to many of the characteristic features of Barth's method. The analytic method is helpful in bringing to expression subtleties and particularly inconsistencies of Barth's theological logic. Nevertheless, one must register a reservation, not only concerning Maurer's efforts, but concerning any attempt to find a justification or confirmation of Barth's characteristic theological concerns by means of a particular philosophical system of thought. The protest against an anthropological root for theology and the consequent polemic against "natural theology" which played such decisive roles in the development of the theological method of the *Kirchliche Dogmatik* must remain casualties of any such undertaking, and this despite Maurer's linguistically won concept of the "anhypostatic semantic." His intention to find a compatibility between Barth's method and post-modern emphases must surely offer a clue as to whether the outcome of such an investigation is a reinterpretation or a dissolution of its object. Like Maurer, we too shall undertake a study of the structure and function of particular aspects of the Barthian method. We shall even feel free to employ the tools of linguistic analysis in identifying the paradigmatic structure of Barth's trinitarian hermeneutic. Unlike Maurer, however, we shall attempt to understand this structure within its own context, which is by no means strictly a semantic one, giving due regard to the external influences which have not only conditioned its development, but its function as well.

The method which is advanced here is sympathetic to the concern with *function*, particularly hermeneutical function, as emphasized by Schmid although better developed by Jüngel and Maurer. We shall seek to identify the functional aspects of Barth's doctrine without abandoning the material context in which these functional aspects are actually exercised. We shall move beyond (or behind) the material context of the doctrine, however, in two respects which seem necessary if a genuine understanding of the function is to be gained. First, the question of the historical background and conditioning of Barth's thought, while hardly a primary concern of the study, will not be allowed to slip out of view altogether. The historical factors are essential for an understanding of why particular emphases surface in Barth's thought and others do not, and often open the way for a greater appreciation of the insights achieved in Barth's thought. The most obvious example is perhaps the perspective given to the protest against "natural theology" when viewed against the "German Church struggle" with which Barth became so intimately involved. Secondly, we shall move beyond the immediate material context of the doctrine in inquiring after the structural elements employed by Barth to bring the doctrine of the Trinity to expression. The inquiry into the structure of Barth's doctrine conducted here is not of course intended in the sense of Maurer's imposition of a structural analysis which is essentially a reinterpretation of Barth's thought in terms of a particular philosophical movement. Rather, the inquiry is restricted to an identification of those philosophical and traditional structures which were taken up by Barth into his trinitarian construction with a view to the particular function and influence exercised by each.

The focus of the investigation is restricted to Barth's *Kirchliche Dogmatik,* although other writings of Barth are referred to in a supplementary way. This decision arises not primarily from a need to limit the amount of literature which can reasonably be made the object of an intensive inquiry, although such a restriction in the case of Barth is certainly appropriate, but rather, reflects the range of influence exercised by the doctrine of the Trinity upon Barth's theological method. It is solely within the *Kirchliche Dogmatic* where the paradigmatic influence of the Trinity doctrine is to be observed to an appreciable degree.

The work is divided into six chapters. *Chapter One* describes in a general way the relationship between Barth's theology and the hermeneutical question. Here we offer an identification of the specific objections which comprised the later Barth's critical stance over and against hermeneutical theology. *Chapter Two* identifies and critically describes the function of the doctrine of the Trinity within the general architectonic of the *Kirchliche Dogmatik. Chapters Three* and *Four* pursue the question of the structural elements operative within Barth's trinitarian hermeneutic. *Chapter Three* considers the problem of tacit philosophical elements, while *Chapter Four* considers the explicit use of traditional elements and their relationship to the event of revelation which is the declared root of the Barthian Trinity doctrine. *Chapters Five* and *Six* return to the material context of the doctrine with inquiries into the primary aspects of its hermeneutical function—responsible talk of God and the interpretation of human existence, respectively.

ENDNOTES

[1]Cf. one of the most recent entries into the wide selection of introductions into Barth's thought: Christofer Frey, *Die Theologie Karl Barths: Eine Einführung* (Frankfurt: Athenäum, 1988), esp. Ch. 1, "Theologie und Lebensgeschichte."

[2](Munich: Kaiser, 1964).

[3]Schmid, 9f.

[4]Ibid., 10.

[5]Tr. from the Dutch by H. R. Boer (Grand Rapids: Eerdmans, 1956 [German tr., 1957]).

[6]Schmid, 11.

[7](Einsiedeln: Johannes, [4]1976 [[1]1951]). ET = The Theology of Karl Barth (New York: Holt, Rinehart & Winston, 1971). Schmid, 11f.

[8]Schmid, 12f.

[9]Ibid., 151.

[10]Ibid., 152–4, 157f.

[11](Tübingen: Mohr, 1965). ET = *The Doctrine of the Trinity* (Grand Rapids: Eerdmans, 1976).

[12]Jüngel, *Gottes Sein*, 22f, 33, 71f. ET, 11f, 21–23, 58–60.

[13]Ibid., 36–41. ET, 25–29.

[14]Ibid., 35. ET, 24.

[15]Ibid. ET, 25

[16]Ibid., 91f. ET, 78f.

[17]It is worthwhile to note in this context the recent work of Bent Flemming Nielson, *Die Rationalität der Offenbarungstheologie: Die Struktur des Theologieverständnisses von Karl Barth* (Aarhus: Aarhus Univ. Press, 1988). Nielson's work is a reflective study which aims to uncover the key structures at work in Barth's theology, both in the dialectic as well as the dogmatic phases of Barth's work. The heart of the book consists of a series of engagements with some of the most recent analyses of Barth's thought. While Barth's Trinity doctrine is not the dominant concern of the study, its pivotal structural role in securing the ontological foundation upon which responsible talk of God must proceed (at least for the Barth of the Dogmatics) is allowed its appropriate weight. Particularly relevant is Nielson's dialogue with Jüngel, where he takes issue with the latter's interpretation of the critical-polemical

dimension of the Trinity doctrine for Barth. While Jüngel is correct in noting the anti-metaphysical function of the doctrine, he actually misses the full significance of Barth's distinction between the divine essence and the divine works, according to Nielson. While Jüngel affirms with Barth the distinction as necessary to an affirmation of the sovereign freedom in which the the Triune God acts, Jüngel does not allow the sufficient weight due to the first moment of this distinction, namely, the immanent Trinty, the free and sovereign God. While the metaphysical polemic is clear and intentional, the end result is not a complete disallowal of talk of God "in and of Himself." Rather, such talk must be taken as one of two mutually related and mutually interpreting lines of thought, both of which are actually necessary for responsible talk of God. Consequently, Nielson sees the convergence of Barthian and Bultmannian emphases noted by Jüngel as a more limited and less significant phenomenon than Jüngel would suggest. Nielson, 159–161.

[18](Frankfurt: Lang, 1989).

[19]The interpretation of Barth's theology from the linguistic frame of reference of the later Wittgenstein is not without precedent. What distinguishes the work of Maurer is the concentrated focus which he brings to Barth's prolegomena, particularly the concept of revelation. Cf. the earlier studies of D. M. Lochhead, "The Autonomy of Theology: A Critical Study with Special Reference to Karl Barth and Contemporary Analytical Philosophy," Ph.D. Diss., McGill Univ., 1967; and A. A. Glenn, "The Relationship Between Theology as a Special Science and Analytic Philosophy with Special Reference to the Theology of Karl Barth," Ph.D. Diss., Northwestern Univ., 1967.

[20]Ibid., 11f.

[21]Ibid., 355.

[22]Ibid.

[23]Ibid., 203f.

[24]Ibid., 131, 153–5.

[25]Ibid., 204.

[26]Ibid., 131f.

[27]Ibid., 154f.

[28]Ibid., 27.

[29]Ibid., 125.

[30]Ibid., 125f.

CHAPTER ONE
Hermeneutics and the Barthian
Cloud of Suspicion

It belongs among the theological truisms of the twentieth century that the theology of Karl Barth is inherently hostile to the contemporary concerns of theological hermeneutics. That Ernst Fuchs began his 1954 *Hermeneutik* with a brief polemic directed against Barth's doctrine of revelation is actually a profound illustration of an "either-or" which has become axiomatic for the theological climate of our time.[1] In spite of the numerous attempts which have appeared over the last two decades to bridge these divergent approaches to the theological task,[2] each continues to be regarded as the critical alternative to the other. An unfortunate effect of this polarization has been its tendency to eclipse the relationship of Barth's theology to the hermeneutical problem as a relationship in its own right, such that when the hermeneutical question arises, Barth is often considered not in terms of a contribution to the discussion, but in terms of a protest against the discussion itself.[3] It is the aim of the present chapter to clarify this relationship between hermeneutics and the theology of Barth in a general way, before proceeding to the more specific question of the hermeneutical significance of Barth's Trinity doctrine. For this preliminary task, we restrict ourselves to an introductory overview of generally recognized focal aspects of Barth's early contributions to (as well as protests against) the hermeneutical discussion in theology.

"Hermeneutics" as a term denoting a particular field of inquiry is of course one which has enjoyed a complex if not desultory history, particularly within the twentieth century. Indeed, it is no longer possible to use the word without careful definition, lest one risk considerable confusion.[4] In Gerhard Ebeling's landmark encyclopedia article, "Hermeneutik," the manifold complexity of the hermeneutical problem is unfolded with concise precision.

According to Ebeling the word's root meanings of "expression," "explanation," and "translation" underwent a decisive transformation in the work of Schleiermacher and Dilthey where the understanding of hermeneutics as a set of rules for the interpretation of varying types of texts was transformed into reflection upon the general process of human understanding presupposed in the interpretive act.[5] This understanding of hermeneutics as the doctrine of understanding forms the basis of the concept as it is widely used in the contemporary discussion, although even here a broader conception is often at work. For as Ebeling points out, this use of hermeneutics is one that comprehends not only the interpretation of texts, but of life, the world, and of human existence itself. Hermeneutics becomes synonymous with philosophy, and for theology becomes synonymous with the problem of method.[6]

As one quickly recognizes, it is possible to "expand" the meaning of a term to such an extent that the effect is far more a loss than a gain in meaning. In the case of hermeneutics, an expanded sense can actually work to overshadow the methodological problem involved in the interpretation of ancient texts, which in modern history has formed the foundation of the hermeneutical problem. Yet, for theology the expanded sense has much to commend it, since as Barth endeavored to remind the theological world in the years of his early phase, theology's concern with the peculiar texts of the Judaeo-Christian tradition is not sufficiently articulated as a strictly historical problem. Its concern is with the mediation of a "content" or a "subject-matter" which the tools of historical-critical research are ill-equipped to convey. This subject-matter which proclaims the salvific acts of God and which seeks on that basis to address the relationship of human beings to God is one which confronts its hearers with a claim to ultimacy. The event of "understanding" in which the human being appropriates this peculiar subject-matter is thus one that involves far more than those aspects of existence which are generally designated the intellect. It is an event which claims the human being in his entirety. It is the reflection on the breadth and depth of this event of understanding which forms the basis of the concept of theological hermeneutics as it is used in this work.

The Prophetic Beginning

It is Karl Barth who set the current discussion into motion as to the proper way to inquire into a text so as to allow the text itself to speak. Above all it was Barth's Römerbrief in both its 1919 and totally revised 1922 editions which comprised Barth's positive statement in this regard. The significance of the Römerbrief for biblical hermeneutics has been the object of considerable discussion and analysis since its appearance over half a century ago and remains a focal point in the contemporary hermeneutical discussion.[7] The outcome of this discussion already bears the marks of a rough theological consensus on the merits and limits of the approach advocated by the early Barth. It is this consensus which we shall seek to summarize in the following paragraphs by identifying three hermeneutical themes which emerged from Barth's engagement with Romans.

The first and most prominent hermeneutical theme emerging from Barth's work was unquestionably the critique of the historical-critical method. The approach to the biblical text described by Barth was one which immediately put itself at odds with the prevailing "scientific exegesis" of the day, and the historical-critical method formed the centerpiece of this prevailing view. In the reviews following [1]Römerbrief this critique was often understood as a denigration of or attack upon the historical-critical method itself, so that one critic could describe Barth as the "abgesagten Feind der *historischen Kritik*."[8] The critique however was intended not as a rejection of the method nor even of its necessity, but rather as a rejection of its claim, whether explicit or implicit, to have sufficiently accomplished the task of interpretation. Barth clarifies the point of the critique in the second edition and narrows its focus to rest upon

a group of commentaries upon Romans which had been published in the years
immediately preceding his own:

> Aber nicht die historische Kritik mache ich ihnen zum Vorwurf,
> deren Recht und Notwendigkeit ich vielmehr noch einmal aus-
> drücklich anerkenne, sondern ihr Stehenbleiben bei einer Er-
> klärung des Textes, die ich keine Erklärung nennen kann, sondern
> nur den ersten primitiven Versuch einer solchen, nämlich bei der
> Festellung dessen "was da steht" mittelst Übertragung und
> Umschreibung der griechischen Wörter und Wörtergruppen in die
> entsprechenden deutschen, mittelst philologisch-archäologischer
> Erläuterungen der so gewonnenen Ereignisse und mittelst mehr
> oder weniger plausibler Zusammenordnung des Einzelnen zu
> einem historisch-psychologischen Pragmatismus.[9]

At the heart of Barth's dispute with the historical-critical method was the claim
of its advocates to have sufficiently undertaken an explanation and thereby an
interpretation of the text. The historical-critical analysis of the text could in
Barth's view be no more than a preliminary though necessary first step in that
direction. Jüngel thus speaks of Barth's hermeneutic at this point as a
"metacriticism." The real criticism of the text is an undertaking which is
different in principle from the historical-critical task and which can begin only
after the critical task is completed.[10]

   If one is to speak of a failure of historical-critical analysis, then for Barth
this means a failure to understand. For understanding becomes the explicit
criterion which allows Barth to restrict the role and value of the historical-
critical method. This, then, is the second hermeneutical theme which was to
emerge from the *Römerbrief*—an elevation of the problem of understanding for
the exegetical task.[11] The sort of explanation offered by historical-critical
analysis was not, in Barth's view, understanding at all.

> Eigentliches Verstehen und Erklären nenne ich diejenige Tätigkeit,
> die Luther in seinen Auslegungen mit intuitiver Sicherheit geübt,
> die sich Calvin sichtlich systematisch zum Ziel seiner Exegese
> gesetzt, die von den Neueren besonders Hofmann, J. T. Beck,
> Godet und Schlatter wenigstens deutlich angestrebt haben. Man
> lege nun einmal z.B. Jülicher neben Calvin. Wie energisch geht der
> Letztere zu Werk, seinen Text, nachdem auch er gewissenhaft fest-

gestellt, "was da steht", *nach* zu denken, d.h. sich solange mit ihm auseinander zu setzen, bis die Mauer zwischen dem 1. und 16. Jahrhundert *transparent* wird, bis Paulus dort *redet* und der Mensch des 16. Jahrhunderts hier *hört*, bis das Gespräch zwischen Urkunde und Leser ganz auf die *Sache* (die hier und dort keine verschiedene sein *kann!*) konzentriert ist.[12]

For Barth, this elevation of the problem of understanding means an emphasis upon the subjectivity of the reader of the text or what Robinson has called, a "basic recognition of the hermeneutical relevance of the subject."[13] The historical-critical method must necessarily distance itself from a text. The historical otherness of the text becomes the focal point of investigation, so that consequently real engagement between the reader and the subject-matter which the text wishes to express is actually impeded since subjectivity is an element which the method strives to eliminate. For Barth it is of paramount importance that the text has something to say which is simultaneously something which we need to hear. Understanding occurs when the reader actually allows himself to hear the subject-matter of the text as phenomena ultimately relevant for himself, so that the "wall" between then and now becomes "transparent." This Barthian concept of understanding must thus be understood in terms of what Jüngel has identified as a "hermeneutic of simultaneity."[14] It is an understanding in which the subjectivity of the reader actually connects with the "subjectivity" of the text. That is, the text ceases to be an object, but becomes a subject addressing a hearing subject. The subjectivity of the reader, "if he understands himself aright,"[15] provides the crucially needed access to the actual content of the text. The historical-critical method fails precisely because it cannot lead to this encounter with the subject-matter of the text, the outcome of which is understanding. Barth declared in the opening paragraph of [1]*Römerbrief*, that if he had to choose between the historical-critical method and the old doctrine of inspiration he would choose the latter.[16] The advantage of the inspiration doctrine was a direct relationship to the problem of understanding in the hermeneutical enterprise, for which the historical-critical method was mere preparation. It belongs to Barth's credit that the subjective process of understanding, understanding not merely of the background, form, or history of a text but of the content which the text wishes to convey, won an enduring place for the theological discussion of the twentieth century.

Hardly separable from the event of understanding, however, is that which is understood, the subject-matter or the content (*die Sache*) of a text, the emphasis of which forms a third hermeneutical theme which emerged from the early phase of Barth's work. In the refined critique of historical-criticism in ²*Römerbrief*, Barth calls for a "*sachlichen* Bearbeiten des Textes."[17]

> *Krinein* heisst für mich einer historischen Urkunde gegenüber: das Messen aller in ihr enthaltenen Wörter und Wörtergruppen an der Sache, von der sie, wenn nicht alles täuscht, offenbar reden, das Zurückbeziehen aller in ihr gegebenen Antworten auf die ihnen unverkennbar gegenüberstehenden Fragen und dieser wieder auf die eine alle Fragen in sich enthaltende Kardinalfrage, das Deuten alles dessen, was sie sagt, im Lichte dessen, was allein gesagt werden *kann* und darum auch tatsächlich allein gesagt *wird*.[18]

Barth declares the subject-matter of a text to be a determinative principle for the interpretation of a text.[19] In the case of Romans, the pressing question is what Paul wants to say. All hermeneutical efforts must be ordered around this question and all else remains secondary. Barth, of course, knew in advance that this subject-matter was one which was related to God. Barth approached the text on the basis of a declared axiom: God is God, and in Jesus Christ human beings are related to this God.[20] This axiom was intended, however, not as a new system of exegesis, but as a self-evident proposition congruent to the text, by virtue of which one is enabled to hear the text speak as it wills to be heard.

It is these three significant hermeneutical themes, the critique of historical-criticism, the elevation of the problem of understanding, and the priority of the subject-matter, which comprise the positive elements within Barth's early contribution to the hermeneutical discussion.[21] Each of these themes were taken up by others in a variety of ways and contexts so that the hermeneutical problem once again came to the forefront of theological discussion. This development was, of course, not one warmly received by Barth, but one with which he came into conflict. It is this second phase of the relation of Barth's thought to hermeneutics to which our overview must now turn.

The Further Development of Theological Hermeneutics
And the Root of Barthian Dissent

If it is Barth who set the contemporary discussion of hermeneutics into motion, it is Rudolf Bultmann who is chiefly responsible for elevating the hermeneutical problem to its present-day place of prominence. Unlike Barth, Bultmann allowed the hermeneutical problem a place of thematic integrity, which he developed systematically in existential-ontological terms borrowed heavily from the early Heidegger.[22]

The most visible and controversial feature of Bultmann's hermeneutic was unquestionably the so-called program of demythologization. Demythologization represented a hermeneutical process which took as its assumption a mythical world-view which conditioned the thought and expression of the biblical texts.[23] Far from removing the mythical elements from the New Testament, however, as the term would seem to imply, demythologization sought a re-interpretation of New Testament mythology in order to discover "the understanding of existence which it enshrines."[24] As significant as demythologization is for the hermeneutical work of Bultmann, it does not in itself take one to the real crux of the hermeneutical problem as he envisioned it.[25] Demythologization is not the root but the out-working of a particular formulation of the hermeneutical task and concern.

Bultmann points to this relation when he says,

> Demythologizing as a hermeneutical method raises the question of the right conceptuality in which interpretation is to be expressed. It thereby points to a science whose business is the methodical development of the understanding of existence that is

given with existence itself—in other words, to philosophy of existence.[26] Bultmann's program of demythologization assumed a set of hermeneutical criteria for the reinterpretation of myth. Developed under the catch phrase of "existential analysis" these criteria represented the existential-ontological foundation upon which the reinterpretation of myth was to proceed. Bultmann found the justification for this form of analysis in the phenomenon of "pre-understanding" (*Vorverständnis*). The interpretation of texts is, according to Bultmann, always guided by a particular formulation of a question, a particular interest of the reader. This understanding is itself not without certain presuppositions, and thereby forms a pre-understanding of the subject-matter of the text.[27] It represents not merely the necessary starting point of an interpretation but, far more significantly, actually exercises a determinative function for the final outcome of the interpretation. Consequently, the task of the interpreter if he is to guide the interpretation to an appropriate outcome is, far from seeking to eliminate the effects and influence of pre-understanding as an undesired prejudice, actually to cultivate and develop the reader's pre-understanding. Bultmann's guiding hermeneutical thesis in this regard is, stated simply, *pre-understanding enables interpretation*.[28] The subject-matter alone is an insufficient ground for the interpretation of a text. Without pre-understanding, there is no understanding in the proper sense. The process of understanding is inescapably determined by the purpose of the query. This purpose presupposes a relationship in the life of the interpreter to the subject-matter brought to expression in the text. In the case of the Bible, the pre-understanding which the reader brings to the text, at least in the church, is a query regarding ones own existence.[29] An ontological relationship is presupposed between the reader and the content of the text prior to the encounter with the text itself. The form of this relation is "an *existentiell* knowledge of God" which "is alive in the form of the inquiry about 'happiness','salvation', the meaning of the world and of history; and in the inquiry into the real nature of each person's particular 'being'."[30] If this is the case, then it stands to reason that an analysis of the existential pre-understanding of the reader in terms of a thoroughgoing analysis of existence itself will better equip the interpreter who seeks the understanding of existence (i.e., the self-understanding) which the Scripture wishes to convey. The analysis of the reader's life-relation to the text thus forms the hermeneutical pre-condition for the possibility of understanding in the modern world.

It is in Barth's dispute with the hermeneutical program set forth here that the contours of the Barthian cloud of suspicion toward theological hermeneutics in general are to be found. It is of course necessary to remember that the Barth engaged in the dispute is not the same theologian who set the whole discussion into motion. Barth the hermeneutical theologian is a figure to be found in the years of dialectical theology, particularly in the pages of both editions of the *Römerbrief* as we have seen above. Barth the hermeneutical antagonist belongs to the years of the *Kirchliche Dogmatik*. The years 1930–31 mark a watershed in this regard, particularly with the publication of *Fides Quaerens Intellectum*, in which Barth's ideas on the fundamental nature of theological method crystallized. In this work Barth articulated what was for him the essential relation between faith, understanding, and a rational, objective conception of the theological object. This essential relation marked a climax and clarification in Barth's thought concerning the impossibility of natural theology, which was to remain an enduring theme for the remainder of his life work.[31] Human understanding of God, that is, the truth of God which is the subject-matter of Scripture, is an event totally dependent upon God's free decision to reveal Himself as He is.

Even more dramatic than the climax of this methodological realization, however, was the new awareness with which Barth interpreted the theological situation and personalities prevailing at that time. Those who earlier had been allies in a common theological struggle now came to be seen as perpetuators of the same errors from which they had sought to free themselves.[32] The intensity of this break is vividly portrayed in a personal letter from Barth to Bultmann in the year 1930 in which Barth charged not only Bultmann, but Gogarten, Schumann and Brunner with a "large scale return to the flesh pots of Egypt."[33] Barth articulates the offense:

> Ich meine damit: Sie sind, wenn mich nicht Alles täuscht, Alle miteinander dabei, den Glauben aufs neue—gewiss in einer sehr neuen und von der Theologie des 19. Jahrhunderts sehr verschiedenen Weise—als eine menschliche Möglichkeit... verstehen zu wollen und damit die Theologie aufs neue der Philosophie in die Hände zu liefern.[34]

It is here in the offense of "faith as a human possibility" that Barth began to recognize his own mistrust of theological hermeneutics. Elsewhere the issue was allowed to take on even larger proportions. Barth realized that what was ultimately at stake was not simply the propriety of a particular anthropological thesis, but much more the preservation of the sovereignty of the divine Word. For the new Barth, there could be no alternative "place" for the event of human understanding, which for both Barth and Bultmann was inseparably bound to the event of faith itself, outside of the "Yes" of God spoken from eternity. To make the event of understanding an independent object of inquiry outside the framework of this "Yes" was to usurp a place reserved only for the Word of God, that is, God's revelation. All of Barth's particular objections against theological hermeneutics may be understood as specific instances of this general principle. The most significant of these particular objections may be brought together under five headings.[35]

(1) *Barth objects to the concept of "pre-understanding" principally on the grounds that it presupposes within the human being, "an ontological existential possibility for the* existentiell *event of faith."*[36] To this extent, Bultmannian hermeneutics represents for Barth a theological starting point which resides in a particular determination of human existence, such that it remains unclear to what extent Bultmann has progressed beyond the liberal inheritance of the nineteenth century (KD I/1, 36). "Pre-understanding," in the Heideggerean form

which Bultmann uses it, orients itself necessarily to human self-understanding. Bultmann, again following Heidegger, analyzes this self-understanding in terms of the possibilities for authentic or inauthentic existence. The event of understanding comes to represent the transition from one state of existence to another.[37] That Bultmann would describe this transition as an "act of God" fails to convince Barth that something other is carried out than an anthropological ontology with a theologically dubious claim.

(2) Insofar as hermeneutical inquiry either tacitly or explicitly assumes an anthropological ground for the possibility of faith, Barth perceives *the threat of natural theology*.[38] If the bridge which hermeneutics proposes to build between human understanding and the subject-matter of the biblical text does not presuppose faith as the externally grounded possibility of that bridge, then for Barth, a theological assertion has already been made which requires the starting point for theological reflection to reside in human understanding (outside of faith) and not in revelation in the proper sense.[39] This is an assertion which is only possible on the foundation of the presuppositions of natural theology, according to which revelation is manifest in creaturliness. And while hermeneutics does not necessarily wish to understand itself as natural theology, this is precisely the direction which its theological logic dictates. The assumptions of natural theology offend against evangelical theology in their failure to take into account the extent of human sin which comes into view only by virtue of God's revelation in Jesus Christ.

(3) *Theological hermeneutics which allows interpretation to be dominated by concepts determined culturally or anthropologically violates the primacy of the subject-matter.* Hermeneutics may actually become in Barth's view a straight-jacket which so confines the interpreter that what for Barth is the most fundamental rule of all hermeneutics, the mandate to openness, is itself violated. This is for Barth a particularly significant critique. It dominates his argument whenever he turns to a critical discussion of the theological function

of hermeneutics. It forms the central point in Barth's dispute with general hermeneutics within the methodological reflections of *Kirchliche Dogmatik* I/2.[40] Hermeneutics holds to preconceived principles regarding what is generally possible. It absolutizes a particular conception of reality which tends to mute those portions of a text which come into conflict with that conception (KD I/2, 812f). Barth counters that it is the one universal principle of hermeneutics that the subject-matter of a text must play the decisive role in bringing the reader to understanding, and this requires an attitude of openness on the part of the reader in which he allows his prejudices and assumptions, indeed his "pre-understanding," to be challenged and even mastered by the text, and not vice versa.[41]

This objection also forms the basis for Barth's critique of Bultmann's theological program in *Kirchliche Dogmatik* III/2 (531–37). Barth finds within Bultmann's hermeneutical tools, particularly the philosophy of existence, the modern "world-view," and the concept of myth, a set of boundaries which are imposed upon the text which violate its identity as a word about God. Barth does not in this context take up a persuasive counter-attack upon the Bultmannian program, but simply raises the question regarding the sufficiency of the hermeneutic in question. If a hermeneutic interprets a text so that all that can be said is restricted to statements about human existence, if it is true that the modern world-view determines what may be ascertained as having "actually happened" in the events which a text describes, and if a concept of myth is employed as a sieve for sorting out authentic from inauthentic language, has one not, asks Barth, so mastered a text as a passive object at the disposal of an active subject, that it becomes impossible for the text to be taken seriously and to speak as it wants to be heard? Barth's objection amounts to a plea that a critical hermeneutic such as espoused by Bultmann not fail to exercise critical judgment with regard to its own assumptions and assertions.

Barth's most sustained polemic against Bultmann's hermeneutical program, however, appeared in the 1952 essay, "Rudolf Bultmann—Ein Versuch ihn zu verstehen." Here the objection to a hermeneutic based upon anthropologically or culturally determined concepts finds its fullest expression. Barth extends his objection that Bultmann has adopted and bestowed canonical status to a particular concept of myth,[42] upon his own modern world-view,[43] and existential philosophy.[44] But he develops a critique of the content of the concepts, as well, in an effort to point up the internal limits of the program. The concept of myth employed is questioned on the grounds of its formal character as opposed to a material definition which Barth would favor. If Bultmann had recognized myth as the portrayal of an eternal truth in the garb of a narrative of the Gods rather than an objectivizing of non-objective realities he would have recognized the essentially non-mythical character of the New Testament kerygma.[45] Barth also contests the sufficiency of existential philosophy to provide an interpretive framework for the biblical text. As much as the subjective emphasis has in its favor, Barth identifies an "abstracting subjectivism" elevated to the level of a systematic principle, which leads to an anthropomonism (*anthropologische Engpass*).[46] Barth also questions the continuing relevance of existential philosophy for the Western world (which for Bultmann had become virtually axiomatic), thereby undermining one of its most persuasive claims to validity.[47] The most serious flaw shared by each of these conceptual tools, however, is the violence which they do to the hermeneutical imperative for an openness to the text itself. Asks Barth,

> Kann man irgend einen Text aus alter oder neuer Zeit verstehen, wenn man—statt seiner Selbsterschliessung offen entgegenzusehen und geduldig zu folgen—mit einer Vorentscheidung über das Mass und die Grenzen seiner Verständlichkeit oder Unverständlichkeit schon an ihn herantritt?[48]

(4) *A theological focus upon hermeneutics diverts theology from its object.* This objection like the one before weighs heavily in Barth's dispute with hermeneutics. For Barth the "translation" work of the interpreter cannot be

carried out effectively when it becomes the primary concern in relation to the text which is being "translated." The text must remain primary. And a good "translation" work is one which will focus all its attention upon the subject-matter which the text wishes to voice and not the conditions under which the understanding of the subject-matter become possible.[49] The latter concern is legitimate only insofar as it is guided by and consequent to the former. Barth energetically applies this critique to Bultmann's hermeneutical program. Bultmann's preoccupation with myth and world-view is a preoccupation with the "cradle" of the New Testament message rather than a focus upon the message itself.[50] It represents an abstraction, an interest in the structural characteristics of statements rather than an interest in the "spirit, object, and scope" of the New Testament.[51] It belongs among the deepest convictions of Barth's own theological program that questions of method must never be allowed to overshadow the object of inquiry. The legitimacy of a philosophical tool as an aid to hermeneutics ends at that point at which the philosophy begins to take on a significance independent of its application (KD I/2, 820–22).

(5) *Hermeneutics threatens to displace the function of the Holy Spirit in the event of revelation.* Barth asks at the conclusion of his Bultmann article, "Ist die Lehre vom *normativen*, gerade mit dem Heiligen Geist konkurrierenden, gerade ihm Schranken setzenden 'Vorverständnis', die der Hermeneutik Bultmanns zugrunde liegt, nicht der Tod *alles* echten und rechten Verstehens?"[52] As will become clearer in later chapters, the doctrine of the Holy Spirit represents indeed the direction of Barth's alternative to a purely formal hermeneutical focus. The question of how God's revelation is received and appropriated by the human being is a question which theology can only answer legitimately in reference to revelation since it is itself a part of the revelation event, that part which is appropriated to the Holy Spirit (KD I/2, 255f). This objection of Barth's, however, is one that is unfortunately often misunderstood. Thiselton,

for example, reads Barth, "so that at times it seems to be implied that the Spirit's communication of the Word of God is somehow independent of all ordinary processes of human understanding."[53] The implication is that Barth allows for a kind of divine magic alongside natural processes. It is indeed true that for Barth the understanding of the subject-matter of the biblical text which leads to faith is an event whose possibility does not lie within human existence itself. It is a possibility which comes from outside (*extra nos*) and which is attributable only to the grace of God. This, however, by no means necessarily implies a magical understanding. What Barth opposes in his objection is a reduction of this event which happens *through* natural human means to a "nothing more than."[54] His opposition is to the dissolution of a particular horizon of meaning whose authenticity is won in faith and proclaimed in the Christian texts and traditions. In this sense one should understand Barth's preference for the "spiritual" explanation of understanding as an alternative wording of his call to openness to the subject-matter of the text. To listen in the power of the Holy Spirit is to listen in an attitude of openness to the biblical claim to proclaim an authentic word about God. Not surprisingly, then, Barth recognizes the necessity of "*der Schule des Heiligen Geistes*" in *all* genuine understanding, even the everyday variety, whether between text and person or between person and person.[55]

The Way Forward

So far we have succeeded in charting to a limited degree the place of Barth's theology in relation to the hermeneutical question. At this point, however, it is a decidedly one-dimensional perspective which we have achieved, a perspective which focuses upon the negative polemical side of the relationship. As is generally recognized, Barth's critique of hermeneutical theology by no means included a rejection of the hermeneutical problem itself nor did it comprise the totality of Barth's response to the problem. It is thesis of this work (one which is also widely recognized) that the positive contribution of (the later) Barth in this regard is to be found in his own interpretation of the doctrine of the Trinity. As we proceed to an interpretation and our own critique of this contribution, Barth's negative critique of hermeneutics will have more to offer than merely an insight into the historical and logical context of Barth's work. It will also provide a methodological starting point for the formation of questions which must test the hermeneutical claims, whether explicit or implicit, which the doctrine of the Trinity makes. In particular, Barth's objection to the intrusion of culturally and anthropologically deter-mined concepts into the interpretive process mandates an inquiry into the conceptual structure of Barth's own trinitarian hermeneutic. The construction which Barth undertakes must be considered from the perspective of the philosophical influences at work, as well as influences rooted in the Christian tradition (which can hardly claim to have preserved itself from culturally and anthropologically determined concepts). Barth's objection to a displacement of spiritual language in favor of existential themes prompts an inquiry into Barth's model in its relation to anthropology and particularly its relation to the pheno-menon of human language which remains unquestionably at the center of hermeneutical reflection. Before proceeding to questions of the structure and content of the trinitarian hermeneutic, however, it will be helpful to consider its hermeneutic function *per se*. To this end we turn to an overview of the "place" of the doctrine of the Trinity within the *Kirchliche Dogmatik*.

ENDNOTES

[1]Ernst Fuchs, *Hermeneutik* (Bad Cannstatt: Müllerschön, 1954), 3–12.

[2]Cf. the efforts of Eberhard Jüngel, a student of both Fuchs and Barth, in *Gottes Sein ist im Werden* (Tübingen: Mohr, 1965). ET = *The Doctrine of the Trinity* (Grand Rapids: Eerdmans, 1976). See also Kurt Lüthi, "Theologie als Gespräch," *Theologie zwischen Gestern und Morgen*, ed. W. Dantine & K. Lüthi (Munich: Kaiser, 1968), 302–32. The work of Friedrich Schmid, *Verkündigung und Dogmatik in der Theologie Karl Barths* (Munich: Kaiser, 1964), also belongs within this category.

[3]Cf. Anthony Thiselton's quick and easy dismissal of Barth as an opponent of hermeneutical theology in what is otherwise a commendable textbook. *The Two Horizons* (Exeter: Paternoster, 1980), 88–92.

[4]See James M. Robinson, "Hermeneutic Since Barth," *The New Hermeneutic*, ed. J. M. Robinson & J. B. Cobb, New Frontiers in Theology, II (New York: Harper & Row, 1964), 1–77. Robinson uses the historical evolution of the word "hermeneutic" as the structure upon which he develops his theme. See also Gerhard Ebeling, "Hermeneutik," [3]RGG, III, 243–5.

[5]Thus for Schleiermacher, hermeneutics is the "Kunstlehre des Verstehens," and for Dilthey, the "Kunstlehre des Verstehens schriftlich fixierter Lebensäusserungen." Cited without notation, Ebeling, "Hermeneutik," 244.

[6]Ibid.

[7]See Ebeling, "Hermeneutik," 261f, for a comprehênsive bibliography through 1958. Many of the responses to the first two editions, as well as the forewords of the first three editions, are reproduced in *Anfänge der dialektischen Theologie, Teil I*, ed. J. Moltmann (Munich: Kaiser, 1962). ET = *The Beginnings of Dialectical Theology*, I, ed. J. Robinson, tr. K. Crim, et al. (Richmond: John Knox, 1968). See also Robinson, "Hermeneutic," 22–32; René Marlé, *Das theologischeRe Problem der Hermeneutik*, tr. N. Rocholl (Mainz: M. Grünwald, 1965), 24–32; Rudolf Smend, "Nachkritische Schriftauslegung," *Parrhesia* (Zurich: Evangelischer Verlag Zürich, 1966), 215–37; Wilfried Joest, "Barth, Bultmann und die 'existenziale Interpretation'," *Theologie zwischen Gestern und Morgen*, 69–87; Rolf Schäfer, "Die hermeneutische Frage in der gegenwärtigen evangelischen Theologie," *Die hermeneutische Frage in der Theologie*, ed. O. Loretz & W. Strolz (Freiburg: Herder, 1968), 430–35; Walter Kreck, "Zur Hermeneutik Karl Barths und Rudolf Bultmanns," *Grundfragen der Dogmatik* (Munich: Kaiser, 1970), 251–4; Nico T. Bakker, *In der Krisis der Offenbarung: Karl Barths Hermeneutik, dargestellt an seiner Römerbrief-Auslegung* (Neukirchen: Neukirchen, 1974); and Eberhard Jüngel, "Theologie als Metakritik. Zur Hermeneutik theologischer Exegese," *Barth-Studien* (Zürich: Benzinger, 1982), 83–98. ET = "Theology as Metacriticism: Toward a Hermeneutic of Theological Exegesis," *Karl Barth: A Theological Legacy*, tr. G. Paul (Philadelphia: Westminster, 1986), 70–82.

[8] [2]*Römerbrief*, x. (= *Anfänge*, 109). The impression, however, was not wholly without support, for not only did Barth dispense with an explicit emphasis upon the historical-critical discussion of the text, but in the opening sentences of the work one reads, "Die Unterschiede von einst und jetzt, dort und hier, wollen beachtet sein. Aber der Zweck der Beachtung kann

nur die Erkenntnis sein, dass diese Unterschiede im Wesen der Dinge *keine* Bedeutung haben." [1]*Römerbrief*, v. (= *Anfänge*, 77).

[9] [2]*Römerbrief*, xi. (= *Anfänge*, 109f).

[10]Jüngel, "Metakritik," 91. ET, 76. Cf. Smend's interpretation of Barth's approach to exegesis as "second naiveté," a thesis which Barth rejected though perhaps misunderstood. Smend, 236f. Jüngel, "Metakritik," 88. ET, 73.

[11]It is of course a theme which was later to be associated less with Barth and far more with Bultmann and the hermeneutical theologians as we shall see below.

[12] [2]*Römerbrief*, xii. (= *Anfänge*, 110).

[13]Robinson, "Hermeneutics," 23.

[14]Jüngel, "Metakritik," 85. ET, 71.

[15]"...wenn wir uns selber recht verstehen." [1]*Römerbrief*, v. (= *Anfänge*, 77).

[16] [1]*Römerbrief*, v. (= *Anfänge*, 77).

[17] [2]*Römerbrief*, xiii. (= *Anfänge*, 111).

[18]Ibid., xiii. (= *Anfänge*, 111f).

[19]This concept is developed into a codified hermeneutical rule in KD I/2, 513–23. See especially 519ff, where Barth speaks of the *souveräne Freiheit* of the subject-matter.

[20] [2]*Römerbrief* xivf. (= *Anfänge*, 113f).

[21]Barth's contributions in this regard, as basic as they are to the hermeneutical discussion, have not gone uncriticized. Particularly Barth's critique of historical-criticism is often reproached as the erection of a damaging dichotomy between scientific exegesis and a "subjective" encounter with the subject-matter of the text. See, eg., Ebeling, "Hermeneutik," 256; Schäfer, 433f.

[22]Among the writings of Bultmann which best represent his New Testament hermeneutic are "Neues Testament und Mythologie," (1941) *Kerygma und Mythos*, ed. Hans Werner Bartsch (Hamburg: Reich u. Heidrich, 1948) 15–53; ET = "New Testament and Mythology," *Kerygma and Myth*, I (London: SPCK, 1953), 1–44; "Das Problem der Hermeneutik," (1950) *Glauben und Verstehen*, II (Tübingen: Mohr, 1952), 211–35; ET = "The Problem of Hermeneutics," *Essays Philosophical and Theological* (London: SCM, 1955), 234–61; "Zum Problem der Entmythologisierung," *Kerygma und Mythos*, II, ed. H.-W. Bartsch (Hamburg: Reich u. Heidrich, 1952), 177–208; ET = "On the Problem of Demythologizing," *New Testament & Mythology and Other Basic Writings*, ed. & tr. Schubert Ogden (London: SCM, 1984) 95–130; *Jesus Christ and Mythology* (New York: Scribner's, 1958).

[23]Bultmann, "Neues Testament u. Mythology," 15f. ET, 1f.

[24]Ibid., 23. ET, 11.

[25]Cf. Bultmann, "Zum Problem der Entmythologisierung," 180. ET, 95.

[26]Ibid., 191. ET, 105.

[27]Bultmann, "Problem der Hermeneutik," 216. ET, 239.

[28]Ibid., 216. ET, 239f.

[29]Bultmann, "Zum Problem der Entmythologisierung," 191. ET, 106.

[30]Bultmann, "Problem der Hermeneutik," 232. ET, 257

[31]"Von einer schöpferischen und normativen Bedeutung der menschlichen *ratio* hinsichtlich der Wahrheit [Gottes] kann somit in keinem Sinn die Rede sein." FQI, 46. "[Die *ratio fidei* bzw. *ratio veritatis*] ist im *Credo* bzw. in der Bibel *verborgen*, und sie muss sich *offenbaren*, um sich uns bekannt zu machen." FQI, 46f. "Ein Modus der *Offenbarung* ist offenbar auch das Ereignis des *intelligere*, des *vera ratione quaerere veram rationem*, das *intus legere*, dem sich auch der innere Text aufschliesst, sofern dabei die Konformität der *ratio* mit der Wahrheit weder im Objekt noch im Subjekt, sondern in derselben offenbarenden Gottesmacht beruht, die dem Glauben als Autorität begegnet und einleuchtet." FQI, 48.

[32]Cf. Eberhard Busch, *Karl Barths Lebenslauf* (Munich: Kaiser, [2]1976), 206-11. ET = *Karl Barth*, tr. J. Bowden (London: SCM, 1976), 193-98.

[33]The letter marked a decisive break in Barth's thinking between himself and the other members of the "dialectical school." *Briefwechsel: Barth - Bultmann*, 100. Tr. from ET = *Karl Barth - Rudolf Bultmann Letters, 1922 to 1966*, tr. G. W. Bromiley (Grand Rapids: Eerdmans, 1981), 58. Cf. Barth's development of the Exodus analogy in "Versuch," 52f.

[34]*Briefwechsel: Barth—Bultmann*, 100f. In a letter to Thurneysen only weeks before Barth identified the efforts of these theologians with "eine Erneuerung des Verhältnisses zwischen Theologie und Philosophie...wie es bei Kant, Hegel, Schleiermacher, De Wette usw. nun wirklich auch schon gedacht war." The critical point is not, however, the presence of philosophical categories, but rather their function. "Es handelt sich mir ja wirklich nicht darum, dass man nicht mit Ehren irgend eine Philosophie im Kopfe haben dürfe, geschweige denn darum, dass es durchaus nicht—und trotz Heiner—die Heideggersche sein dürfe. Aber die Kerle wollen sich doch alle vor der Philosophie in Sicherheit bringen, statt mit dem lieben Gott mit irgend einer 'Möglichkeit' anfangen, dem Ärgernis der Theologie mittelst irgend eines 'Vorverständnisses' oder eines Tricks zum Ad-absurdum-Führen der Heiden ausweichen und so fein heraus sein." *Briefwechsel: Barth - Thurneysen*, II, 700, 701f.

[35]Barth's posthumously published letters reveal an even deeper antipathy toward hermeneutical theology (including the so-called "new hermeneutic" with which Barth refused to enter into a sustained dialogue) than is revealed in any of his published writings. See *Briefe: 1961 - 1968*, 109, 147f, 158f, 217, 231, 513f. Barth's apparent restraint from public and sustained critique is explainable in light of Barth's rule restricting theology's focus to its "subject-matter" (*zur Sache selbst!*). Cf. Barth's advice to Oscar Cullmann not to polemicize

the Bultmannians as often as he does since it gives them more attention than they deserve. "Ich habe vielfältig die Erfahrung gemacht, dass man die theologisch Widerwärtigen am besten damit bekämpft, dass man—mit Ausnahme gewisser momentaner Blitzlichter—an ihnen vorbei gelassen ('Du bereitest vor mir einen Tisch im Angesicht meiner Feinde' Ps. 23,5) sein eigenes Verslein aufsagt." Ibid., 236f.

[36]KD I/1, 36 (Translation mine).

[37]"Versuch," 37f.

[38]Barth makes this connection in the decisive letter to Bultmann (See note 33, above): "Wo man so mit der Möglichkeit einer natürlichen Theologie spielt, so eifrig ist, die Theologie im Rahmen eines untheologisch gewonnenen Vorverständnisses zu treiben, da kann es gar nicht anders sein, als dass man in solchen Verkrampfungen und reaktionären Winkeln endigt, die um nichts besser sind, als die Liberalismen der Anderen." *Briefwechsel: Barth - Bultmann*, 101.

[39]Cf. Barth's critique of F. Gogarten's anthropological theses in KD I/1, 130-36.

[40]Barth denies the possibility of a special biblical hermeneutic over and against general hermeneutics. KD I/2, 515. General hermeneutics has in practice, however, lost sight of its most basic principle, namely, that interpretation must proceed on the basis of a fundamental fidelity to the object which the words of a text seek to bring to expression. In this regard biblical hermeneutics offers a needed correction to general hermeneutics. KD I/2, 812-15.

[41]Cf. also KD I/2, 818-25, in which Barth lays down principles for maintaining the sovereign freedom of the subject-matter when one legitimately employs a philosophy or "scheme of thought" as a tool or aid to hermeneutical reflection.

[42]"Versuch," 30-4.

[43]Ibid., 31.

[44]Ibid., 35-41.

[45]Ibid., 31f.

[46]Ibid., 12f, 38f.

[47]Ibid., 38f.

[48]Ibid., 30.

[49]Ibid., 8.

[50]Ibid., 7f.

[51]Ibid., 27.

[52]"Versuch," 52.

[53]Thiselton, 89. One wonders if Heinrich Ott is not also speaking of Barth when he speaks of this appeal to the Holy Spirit against hermeneutics as a "'pious' objection, designed to make light of the hermeneutical problem." "What is Systematic Theology?" *The Later Heidegger and Theology*, New Frontiers in Theology, I, ed. J. M. Robinson & J. B. Cobb (New York: Harper & Row, 1963), 81.

[54]Cf. Barth's repudiation of a magical conception of the Spirit's role in KD IV/2, 382-4.

[55]"Versuch," 51f.

CHAPTER TWO

The Place of the Doctrine of the Trinity
in the *Kirchliche Dogmatik*

In the present chapter we are concerned with Barth's doctrine of the Trinity in its integration within the total theological context and development of the *Kirchliche Dogmatik*. To speak of the "place" of a doctrine is to speak of far more than its mere position within a particular dogmatic theology, although the position may indeed play a significant role in determining the "place" of a doctrine. To speak of a doctrine's "place" is to speak of its relationship and function with regard to the total presentation. The terms "relationship" and "function" imply an acknowledgment of the fact that no theological *locus* may be developed in complete isolation from all others. While this need not imply the phenomenon of a "theological system," the perennial question of whether Barth has in fact constructed the *Kirchliche Dogmatik* on the basis of a system (and if so, how it may be characterized) would appear to present itself as a necessary consideration before any final judgment regarding the relationship of one doctrine to the whole can be made. This question will be taken up in due course, following an analysis of Barth's declared understanding of the peculiar task of the doctrine of the Trinity. Before proceeding further, however, it is necessary to reflect briefly on the place which the doctrine has occupied in the dogmatic tradition.

The Place of the Doctrine in the History of Dogma

What follows does not intend to provide even a summary of the rich and complex history of the doctrine of the Trinity within the history of Christian dogma. Indeed, a complete and systematic account is an ambitious project which few are qualified to carry through and which need not be undertaken here.[1] Our present concern is rather to draw together in as brief a form as possible a handful of broad and generally recognized observations concerning the different roles which the doctrine has played throughout its history. This will provide a certain background which will highlight the distinctive place of the Barthian doctrine.

The doctrine of the Trinity has enjoyed varying degrees of popularity within the history of the Church. One may speak of periods of vigorous trinitarianism, periods of trinitarianism in decline, as well as periods of outright rejection. The peculiar place of the doctrine within the doctrinal schemes of a given age have varied accordingly. At no moment, of course, in the history of the doctrine has the Church come to unanimity with regard to either the content or the place of the doctrine. If the fourth century were to be categorized as the period of vigorous trinitarianism *par excellence*, one would also have to take note of the counter christologies and theologies which were the object of trinitarian polemic and thus a source of life to trinitarianism itself. Nevertheless, this threefold means of categorizing the Church's historical attitude toward the doctrine will provide a useful abstraction for considering its variety of functions within Christian dogma as a whole. While each designation may apply especially well to a particular period, the amount of overlap is considerable. One can fairly say that each brand of trinitarianism is to be found in at least some degree in every epoch of Church history.

Vigorous Trinitarianism

Within theological epochs or movements that have insisted on a high place for the doctrine, trinitarianism has usually assumed one of three broad roles:

(1) The earliest function of the doctrine of the Trinity was that of a *doxological summary of the history of salvation*. This is what R. Jenson has termed "primary trinitarianism," intending thereby the use of trinitarian language in Christian worship prior to the doctrine's actual codification.[2] It

developed on the basis of reflection upon the data of revelation, particularly the resurrection of Christ, the proclaimed promise of salvation, and the belief that God had poured his Spirit out upon the Church. It was the result of reflection on the soteriological function of the Christ event and the outpouring of the Holy Spirit, a function which only God Himself could assume.[3] When employed in this sense the doctrine functions as "the doxological response of faith to God's historical, salvific act in Jesus Christ through the Holy Spirit."[4] Its primary place is Christian worship. The doctrine represents the answer of faith to the Lordship of Christ and to the presence of God in the Church through the Holy Spirit. It is a summary in a single formula of the Christian community's praise of those who have executed God's salvific acts, that is, the Father, Son and Holy Spirit as the one Lord and God. Its boundaries are the Scriptures as it seeks to respond to the witness it finds there without thereby rendering a new or additional witness to revelation.

A doctrine of the Trinity which assumes this role need not eschew all talk of the divine being. The doctrine may occupy a dual place, affirming on the one hand the acts of God in history in Jesus Christ and the Holy Spirit, while on the other affirming that the God who has so acted is Himself Father, Son and Holy Spirit. A doctrine of the Trinity which functions doxologically and soteriologically may indeed affirm an immanent just as well as an economic trinity. Nevertheless, a thoroughgoing doxological and soteriological trinitarianism avoids the path of speculative metaphysics. Many of the great trinitarian theologians have urged caution in a vein similar to that of Gregory of Nyssa: "He whose curiosity rises above the Sun passes also by the thought of the Father"; for such "faith is...vain, the message empty, baptism pointless, and the pains of the martyrs for nothing."[5] It was precisely the speculative orientation of much trinitarian theology which lay behind the reserve which the Reformers expressed toward the doctrine. Typical of this reformation sentiment was the insistence of Luther that investigation concerning the Trinity be restricted to the Scripture. Further inquiry was ill advised.

> These, then, are the differences between the [trinitarian] Persons as given to us in the gospel. Whoever wishes to do so can ponder on it further, but he will find nothing of greater certainty. Therefore we ought to stay with this in all simplicity and be satisfied with it, until we arrive in heaven, where we shall no longer have to hear it or believe it, but clearly see and apprehend it.[6]

(2)   By no means, however, have theologians of the Trinity always observed such discretion. Indeed the doctrine has often come to occupy a place beyond that of reflection upon salvation history, one which may be termed *metaphysical speculation on the being of God*. A doctrine of the Trinity which exercises this function does not understand itself so much as a summary of the testimony of Holy Scripture as it does a revealed ontology of God which affords reason the opportunity to advance the human striving for knowledge of the divine. The metaphysical function of the doctrine has roots deep within the dogmatic tradition, extending back to the trinitarian disputations themselves.[7] The speculative function received a strong impetus from the work of Augustine, particularly with his doctrine of the *vestigia trinitatis*. Trinitarian speculation dominated trinitarian thought in the Middle Ages such that Thomas was able to logically deduce the threefoldness of the divine being simply on the basis of the theological assumption that God knows and wills. Thomas did not, however, go so far as to derive the Trinity by means of unaided reason alone. Unlike the assertions of God's nature and existence, the divine Trinity was not held by Thomas to be derivable within the limits of natural theology, but rather required the communication of divine truth.[8]

(3)   A third role which the doctrine of the Trinity has often assumed during periods of vigorous trinitarianism is that of *polemical tool* or *agent for resolving controversy*. This was a dominant function of the doctrine in the formative era of the third and fourth centuries. If the creeds of Nicaea and Constantinople represent the foundations of all later trinitarian development, then the

polemical place of the doctrine is well established within its history. The controversies with the Arians at Nicaea and with the Pneumatomachians and other groups that denied the full divinity of the Spirit at Constantinople were the most significant factors in shaping the language of the resultant creeds.[9] When the doctrine of the Trinity assumes this role it is employed with a view more to what it denies than what it affirms. The precise form which the doctrine assumes will depend in part on key relationships which are forged with competing lines of theological thought. Consequently, the polemical doctrine may often be found to be in disharmony with itself and the theological line of thought in which it finds its home.

Trinitarianism in Decline

The doctrine of the Trinity has often been allowed to assume a less prominent role within Christian theology. Far from being the pinnacle of the Doctrine of God or of the whole of Christian theology it has taken on an auxiliary function; it has slipped to what Welch has called a "doctrine of the second rank."[10] As a doctrine in decline the Trinity has assumed multifarious forms and functions. Two are noted here for their prominent place in the history of dogma.

(1)   Within the great theological syntheses of the scholastic era, the truth of the doctrine of the Trinity was steadfastly affirmed. Its actual place however was one of lessened significance. This was a consequence of what Rahner has referred to as the "isolation of the Doctrine of the Trinity in piety and textbook theology [Schultheologie]."[11] This situation has in fact continued even into the modern era. Rahner observes that the doctrine of the Trinity has lost its relevance for average Christians, who in their practical lives are "almost mere monotheists."[12] Were the doctrine of the Trinity to be rejected as false, the dominant portion of theological literature could remain unchanged. The root of the problem is for Rahner to be found within the structures of the doctrine's

classic formulation. Rahner pinpoints the Augustinian rule *opera Trinitatis ad extra sunt indivisa* and the consequent allocation of predicates only as "appropriations" as factors in the failure of theology to take seriously the triune divisions in God. Structural failings have contributed to disconnectedness between the Trinity and the other doctrines of the traditional dogmatic system.

> To put it crassly, and not without exaggeration, when the treatise is concluded, its subject is never brought up again. Its function in the whole dogmatic construction is not clearly perceived. It is as though this mystery has been revealed for its own sake, and that even after it has been made known to us, it remains, *as a reality*, locked up within itself. We make statements about it, but as reality it has nothing to do with us at all.[13]

The disconnectedness of the doctrine within the total dogmatic context owes in part to the traditional ordering (beginning with Thomas) of the article "*de Deo Trino*" only after the article "*de Deo Uno*".[14] The result is that one begins not with the God of salvation history, the God experienced in His relations to his creatures, but with a "philosophical and abstract" doctrine of God.[15]

The doctrine of the Trinity which loses its place within the total theological scheme will concomitantly lose the ultimacy of its relevance for Christian living and experience. It runs the risk of becoming one *credendum* within a series of other *credenda*. While it may well be exonerated as revealed truth, the depth of meaning can be no more than one dimensional. The range of its meaning becomes restricted to a heavenly sphere far removed from the exigencies of Christian life.

(2)   A second place which the doctrine has found within those lines of thinking that afford it no more than secondary status is its function as analog to a philosophically derived trinitarian principle of form. This is the place which the doctrine has assumed within the great variety of modern *philosophical trinitarianism*. Perhaps the most celebrated instance has been the series of efforts to construct a theological trinitarianism on the foundation of Hegel's

philosophy of religion. Hegel's doctrine of self-differentiation of the Absolute Spirit fails to correspond to the Christian doctrine at a number of significant points.[16] Nevertheless, Hegel's program appeared to offer a means to Christian theology of preserving many of the Trinity's basic concepts. At a time when the doctrine of the Trinity seemed to be rapidly falling out of favor, a number of theologians sought a synthesis of theology with Hegelian philosophy with the intention, among other things, of providing a new interpretation and thereby a revival of the trinitarian doctrine. I. A. Dorner is among the most significant of these.[17] According to Dorner, the doctrine of the Trinity together with the Incarnation are the consequence of the insight of faith. Yet, the observation that Dorner finds the ground for the immanent Trinity in speculative thought would seem to be held off only by assertion.[18] It is constituted at a distance from the economic Trinity, that is, at a distance from God's saving presence in Jesus Christ and the Holy Spirit, and not in continuity with it.

While the attempts of Dorner and others signaled the attempt of a retrieval of trinitarian language, the shifting basis into speculative thought would appear to have put the vitality and relevance of the distinctively Christian doctrine into question. A lessened role and place for the doctrine was inevitable as the doctrine could be afforded no more prominence than is ever afforded the fruits of speculative thought.[19]

Rejection of the Doctrine of the Trinity

It might seem strange that one can speak of the place of a doctrine for a pattern of theological thinking which explicitly rejects it. Yet no Christian theology rejects the doctrine without due reason, and thus even in its rejection there is consciousness of the historical phenomenon of the doctrine and its place and function (even though this place and function is determined to be irrelevant for Christian faith).

There is actually no time in the history of the doctrine that it has not been challenged on one level or another. The conceptions of the Trinity and its place which have led to its rejection are as numerous as the positive conceptions of the doctrine which led to its inclusion in orthodox (or not so orthodox) thinking. For the purposes of the present inquiry it is sufficient to consider only the modern rejection of the Trinity and indeed only two broad conceptualizations of the place of the doctrine which have led to this rejection. These two understandings of the doctrine and subsequent critiques are logically distinct from one another, yet quite compatible as well. Thus one is seldom found without the other.

(1) A dominant line of critique that has capitalized on the speculative role of the doctrine may be traced largely to the Schleiermacher / Ritschl / Harnack theological line. Schleiermacher was not himself a representative of the rejection of trinitarian theology. He did not himself explicitly reject the doctrine. His much celebrated relegation of the Trinity to a concluding appendix in *Der christliche Glaube* was, however, indicative of the declining significance of the doctrine within Enlightenment Christianity. And his incisive criticism that the doctrine is not "an immediate utterance concerning the Christian self-consciousness but only a combination of several such utterances,"[20] set the stage for a rapid decline of the doctrine which led to its eventual rejection by much of the liberal theology of the nineteenth and early twentieth centuries with which Schleiermacher is closely associated. The identification of the doctrine with speculative theology was intensified in the writings of Albrecht Ritschl, which were in part influenced by Kantian epistemology and its consequent metaphysical agnosticism.[21] All talk of God in Himself or divine relations was not only deemed irrelevant, but indeed unavailable to human thought. Ritschl's view was radicalized by Harnack who held the doctrine to be a perversion of the simplicity of the gospel. Speculative doctrines such as the

Trinity are suspect for their tendency to displace fundamental religious interest which will focus not so much upon the person as the commands of Jesus.[22]

(2) A second line of critique has its roots in the rise of historical conscious-ness and attaches itself to a historical-critical analysis which would explain the doctrine almost entirely in terms of historically conditioned factors. With the rise of biblical criticism in the eighteenth century, many of the roots of trinitarian theology, particularly Jesus' utterances regarding himself in the fourth Gospel, fell into question.[23] Not only the rise of biblical criticism, but also the increasing awareness of social, cultural, and political factors which had conditioned the history of dogma increased the suspicion that the doctrine represented the culmination of years of church and state politics, power struggles, and social and economic influences, all of which came to bear on certain early dilemmas within Christian theology through the thought forms of Hellenistic philosophy. A one-sided focus on the doctrine's historically conditioned character resulted in a radical questioning of its continuing relevance for the modern era.[24]

The Place of the Doctrine in the *Kirchliche Dogmatik*

With the publication of the first half-volume of the *Kirchliche Dogmatik*, vigorous trinitarianism became a present reality for twentieth century Christian thought.[25] Whether or not one is inclined to agree with G. T. Thomson, translator of the first English edition of the work, that Barth has written "the greatest treatise on the Trinity since the Reformation,"[26] or with the editors of the second edition who extended the acclamation to Augustine's *De Trinitate*,[27] Barth shifted the doctrine to a place of prominence which it has seldom enjoyed in post-enlightenment Protestant theology.

Barth's chief innovation in trinitarian thought lies in the new home which he hammered out for the doctrine, namely, its place among the prolegomena to Christian theology. It is this place upon which we must focus if we are to appreciate Barth's intention in retrieving the doctrine to a place of theological eminence. Before proceeding in this direction, however, it will be helpful to consider Barth's doctrine in light of each of those "places" associated with vigorous trinitarianism which were outlined above: the doxological summary of salvation history, polemic, and speculation.

The Trinity Doctrine as Doxological Summary of the History of Salvation

That doxological context is an essential aspect of the character of Christian theology is a conviction at which Barth arrived early in his career and one which he emphasized frequently in his life-long debate with Neo-Protestantism.[28] The task of dogmatics is not strictly speaking the task of worship. Each functions differently.[29] Yet the two undertakings stand in a relationship of essential continuity, so much so that Barth is able to speak of a "churchly attitude" (KD I/2, 939) as a concrete demand to which dogmatic method is subject. The situation to which dogmatics orients itself is the situation which faces the Church. Dogmatics stands together with the Church in a "fellowship of prayer" (939). Each is seeking in its own way and in a relationship of cooperation to hear and proclaim the Word of God.

> [Die Dogmatik] muss schlechterdings mit [der Kirche] zusammen Gott danken und preisen für die Wohltat seiner Offenbarung und Versöhnung, mit ihr zusammen vor Gott Busse tun für alle die Verfehlung, deren sich die ganze Kirche dieser Wohltat gegenüber dauernd schuldig macht, mit ihr zusammen bitten um den Heiligen Geist und das heisst: um die Möglichkeit eines neuen besseren, entschiedeneren Hörens und dann auch Sagens seines Wortes.[30]

The doxological context for which Barth strives is likewise reflected in his formulation of the doctrine of the Trinity. It is reflected in the revelation formula which stands at the very root of the doctrine as Barth wants to develop it: "God reveals Himself as Lord". The theme of Lordship is one that may be followed consistently through every step of the lengthy development of the doctrine of the Trinity.[31] The immediate object of doxology not only for the doctrine of the Trinity but for all of theology is nothing else than God in His revelation. The doctrine is the result of the Church's reflection upon the Lordship which is the content of that revelation. This reflection takes the form of an "analysis" of revelation (KD I/1, 309f).[32] The doctrine adds nothing of material content to revelation, but rather seeks to understand revelation as the Scripture bears witness to it.[33]

The event of revelation which the Church has pondered and which forms the basis of Barth's doctrine is the event of Jesus Christ (122f). It is the analysis of what happens and what has happened in Jesus Christ in both its objective and subjective aspects which yields the Revealer, Revelation, Revealedness triad which stands at the root of the doctrine. Consequently, it is a doctrine oriented toward the history of salvation—not only God in his acts and his speech, but the God who acts and speaks for us. "Die Trinitätslehre sagt..., dass und inwiefern der, der sich nach dem Zeugnis der Schrift Menschen offenbart, unser *Gott*, dass und inwiefern er *unser* Gott sein kann" (403). The doctrine of the Trinity is as much a summary of the event of human redemption as it is a summary of revelation itself.[34] For, "Offenbarung ist ja auch nicht verschieden von der Person Jesu Christi und wiederum nicht verschieden von der in ihm geschehenen Versöhnung" (122).

The history of salvation also offers the material with which Barth develops the doctrine more fully. With a spirited employment of the Rule of Appropriations, each of the three trinitarian Persons is developed by means of particular works of God which are "appropriated" to the respective person.[35] Thus it is *per appropriationem* that the Father is the Creator, the Son the Reconciler, and the Spirit the Redeemer. It is appropriate and necessary to speak of the second Person of the Trinity when one speaks of the incarnation, just as it is appropriate and necessary to speak of the third when one speaks of the presence of God in the Church. The appropriations, however, are an "improper" (*uneigentlich*) (but nevertheless true and necessary) way of speaking.

They can only be employed in light of the trinitarian rule, *opera trinitatis ad extra sunt indivisa*, which affirms the unity of God in all of His outward acts. The appropriations of particular moments of God's salvific history with the world are an improper way of speaking because no trinitarian person acts alone outside of the being of God. It is always God in his unity, as Father, Son, and Spirit, acting indivisibly.[36] Each of the three Persons participates in the other two, and none of the three can be without the others (390).

There remains still another side to the relationship between Barth's doctrine and the doxological summary of salvation history. While salvation history forms the root of our knowledge of the doctrine, it in no way is the ground of the doctrine itself. The ground of the doctrine resides in the being of God Himself (328f). Barth wants to understand the acts of God not only in continuity with, but in identity with the being and nature of God.

> Wesen und Wirken Gottes sind ja nicht zweierlei sondern eins. Das Wirken Gottes ist das Wesen Gottes in seinem Verhältnis zu der von ihm unterschiedenen, zu schaffenden oder geschaffenen Wirklichkeit. Das Wirken Gottes ist das Wesen Gottes als das Wesen dessen, der (NB. in freier Entscheidung, begründet in seinem Wesen, aber nicht genötigt durch sein Wesen) der Offenbarer, die Offenbarung, das Offenbarsein oder der Schöpfer, der Versöhner, der Erlöser ist. In diesem seinem Wirken ist uns Gott offenbar.[37]

Thus what God is in His revelation, He is already in the eternity of His inner life. It is for Barth far more accurate to describe salvation history as rooted in the eternal Trinity, than vice versa. God in Himself is an inconceivable reality for human thought and experience. But the distinctions which we experience in the event of God's self-revelation act as a "pointer" (*Hinweis*) to the distinctions within the eternal being.[38]

The Doctrine of the Trinity as Polemic

In the first volume of his *Dogmatics*, Emil Brunner described the place of the doctrine of the Trinity in the theology of Barth in this way:

In [Barth's] view, the outstanding, and indeed the *absolutely decisive importance* of this doctrine lies in the fact that in it he sees the basis for his main concern, the contrast between the speculative *theologia naturalis* and the theology which from beginning to end, in accordance with revelation, is orientated towards Jesus Christ alone.[39] (emphasis mine)

It is in Brunner's analysis the polemical function of the doctrine which determines its place for Barth. "Hence he sets the doctrine of the Trinity at the beginning of his work and has no use for a theology in which the Being of God in general...is dealt with first of all."[40]

Robert Jenson is another who has noted the strong polemical character of the doctrine as Barth has formulated it. Jenson interprets Barth's doctrine in continuity with a set of motifs that Barth brought to expression in his 1922 *Römerbrief*—notably, the polemic against religion and against a theology of static categories.[41] These themes are carried over into the doctrine of the Trinity by means of the doctrine's essential function which Jenson suggests is that of "identification".[42] Taking seriously Barth's thesis that the doctrine of the Trinity is the biblical answer to the question, "Who is God in his revelation?" (KD I/1, 136, 311–13, *et passim*), Jenson suggests, "The function of the doctrine is to *identify* which being we are going to be talking about in our theologizing."[43] By using the doctrine as a set of descriptions to identify God, Barth has actually given the doctrine the logical function of a proper name. It is "the fundamental identifying description" of God as the one who is revealed in Jesus Christ.[44] The implication is that neither the revelation in Jesus Christ nor the doctrine of the Trinity may be simply attached to a preconceived concept of God; rather, the reverse is true -- the definitive starting point for a concept of God is the doctrine of the Trinity which itself emerges from an analysis of revelation. The consequence for Barth is that he is able to safeguard the concrete object of theology against the intrusions of natural theology. The second motif, the critique of static categories in theology is accomplished by the particular form which Barth gives the doctrine. This is the actualistic notion of God which the

Trinity doctrine brings to expression, so that "God comes to be understood not as a transcendent thing but as a transcendent happening, and his transcendence therefore understood not as his timelessness but as his radical temporality."[45]

That the doctrine of the Trinity occupies a polemical place in the *Kirchliche Dogmatik*, is affirmed by the author himself. Barth characterizes the "Meaning of the Doctrine of the Trinity,"[46] that is the meaning inherent to the doctrine in the Church's formulation of it, as a twofold rejection. On the one hand, the doctrine signifies the rejection of subordinationism, the belief that the Son and Spirit, while somehow participating in the deity of the Father, do not share in its fullness. They are lesser beings (KD I/1, 401f). Barth sees at the core of subordinationism an objectification of God which denies His subjectivity. This entails a denial of revelation and a displacement of the category of divine subjectivity into the realm of anthropology. On the other hand, the doctrine of the Trinity signifies the rejection of modalism, the notion that the real God lies somehow behind the divine economy of Father, Son, and Spirit (402f). God's being is a reality beyond the trinitarian persons. For Barth this error too is an objectification of the being of God, which entails a denial of the "one true God" (403). The way of modalism is the way of mysticism, leading to a God beyond the God who reveals Himself, but leading ultimately to "man alone with himself" (403). In this way Barth identifies the ancient heresies of subordinationism and modalism with contemporary equivalents, either of which could be tied to his critique of Neo-Protestantism with little difficulty. On each of these polemical fronts Barth seeks to challenge any attempt to think of God without taking seriously the theological fact of revelation. It is the self-revelation of God in Jesus Christ that is the norm and object of theology, and there is no possibility of its circumvention. The anthropological route can be no more than a false mysticism or fruitless speculation.[47]

The polemical place of the doctrine for Barth is thus well established. Whether one can agree with the assessment of Brunner, that the "absolutely decisive importance" of the doctrine lies in this aspect will have to await further inquiry into the varieties of places which the doctrine occupies in the *Kirchliche Dogmatik* and an overview of its function within the work as a whole.

The Doctrine of the Trinity as Speculative Metaphysics

It has already become clear from the preceding discussion that Barth has sought a role for the doctrine of the Trinity which is not only *not speculative*, but which is actually *anti-speculative* in character.[48] God's historical revelation is the source and boundary of the doctrine.[49] There can be no question of deriving a Trinity from a given anthropology or cosmology. The doctrine of the Trinity is read off the "fact of revelation" (309). It is an interpretation or analysis of revelation (325). The point of the interpretation is to identify concretely the God who in turn has revealed Himself in that revelation.[50] This identification function of the doctrine is what forms its anti-speculative character. For without the doctrine of the Trinity to constantly identify the God with whom faith and theology have to do, the possibility is left quite open for some other source to provide a model or concept of God which usurps the role that only revelation can play.[51] The doctrine of the Trinity functions for Barth as a guard for Christian theology to insure that talk of God is always talk of the Father, Son and Holy Spirit revealed in Jesus Christ.[52]

It might be objected that all talk of an anti-speculative function of the doctrine stands in serious tension, if not outright contradiction, with Barth's efforts to carry the doctrine of the Trinity into the inner life of God and to read the immanent Trinity on the basis of the economic Trinity. Barth does indeed carry the triune distinctions of revelation into the eternal life of God in Himself. This he is able to do so partly on the basis of his thesis noted above of the identity of God's essence with his works.[53] While the problem of the relationship between the immanent and economic trinity is a theme that will be taken up more fully in a later chapter, it is perhaps helpful at this point to observe that what Barth undertakes in this regard is neither an effort to move beyond revelation into the inner life of God, nor a simple equation of revelation with the inner life of God as would seem to be the case with Rahner's thesis of identity.[54] For the question of the trinitarian distinctions as descriptive of the eternal being of God is a question posed by the revelation itself (392f). Revelation itself points in this direction since God's revelation is His *self*-revelation. And the doctrine of the Trinity is accordingly not merely an interpretation of revelation, but also "eine Interpretation des in der Offenbarung sich offenbarenden *Gottes*" (328f). Moreover, the doctrine does not impose itself upon the incomprehensibility of God.

> [Die Schrift] zeigt uns Gott in seinem Wirken als Offenbarer, als Offenbarung, als Offenbarsein oder als Schöpfer, Versöhner und Erlöser, oder als Heiligkeit, Barmherzigkeit und Güte. In diesen Unterschieden können und sollen wir der Unterschiede der göttlichen Seinsweisen in der uns zugemessenen und angemessenen Wahrheit einsichtig werden. Die Schranke unseres Begreifens liegt darin, daß wir, indem wir diese Unterschiede *begreifen*, die Unterschiede der göttlichen Seinsweisen selber *nicht begreifen*.[55]

The economic trinity does not exhaust the immanent trinity. The conceptuality of God gained in the doctrine of the Trinity remains a "creaturely" conceptuality. The possibility of its simultaneously being a true conceptuality lies not in the capacity of human reason to comprehend the divine but in the grace of God, a thesis brought to expression in Barth's notion of the *analogia fidei*. The conception of theological language which presses itself at this point is, of course, not without its own peculiar set of problems, problems which will require careful consideration at a later moment.

In sum, it is clear that Barth intends to exclude the speculative place which the doctrine of the Trinity has sometimes occupied from his own theological scheme. The doctrine performs rather an anti-speculative function by setting criteria for authentic theological language—not by disallowing talk of God in Himself, but by disallowing all talk of God which is not rooted in the concrete object of theology, God's self-revelation in Jesus Christ.[56]

The Doctrine of the Trinity as the Content of Prolegomena

The most striking feature of Barth's trinitarianism is the place which he expressly assigns the doctrine. It is found at the beginning of the massive *Kirchliche Dogmatik*. Yet its significance consists not simply in its position as a first dogma or as the beginning of the doctrine of God, but rather in its place within the prolegomena. That is, the doctrine is designated within the Barthian scheme not merely as a piece of material dogmatics, not even as the chief doctrine of dogmatics, but as the presupposition upon which dogmatics must proceed. It is here where the historical novelty of Barth's accomplishment lies. It signals a new place for the doctrine, which as Ebeling says, "has never before been the case."[57]

The full implications of Barth's decision in this regard, however, are not immediately clear. It remains to be seen in what sense the function of the doctrine is actually formed by its place among the prolegomena. It also remains to be seen in what sense the function of prolegomena is influenced by Barth's doctrine of the Trinity. Before identifying the precise relationship between the doctrine and the prolegomena, it is necessary to uncover Barth's distinctive understanding of the theological task of prolegomena, the question to which we now turn.

Prolegomena—The Doctrine of the Word of God

Barth defines prolegomena as "den Versuch einer expliziten Rechenschaftsablage über den besonderen Erkenntnisweg, der in der Dogmatik begangen werden...soll." (KD I/1, 24). The consistent motif is the explication of the path of knowledge which is peculiar to theology as a scientific discipline. Yet this may not be understood in a strictly epistemological sense. Barth offers as a paraphrase of the same definition, the ascertainment of the particular point, "von dem aus in der Dogmatik gesehen, gedacht und geurteilt werden soll" (24). Thus in Barth's understanding we have to do with a fundamental perspective, an interpretive framework very much like what is referred to in the contemporary philosophy of science as a "paradigm."[58] It is a path to knowledge in the sense that without this fundamental perspective a further material gain for the discipline is out of the question.

It is axiomatic for Barth that this fundamental perspective is gained from within the horizon of Christian theology itself and not from an external source.

> Prolegomena zur Dogmatik sind nur möglich als ein *Teilstück der Dogmatik selber*. Die Silbe Pro- in dem Wort Prolegomena ist uneigentlich zu verstehen: es handelt sich nicht um die *vorher*, sondern um die *zuerst* zu sagenden Dinge.[59]

There is no "place" outside or above the dogmatic undertaking from which it may be viewed and assessed. Prolegomena are worked out within the boundaries of dogmatic theology, which for Barth means within the boundaries of faith and the Church. The reason for this necessity is for Barth rooted in the very character of Christian theology, a character which Barth expresses in the actualistic category of "event."[60] The character of dogmatics is thus equivalent to that of the Church, namely as *actus purus*, not a continually present phenomenon, but an event contingent only upon the free decision and grace of Jesus Christ (41).

A number of alternative conceptions of the task of prolegomena are excluded by the Barthian definition. Prolegomena is not an exercise in apologetics (25–30). Apologetics is suspect precisely for its attempt to establish a ground for theological statements outside the realm of faith, thus losing sight of the object which theological statements seek to bring to expression. Nor is the question of existence or an analysis of human "pre-understanding" the appropriate task of theological prolegomena (35–39). Such undertakings, evident from Schleiermacher to Bultmann, are implicitly seeking to ground the possibility for faith within human existence, or as the case may be, within a given ontology or anthropology. Barth is equally critical of what he identifies as the distinctly Catholic prolegomena (39–41). Catholic theology seeks to ground itself in the entities of Scripture, tradition and in the teaching office of the Church, which together form an objective principle of knowledge, which the *fides catholica*, the subjective principle of knowledge, then accepts. Barth protests that the continuity in this movement from objective to subjective principles of knowledge incorporates a manifestation of the *analogia entis*, such that God's gracious act is dissolved into a human undertaking.

For Barth then the task of prolegomena to theology is to provide an account of its language on the basis of the object which it seeks to bring to expression.[61] Its character is unabashedly circular. For Barth there is no question of an external foundation which would provide the necessary perspectives and methodological principles appropriate to the theological task. Prolegomena is inescapably drawn from that which it precedes.[62]

The act of giving an account (*Rechenschaftsablage*) of theology's peculiar language, which is the special task of prolegomena, includes for Barth the exercise of critique and correction of that language (43). Critique and correction, however, are possible only on the basis of criteria. And if prolegomena is to operate only within the boundaries of the dogmatic task itself, then it follows that the criteria must be determined on the basis of that task, or rather, on the basis of its subject matter. Barth identifies this criterion as the Word of God (42f). Barth intends thereby to maintain a certain parallel to Protestant scholasticism for which typically prolegomena meant a definition of the theological task followed by a *locus* on Scripture and a *locus* on God, the *principium cognoscendi* and the *principium essendi* respectively.[63] At the same time he must be careful not to commit the same error for which he has taken Catholic theology to task. It is insufficient simply to begin with a doctrine of Holy Scripture as was generally customary in the dogmatic tradition. One must begin with the ontically prior question of the God whose revelation in Scripture makes that Scripture holy in the first place.[64] The ontically prior *principium essendi* must precede the *principium cognoscendi*.

Barth's Doctrine of the Word of God is far more then than a Scripture principle, even though Barth contends that the Scripture is the decisive criterion upon which the doctrine is developed, and even though a doctrine of Scripture is included as a portion of the Doctrine of the Word of God.[65] The Word of God means for Barth the reality that God speaks to humankind.[66] It is the comprehensive category with which he brings to expression the Christian claim to revelation. And for theology it is the objective norm to which all theological statements are subject.[67]

The Word of God has manifest itself to the Church in three forms: the Word written in the Scripture, the Word proclaimed, and the Word revealed in Jesus Christ. Together these three forms compose the comprehensive reality of God's revelation, and the treatment of each of these forms comprise the dominant part of Barth's prolegomena to the *Kirchliche Dogmatik*. Barth brings each of these three forms of the Word of God to expression in terms of a linguistic character,[68] in actualistic categories,[69] and often in the categories of personalism.[70] In each of its three forms (and always through one of its forms) the Word of God is an event of personal encounter in which the person is addressed by God in his revelation. But the three forms are neither equal nor interchangeable—a clear priority exists. The written Word of God is superior to the Word proclaimed.[71] The written Word has "imposed itself" upon the life of the Church as the norm by which its proclamation is to be judged (109–11). Superior to both the written and proclaimed Word is the revealed Word.[72] While the other two forms can be God's revelation indirectly, God's Word as revelation is rooted only in itself as direct revelation. The revelatory character of the first two forms is derived from the third, the actual revelation of God in history. It is within the context of this third form of the Word of God, that the doctrine of the Trinity assumes its decisive function within the prolegomena.

The Doctrine of the Trinity as the Analysis of the Concept of Revelation

As the above discussion has indicated, Barth identifies the criterion for critique and correction in theology with the doctrine of the Word of God. The task of prolegomena, which consists formally in the elaboration of the criterion, will consist materially in an analysis of the threefold Word. Accordingly, an explication of theology's peculiar path of knowledge means for Barth an elaboration of the doctrines of Holy Scripture, Church Proclamation, and of Revelation. It is consistent with a well established Barthian motif, that he selects the analysis of revelation as the first in this series of three discussions, since revelation provides the ground for Scripture and proclamation. Revelation is the ontically prior reality, and Scripture and proclamation are merely noetically prior.[73]

The first material task of the prolegomena then is an analysis of revelation. In practice this means an analysis of the *concept* of revelation. Dogmatics is unable to deal with the actual reality of revelation (308f). The actual reality is bound up with the redemptive past and the eschatological future. It is realized in the present only by means of the *concept* of revelation. This relativizing of revelation is, however, simultaneously balanced by the way in which Barth is able to speak of the *Faktum* of revelation (309f). The fact of revelation is the reality which ontically precedes faith, and consequently the dogmatic task. Prolegomena and indeed the whole of dogmatics assume the acknowledgment of God's self-revelation to which the Scripture bears witness. The possibility of proceeding on the basis of a concept of the possibility of revelation or the belief in revelation, as though it were a hypothesis to be confirmed, are excluded by Barth's interpretation of the method of theology.[74]

Barth identifies the doctrine of the Trinity with an analysis of the "fact of revelation".

Die Analyse dieses Faktums als solche wird nichts anderes sein
können als eine Entwicklung dessen, was in der Dogmatik aller
Zeiten unter dem Namen der Lehre von der göttlichen *Trinität*
seine eigentümliche Rolle gespielt hat. Die Antwort auf die Frage
nach der inneren Möglichkeit dieses Faktums wird gegeben einer-
seits durch die grundlegenden Sätze der *Christologie*, anderseits
durch die grundlegenden Sätze über die Wirksamkeit des *Heiligen
Geistes*. (309)

A thorough treatment of the doctrine of the Trinity, thus stands at the
beginning of Barth's lengthy chapter on the "Revelation of God," followed by
a section on the incarnation of the Word and another on the outpouring of the
Holy Spirit. Together these discussions form what for Barth is the appropriate
content of theological prolegomena and what is in effect the whole of
dogmatics *in nuce*.

The concept of revelation for which the doctrine of the Trinity is the
appropriate analysis is summarized by Barth in the formula, "God reveals
Himself as Lord."[75] The formula represents a summary of the whole biblical
witness to the God who reveals himself in history through his word and deed.
Emphasis falls squarely upon the assertion that revelation is to be understood
as God's act and as God's word. Revelation moves in a single direction—from
God to humankind.[76] The revelation formula represents a summary of the fact
of revelation. It is the ground of the doctrine of the Trinity insofar as
revelation is the ground of the doctrine (329), and indeed, for Barth, there can
be no other ground for the doctrine outside of revelation.[77]

This is not to say, however, that Barth derives the doctrine of the Trinity
on the basis of the formula.[78] He would appear to see the doctrine given with
the revelation itself. Correct interpretation of God's revelation requires that it
be interpreted as the ground of the doctrine of the Trinity.[79] Scripture bears
witness to revelation in such a way that our understanding of the God who
reveals himself there can only be in terms of the Trinity doctrine. Therefore,
the revelation formula "God reveals Himself as Lord" is and must already be

formulated in such a way as to contain the doctrine of the Trinity which its analysis will reveal.[80]

The analysis of revelation proceeds by putting the right questions to revelation. The right questions arise for Barth from the "fundamental problems" which Scripture itself places before us (311).[81] The foremost problem consists in the claim to uniqueness which revelation makes. For Barth, this translates into the demand that revelation must be understood primarily in terms of its subject, namely, in terms of the God who reveals himself. Theology asks, "Who is the God who reveals himself?" The line of inquiry moves inexorably to a second question: "How does God actually reveal himself?", and finally to a third: "What is the consequence or effect of revelation for the person?" The analysis concludes that it is the same God in undisturbed unity who is at once Revealer, Revelation, and Revealedness (315). On this basis Barth justifies his thoroughgoing treatment of the Trinity at the very beginning of the *Kirchliche Dogmatik*.

> Dies ist der zunächst bloss anzugeigende Sachverhalt, durch den
> wir uns angewiesen sehen, die Lehre von der Offenbarung mit der
> Lehre von dem *dreieinigen* Gott zu beginnen. (312)

The doctrine of the Trinity functions then for Barth as an analysis of the fact of revelation. As analysis, however, it can make no claim for identity with revelation (325). The doctrine of the Trinity is a "work of the Church." It is a document, a text, which has arisen in the history of the Church, which relates only indirectly to the text of the revelatory witness. It relates to the revelatory witness as an "interpretation," a "translation," and an "exegesis." Thereby Barth intends to secure the "distance" which exists between the doctrine and revelation and between the doctrine and the Scripture (325).

This relativizing of the doctrine by no means implies its arbitrariness. While not directly identical with revelation, it is nevertheless "indirectly identical" (326). It is an interpretation, but it is a "correct" (*zutreffende*) interpretation (327). The doctrine of the Trinity is a "necessary" and "appropriate" (*sachgemäss*) analysis of revelation (326).

To summarize, Barth employs the prolegomena to establish the comprehensive norm for theological speech. This norm, the Word of God, is in its direct and most authentic form the self-revelation of God in Jesus Christ. The doctrine of the Trinity is the single most appropriate exegesis of the revelation event. Its analysis yields an unmistakable threefold schema which identifies God as the Revealer, the Revelation, and the Revealedness. This threefold repetition of God justifies a further inquiry into the doctrine of the Trinity as the necessary and appropriate interpretation of revelation, which is of course identical with the self-revealing God Himself.

In this early methodological phase of Barth's discussion of the doctrine in which justification is sought for its role as the dominant content of the prolegomena, the doctrine would appear to function almost solely as a heuristic or even rationalistic device which prepares the way for a dogmatic theology which will simply move through the three traditional articles of the creed. There would appear to be justification for Pannenberg's suggestion that in contrast to his declared intentions Barth is actually developing a speculative doctrine of the Trinity, based not on the findings of exegesis or the relationship between Jesus and the Father which exegesis points up, but on the "innere Logik des Offenbarungsbegriffs".[82] This is true, however, only if the analytical discussion is taken in isolation from the material discussions which follow in §§ 10–12, entitled God the Father, God the Son, and God the Holy Spirit, respectively. While the procedure there is no less analytical, the biblical narrative of salvation becomes far more prominent in providing language and categories for bringing the Trinity doctrine to expression. This is equally true for the role which the doctrine plays in later volumes of the *Kirchliche Dogmatik*.

Thus far, it is only the formal place of the doctrine that has been the object of focus. It remains to be seen how the place of the doctrine in the prolegomena actually functions in relationship to the remainder of the *Kirchliche Dogmatik*, thus giving a view to the actual content and effect of the trinitarian perspective. We must turn to an overview of the function of the doctrine within the whole of the work if we are to bring this crucial aspect to light.

Place of the Doctrine in the Remainder of the *Kirchliche Dogmatik*

In the foregoing discussion we have developed the distinctive approach of Barth to the problem of prolegomena as the construction of a fundamental perspective or paradigm which consists of the necessary assumptions and axioms for the dogmatic task. Prolegomena perform theology's obligatory task of giving account of its language and disciplinary method. The criterion which it employs must however come from the content of the dogmatics for which prolegomena prepare the way. This criterion is the Word of God, and its explication leads inevitably to the doctrine of the Trinity. We are thus justified in speaking of a trinitarian paradigm, the construction of which is the peculiar task of the prolegomena. But a paradigm is not an end in itself. It rather offers a fundamental perspective through which one is enabled to bring order to a given field of data or experience.

A certain understanding of how this paradigm operates for Barth has already been gained by considering the traditional "places" of the doctrine of the Trinity and their relevance for the *Kirchliche Dogmatik*. There a number of aspects became clear: the doxological and soteriological orientation of the doctrine, its critical function of defending against natural theology and abstraction in talk of God, and its anti-speculative character. Each of these may be understood as particular functions of the fundamental perspective formed by the Trinity doctrine. It now remains to be seen how this perspective is actually operative within the *Kirchliche Dogmatik* as a whole.

Trinitarian Aspects of the *Kirchliche Dogmatik* as a Whole

Any overview of the *Kirchliche Dogmatik* which is not a book in itself must necessarily be selective. While comprehensiveness is not possible within the space allowed this discussion, it is worthwhile to select a few of the more significant doctrinal developments of the work and consider them in light of the trinitarian paradigm for which Barth lays the foundation in the prolegomena. *(1)* Following his development of the Trinity doctrine in its many formal aspects, Barth turns to a material consideration of the Father, Son, and Holy Spirit in I/1, §§ 10–12 respectively. The trinitarian perspective (including the rules of "appropriation") is determinative for the entire discussion. God the Father is known not initially as the Creator nor even as "our Father" except by virtue of his revelation as the Father of Jesus Christ (412f). The Father is He who reveals in the event of revelation. The Father reveals Himself to humanity preeminently upon the cross (411); He is the "Lord of our existence" (409), the one who sets human existence radically into question (407). By appropriation we are able to speak of Him as Creator (415). If the Father is known only through Jesus Christ, then Jesus Christ is likewise Himself Lord (419). He is the revelation in which the Father has revealed Himself. The revelation of Christ is the *self*-revelation of God. By appropriation He is known to us as reconciler (465). The Holy Spirit designates the event in which a person comes to acknowledge revelation (470). The Holy Spirit is the subjective side of revelation (472). The divinity of the Holy Spirit is evidenced in the fact that the possibility of redemption is not a possibility for human existence. The certainty of redemption lies solely in the promise of God (481f). Just as God makes himself known through each of these Modes of Being in his revelation, so he is eternally the triune God. God can be Father, Son, and Holy Spirit in His revelation, because He is already Father, Son, and Holy Spirit antecedently in Himself (411, 435, 489f).

Each of the remaining moments of the prolegomena are likewise considered from the vantage point of the trinitarian perspective. The doctrine of the triune God provides the ontological assumption upon which the following dogmatic sections proceed. In §13 Barth articulates the doctrine of the incarnation as not only the objective reality of revelation but also as the objective possibility of that reality. That revelation is possible is read off from the fact of its occurrence and not from any "higher" perspective. Yet the whole argument proceeds on the basis of the trinitarian perspective which was established in the previous paragraphs. The incarnation is taken up not as an event concerned solely with the second Person of the Trinity—It is not purely an exposition of christology. The incarnation is an event *appropriated* to the Son in recognition that it is a work executed in the unity of Father, Son, and Spirit (KD I/2, 36–9). The trinitarian theology allows Barth to ground the possibility of the incarnation in an eternal reality in the life of God (34f).

An initial ecclesiology is presented under the rubric of the out-pouring of the Holy Spirit as the "*subjective* possibility" of revelation (874). Thereby the life of the Church is presented in a corresponding way in thoroughgoing trinitarian categories. The Church is so to speak the space, the arena of the subjective reality of the revelation. The answer to the question of what fills this space, that is, what the Church actually is, is the outpouring of the Holy Spirit (242). The sacraments constitute an "objective side" in which the subjective reality of revelation, the Holy Spirit, comes to expression (253). Even ethics, the expression of the love of God in the believer, is grounded ultimately in the doctrine of the Trinity. It is the love of God in Himself, the fellowship of love which is the Father, Son and Holy Spirit, that enables the believer to love (415).

The doctrine of the Trinity informs the detailed discussions of the two other forms of the Word of God. The "objective possibility" of the Word of God for the Church is the Scripture (874). The authority of Scripture resides

not in itself *per se* but in the witness which it offers to the triune God (510f).
The "subjective possibility" of that reality resides in the reality of proclamation
(874). It is likewise the witness to the revelation itself which bestows authority
and dignity on the preaching event.

(2)   The trinitarian perspective also informs the doctrine of God in a number
of ways beyond the explicit discussion of the trinitarian titles. Most prominent
is the framework it forms for Barth's theological epistemology. Not only does
the doctrine identify the God who is the object of theological inquiry, but it
grounds the possibility of human knowledge about Him. God is object first of
all to Himself as the God who knows Himself in the Trinity. This is Barth's
notion of "primary objectivity" (KD II/1, 14–18). The knowledge of God which
comes to the believer by way of revelation is a "secondary objectivity." The
"primary objectivity" enables and authorizes the free decision in which God
becomes secondarily objective to human beings.[83] "Ist das wahr, dass Gott vor
dem Menschen steht, sich dem Menschen zu erkennen gibt und vom Menschen
erkannt wird, dann ist das daraufhin und darin wahr, dass Gott der Dreieinige
ist, Gott der Vater, der Sohn und der Heilige Geist" (52).

The doctrine of God proper is likewise developed on the trinitarian field
of reference. The doctrine of the Trinity stands against any effort to draw a
concept of God from any source other than His act of revelation in which He
reveals Himself as Father in the Son through the Holy Spirit (293). There is no
other source from which a doctrine of God may be derived than the doctrine
of the Trinity (292f). Each of the divine attributes must root itself in revelation
and thus in the Trinity if it is to be an authentic theological expression. The
omnipresence of God, for instance, means not an abstract infinitude, but the
realization that God is "present" to the creature in a "togetherness" at a
distance (527). This presence and the spatiality which it implies is possible
because God is eternally present to Himself as the triune God in his own

"spatiality" (527). Likewise, the divine omnipotence and eternity must each correspond to a feature of the triune God of revelation.[84]

(3) Barth's doctrine of Election forms perhaps one of the most thoroughly trinitarian sections (outside of the prolegomena) of the entire *Kirchliche Dogmatik*.[85] Barth's reinterpretation of the traditional doctrine dispenses with the dark mystery of an arbitrary election in an eternal divine decree. In its place is the doctrine of the election of grace in which Jesus Christ is both the electing God and the elect man (KD II/2, 110). The doctrine of Election as Barth has formulated it comes to expression by means of a trinitarian drama, forming a bridge between eternity and temporality and between the divine essence and the history of salvation. It is God's election in eternity, an event in the triune life, played out among the trinitarian Persons, which forms the foundation for the drama of reconciliation of humanity in Jesus Christ.

> Es war im Anfang die Wahl des *Vaters*, diesen Bund mit dem Menschen darin wahr zu machen, dass er seinen Sohn für ihn dahingab, um selbst Mensch zu werden zum Vollzug seiner Gnade. Es war im Anfang die Wahl des *Sohnes*, der Gnade gehorsam zu sein und also sich selbst hinzugeben und Mensch zu werden, damit darin jener Bund seine Wirklichkeit habe. Es war im Anfang der Beschluss des *Heiligen Geistes*, dass die Einheit Gottes, die Einheit des Vaters und des Sohnes durch diesen Bund mit dem Menschen nicht gestört, geschweige denn zerrisen, vielmehr um so herrlicher werde, dass die Gottheit Gottes, die Göttlichkeit siener Freiheit und seiner Liebe eben in diesem Hingeben des Vaters und in seinem Sichhingeben des Sohnes sich bestätigen und bewähren solle. (109)

The significance of the trinitarian drama for Barth's Doctrine of Election is to be found in its ability to demonstrate that God's grace which results in reconciliation is not simply a decision of divine benevolence. Rather, it is the outworking of the very nature of God (cf. 129).[86]

(4) The doctrine of Creation is likewise developed in a thoroughly trinitarian context. Creation is first among the outward works of God. Its significance for Barth lies in its place among the series of God's works which constitutes His

covenant of grace, the divine plan for the salvation of humanity (KD III/1, 45f). Creation is the "outward ground" of the covenant of grace, the prepared space or stage where the historical drama of salvation occurs (44–6). This interpretation of the doctrine of Creation derives from the trinitarian perspective from which Barth views it. "Die entscheidende Verankerung der Erkenntnis der Zusammengehörigkeit von Schöpfung und Bund ist die Erkenntnis, dass Gott der Schöpfer der *dreieinige* Gott ist, Vater, Sohn und Heiliger Geist" (51). Because the doctrine of the Trinity affirms that the Creator God is also in His essence the loving, electing, and reconciling God, then creation will be understood as a moment along the path of God's plan of salvation. The Trinity would stand against any attempt to interpret creation as a general concept significant in its own right (51).

As if the trinitarian context of the doctrine does not come through clearly enough in its basic statement, Barth offers a reflection on the doctrine in light of the trinitarian rule *opera trinitatis ad extra sunt indivisa*, that is, in light of the unity of the outward works of the triune persons (52–63). The Father is identified *per appropriationem* in the confessions of the Church as the Creator. As the one who eternally begets the Son and breathes forth the Spirit, He is thereby appropriately designated Lord and Creator of all things. But creation is "through the Word." It is in His love for the Son that the Father created and loves the world. The real ground of creation is to be found in the light of the incarnation and the cross, in that the real purpose of creation becomes manifest (53f). The Holy Spirit relates to creation in that in the Holy Spirit God's being for the creature and the creature's being for God become possible. In the Spirit the fellowship of Father and Son are realized. Thus in the Spirit the whole reality of God's fatherly mercy, His self-revelation, His self-glorification in the Son, the promise, the power of the Gospel, and the whole order of the relation between the Creator and the creation find their pre-existence. The creature then in a sense pre-exists in the Holy Spirit, for the

Spirit makes that existence possible in and through His special trinitarian function.[87]

(5)   Barth's Anthropology also shows evidence of interpretation from the perspective of the trinitarian paradigm. The christological ground of anthropology in the *Kirchliche Dogmatik* is widely recognized. Thus, when Barth considers men and women in their relationships to others, self, and time, it is Jesus Christ in His relatedness that is the theme. The being of the man Jesus, is a being for others (KD III/2, 243ff). That Jesus is the man for others is a mystery rooted in the mystery of God Himself. Jesus' relation to others is an outward repetition of a relationship which exists in the inner life of God. The relation of Jesus to others is the image of God's inner relation. The love of God in his trinitarian inner-life, a love between others, is the origin (*Urbild*) and source of the basic I and Thou human relation (260). The possibility of human love finding expression is thus a possibility rooted ultimately in the triune God.

(6)   The trinitarian perspective guards the doctrine of Providence against arbitrary speculation upon God's activity in the world. The God of providence is the trinitarian God (KD III/3, 132–4). He is as Father, Son, and Spirit eternally love in Himself. His will and his works in the world will reflect his eternal nature of being for the other, and thus the mercy and grace revealed in Jesus Christ. A doctrine of Providence must reflect this understanding of God if it is to be genuinely Christian.

(7)   The interrelationship between the doctrine of Reconciliation and the doctrine of the Trinity is sufficiently extensive as to defy brief summary.[88] At the outset of his discussion of the doctrine of Reconciliation Barth calls upon the doctrine of the Trinity to identify the God who is reconciling and to identify Jesus Christ from the very beginning as the divine and eternal Son of God (KD IV/1, 140–3). The event of reconciliation in Jesus Christ is portrayed as an event in correspondence with God's own inner history (222f). The

humanity of Christ, like the divinity, is also the consequence of a trinitarian determination (KD IV/2, 33). It is rooted in the election of grace executed by God in eternity, a divine decision prior to all others in its significance. In the context of the doctrine of Reconciliation Barth offers a reflection on a Christian view of history, which means of course a trinitarian view of history (372ff). The history of God with the world through Jesus Christ is a "little history" which in fact forms the heart of all world history—the rest is mere accompaniment (373). Three decisive features emerge from the specific Christian history: (1) the existence of the man Jesus as the foundation and beginning of this history, (2) the Church, that is, the Christian community as the goal of this work of God begun in Christ Jesus, and (3) God's self disclosure as transition between the two (375f). Thus in each of these three decisive factors of history, one encounters God himself—three times God. A formal correspondence to the doctrine of the Trinity emerges, even though there is no material correspondence except in the third factor which would correspond to the Holy Spirit. Barth identifies the formal correspondence in the following schema which corresponds to the three named factors: God as origin, God as goal, and God as the reality of transition between the two (375–77). God as the origin of this history in the existence of Jesus Christ which already includes its goal corresponds to God the Father in his trinitarian life as *fons et origo totius Deitatis*. And the second factor, i.e., the goal which corresponds and refers back to its origin of that history, is analogous to the Son who in the eternal inner life of God simultaneously is loved by the Father and loves the Father in return. In the third factor we have to do with the Holy Spirit, who performs a mediatory function both in the case of the *opus trinitatis ad extra* or salvation history and in the case of the *opus ad intra* whereby the mutual love of Father and Son is mediated through the Spirit. It is this third material correspondence which confirms for Barth the correspondence between the form or structure of that history with God's trinitarian essence. Barth claims that we cannot think of this history as a whole without being stimulated and invited to think of the triune God (378f).

(8) The final planned volume of the *Kirchliche Dogmatik*, the doctrine of Redemption was never written. The pneumatology and ecclesiology which it would have treated, however, are significantly anticipated in a number of key sections within the work. The doctrine of the Church is formed by the trinitarian perspective such that Christian talk about the Church must simultaneously be talk about the Holy Spirit. The gathering of the Church is the work appropriated to the Holy Spirit (KD IV/1, 722f, 726f). The Church is indeed a concrete, historical, and human phenomenon, but it is a phenomenon which occurs in so far as the Church is awakened or given birth by the Word of God (728f). The trinitarian perspective informs Barth's doctrine of the Church in such a way that it can only be thought of in terms of its transcendent roots, as an historical manifestation of the trinitarian drama of reconciliation.

The foregoing has presented but a few of the significant lines of thought within the *Kirchliche Dogmatik* in an attempt to illustrate the effects of the trinitarian paradigm in some of their more overt forms. Certain functions in particular have emerged numerous times: (1) The trinitarian paradigm identifies concretely the God with whom theology is concerned. This identifying function stands as a guard against foreign, abstract, and speculative concepts which threaten the uniquely Christian understanding. (2) By locating the ground of God's salvific acts within God's triune being and essence, talk of God is oriented soteriologically. (3) The eternal trinitarian drama which the paradigm presupposes forms the background against which the historical drama of salvation must be interpreted and within which it finds its ultimate ground.

The Problem of Trinitarian Systematization in the *Kirchliche Dogmatik*
The suggestion of a fundamental perspective of any type in the *Kirchliche Dogmatik* raises in an acute form the problem mentioned at the beginning of

the chapter, namely, the problem of systematization in the *Kirchliche Dogmatik*.[89] Barth himself has harsh words for dogmatic theologies which seek to forge an internal set of relationships by means of a dogmatic system, a concept which Barth understands as "ein unter Voraussetzung einer bestimmten *Grundanschauung* mit Benützung bestimmter Erkenntnisquellen und bestimmter Axiome aufgebauter, in sich abgeschlossener und voll-ständiger Zusammenhang von Grundsätzen und Folgesätzen" (KD I/2, 963). Dogmatic systems as such not only deprive the theologian of his relative autonomy in his efforts to interpret the Word of God, but moreover, "im dogmatischen System bekommt die vorausgesetzte Grundanschauung unvermeidlich die Stellung und Funktion, die nach allen unseren Überlegungen allein dem Worte Gottes zukommen kann" (964). Barth expressly denies that he has used the Trinity as the basis of a system from which doctrines may be derived.[90] Even the architectonic of the work as originally planned which divided the work into the doctrine of God, followed by the doctrines of Creation, Reconciliation, and Redemption is according to Barth derived not from the doctrine of the Trinity but from the same "fact of revelation" from which the Trinity doctrine itself is derived (983). Barth's aversion to systematization is rooted in his principle of the "theonomy" of the dogmatic task, according to which theological method must respect the freedom and lordship of revelation. Systematization effects a violation of the theonomy principle (958, cf. 911). The Word of God is not reducible to any human principle or dogma. The use of a principle or doctrine or even a *concept* of the Word of God as the centerpiece of theology means the selection of an arbitrary foundation upon which the theological work will falter (964f, 968).

This vigorous aversion to systems would appear to stand in serious tension with our own thesis that Barth has developed a trinitarian paradigm which offers a vantage point for ordering and understanding theological statements. The problem, however, arises largely from an ambiguity surrounding the word "system." When pressed by a student regarding the apparent "syste-

matic" character of the *Kirchliche Dogmatik*, it was the ambiguity of the word
to which Barth immediately pointed:

> We must distinguish at least three uses of the term "systematic": (1)
> systematic as regards orderly and thoughtful organization of
> material; (2) systematic in that it claims to be exhaustive in its
> interest, believing that revelation has something to say to all areas
> of life; (3) systematic in the sense of being derived from a main
> principle or group of principles. I will admit that the *Church
> Dogmatics* is systematic in the first two senses, but not in the last.[91]

What appears on the surface a rather casual delineation couched in everyday
language actually offers a profound insight into the "systematic" character of
the *Kirchliche Dogmatik*. This is evident if we compare Barth's remarks to a
more scientific classification of the variety of "systems" which are possible for
theological thought. Joest distinguishes three dominant types: a deductive
system, a "unified thematic" which is essentially non-systematic in character
although unified by a common theme, and a system of classification (*Zu-
ordnungsystem*).[92] The deductive system derives a comprehensive set of
statements on the basis of a given set of definitions and axioms. Mathematics
is the obvious model for deductive systematization. Barth clearly rejects this
kind of system as an option for Christian theology, although as Joest points out,
in a strict form it has hardly ever been realized in theology.[93] The second
possibility, that of the unified thematic assumes in theology the form of a series
of themes (*loci*), the ordering of which is determined by a methodological
principle or pattern such as a generally recognized confession of faith, the
development of Scripture as a whole, or the history of salvation. Barth
identifies his own methodological choice with this pattern:

> Wir haben zu der Methode der *Loci* zurückzukehren, die die
> Methode *Melanchthons*, aber auch die *Calvins* gewesen ist und die
> von den fortgeschritteneren Zeitgenossen des *J. Gerhard* und *A.
> Polanus* zu Unrecht als unwissenschaftlich beiseite gestellt wurde.
> Gerade sie ist die in der Dogmatik allein wissenschaftliche
> Methode. Eben die *Loci* der älteren Orthodoxie waren nämlich
> noch solche dogmatische Grundsätze, die aus keiner höheren Ein-
> heit als eben aus der des Wortes Gottes selbst hervorgehen, keine

höhere Synthese als eben die des Wortes Gottes selbst zum Aus-
druck bringen wollten, die in keiner höheren Systematik als
wiederum der des Wortes Gottes selbst begründet und zusammen-
gehalten waren. (973)

The third possibility offered by Joest is the system of classification. Like
the deductive system, one or more basic ideas are explicitly stated. The rest of
the "system," however, does not necessarily derive from these basic ideas. Other
sources are also possible. The systematic character is won by classification, such
that theological statements "are understood, interpreted, and set into relation
with one another" in light of the basic idea(s).[94] The collective statements of the
"system" form a "context of reference" in the middle of which stand the basic
ideas.

While Barth would want to identify the *Kirchliche Dogmatik* with the
second possibility, the evidence would place it closer to the third. The
classification system is actually quite compatible with his own admission "as
regards orderly and thoughtful organization of material" as well as the claim to
comprehensiveness.[95] His rejection of any organizing principle other than the
Word of God (968) would seem, however, to require further explanation. It is
accountable on two fronts. First, even though Barth is quite conscious of the
infringement upon the freedom of the theologian which a deductive system
entails (963), he would appear to underestimate the infringement which occurs
simply by means of an "orderly and thoughtful organization of the material".[96]
In the language of our own thesis, Barth would appear to underestimate the
paradigmatic function of the doctrine of the Trinity which he develops in the
first half-volume of the *Kirchliche Dogmatik*. Secondly, it is apparent that in his
polemic against systematization in theology there is a certain confusion between
the source of theology as expressed in ultimate terms and the human devices
which are employed for bringing a concept of ultimacy to expression. This is
ever so surprising in light of his emphasis upon the human and limited
character of every dogmatic statement. There is no dogma of the Church which

more than approximates what Barth has described as the "eschatological concept" of dogma (967). Dogmatics is "ein *menschlicher* Akt..., der in sich keinerlei Gewähr für die Richtigkeit der in Frage stehenden Aneignung bietet, der in sich vielmehr fehlbar und also selber der Kritik und Korrektur, der nachprüfenden, überbietenden Wiederholung bedarf" (KD I/1, 13). Nevertheless, Barth is able to speak of such a thing as "pure doctrine" as a possibility for dogmatics. For "reine Lehre ist ein Ereignis" (KD I/2, 859) which happens by grace of the Word of God. It is difficult to see, then, as Barth is forced to maintain, how a limited, human principle of organization is able to silence the Word of God, when limited, human dogmas are able to become vehicles of its expression. Barth's justifiable reserve toward a deductive system would seem to have effected a radicalization of his anti-system polemic, one consequence of which is an unwillingness on his part to recognize the subtle systemizing dynamic of his own "orderly and thoughtful organization," an important part of which is the trinitarian paradigm.

The doctrine of the Trinity does not of course form the only fundamental perspective at work in the *Kirchliche Dogmatik*. It is not the singular key for interpreting the work of Barth. It stands alongside other fundamental or axiomatic truths which wax and wane in their relative influence upon the dogmatic stuff. At times the trinitarian perspective would appear to diminish while christology alone comes to the fore.[97] At other points Barth's Scripture principle seems to become the dominant perspective. The view defended here, however, is that the trinitarian paradigm is a pervasive perspective which informs the formation of thought at a number of crucial junctures throughout the *Kirchliche Dogmatik*. That this operation is hermeneutically significant is the thesis which occupies the remainder of our discussion.

The Hermeneutics of Place

That the peculiar place which Barth assigned the doctrine of the Trinity is a hermeneutically significant decision is an observation often noted by Barth's commentators. Jüngel speaks of the placing of the doctrine at the beginning of the whole Dogmatics as a "hermeneutical decision of the greatest relevance."[98] This is evident to Jüngel not only because the doctrine of the Trinity is placed where one would expect to find a hermeneutical reflection in a dogmatic theology, but also because Barth's trinitarian prolegomena offer a foundation and starting point for the entire theological task as well as a starting point for a distinctively Barthian hermeneutic.[99] The theological foundation and the hermeneutic are of course by no means separate subject matters in the prolegomena, but rather two complementary descriptions of a single subject matter. The hermeneutical relevance of the theologian's efforts to give an account of his method and presuppositions is a frequent theme of contemporary hermeneutical theology. Gerhard Ebeling has pleaded for an understanding and employment of "hermeneutical theology" in just such a way:

> [Das Stichwort "hermeneutische Theologie"] meint also nicht eine Teildisziplin oder einen speziellen Stoffbereich, auch nicht ein beliebiges Sonderinteresse. Es will vielmehr auf etwas hinweisen, was eo ipso zur Theologie gehört und bei jedem Theologietreiben wirksam ist. Selbstverständlich wird nicht behauptet, damit sei über das Wesen von Theologie alles gesagt. Es könnten entsprechend auch andere Wesensmerkmale hervorgehoben werden. Aber es wird in der Tat beansprucht, damit werde, jedenfalls unter den gegenwärtigen Erfordernissen und Möglichkeiten theologischer Rechenschaft, die Wurzel theologischer Problematik am tiefsten und deshalb auch die Weite theologischer Aufgabe am umfassendsten auf den Begriff gebracht.[100]

What Ebeling considers the proper content of this hermeneutical task diverges considerably of course from Barth's own prolegomena. Yet, the formal delineation is remarkably similar.

The intention of the foregoing discussion has been to suggest in concrete terms the hermeneutical significance of Barth's placement of the doctrine of the Trinity. We have described this significance in terms of a trinitarian paradigm—a fundamental perspective drawn from the content of dogmatics itself which offers the necessary context in which all further theological expression must be placed. By using the word "paradigm" to describe the comprehensive hermeneutical significance which Barth attaches to the doctrine it is hopefully clear that we have already ventured an interpretation of Barth's own re-interpretation of the Trinity doctrine. While the concept is itself external to Barth's thought, coming rather from recent developments in the philosophy of science, its intention is to emphasize a particular feature which we believe is internal to Barth's prolegomena and which has received far less attention than it deserves. In Thomas Kuhn's landmark essay, *The Structure of Scientific Revolutions*,[101] he defines paradigms as expounded bodies of theory, which historically have shared two characteristics:

> Their achievement was sufficiently unprecedented to attract an enduring group of adherents away from competing modes of scientific activity. Simultaneously, it was sufficiently open-ended to leave all sorts of problems for the redefined group of practitioners to resolve.[102]

A paradigm for science may mean a comprehensive system which deduces universal constants as in the case of Newtonian physics or may consist simply of a quantitative law, such as Boyle's law relating gas pressure to volume, or Joule's formula relating generated heat to electrical properties.[103] A paradigm forms the basis for the rules and principles employed by a science. It is more fundamental than particular rules or principles, and a plurality of conflicting rules are in principle possible on the basis of the same paradigm. The paradigm offers not only the criteria by which problems facing a discipline are solved, but it also defines the problems themselves. For as a fundamental perspective it functions to define the horizons which comprise the investigator's field of perception. A problem is a problem only insofar as it is visible within that given field.

This concept of paradigm points the way to the problem of verification. How does one prove a paradigm? In the history of science the question is one

that rarely finds an application. Paradigms are not disproved so much as they
are replaced. For as Kuhn explains,

> Paradigms gain their status because they are more successful than
> their competitors in solving a few problems that the group of
> practitioners has come to recognize as acute. To be more success-
> ful is not, however, to be either completely successful with a single
> problem or notably successful with any large number. The success
> of a paradigm—whether Aristotle's analysis of motion, Ptolemy's
> computations of planetary position, Lavoisier's application of the
> balance, or Maxwell's mathematization of the electromagnetic
> field—is at the start largely a promise of success discoverable in
> selected and still incomplete examples.[104]

It is the heuristic success of a paradigm which in the end acts as its principle
of verification or falsification.

It is this heuristic dimension of Barth's Trinity doctrine and its hermeneutical employment within the *Kirchliche Dogmatik* which we hope to emphasize
by speaking of it in paradigmatic terms. This aspect of the doctrine of the
Trinity is consistent with his own description of the doctrine as a "critical
principle" which is simultaneously a "working hypothesis."[105] Moreover, this
interpretation of the doctrine has the advantage of avoiding what has become
the post-modern critical nemesis of Barth's revelational theology, namely the
charge of "revelational positivism."[106] The doctrine of the Trinity as hermeneutical paradigm cannot be regarded as a set of givens (*posita*) without any prior
ground or relation to human life or experience which enter into theology
demanding obedient acknowledgement. It will be the object of the remainder
of this work to demonstrate that the relationship to experience (via philosophy,
tradition, language, and the question of human existence) is integral to the
Barthian paradigm, even though it refuses to allow general experience to
become the field from which theological truth is derived. Barth's Trinity
doctrine does not drop from heaven with the grim ultimatum "Believe or
perish." Rather, it presents itself as an invitation to faith to understand its
cognition and talk about God in a particular way, the verification of which

depends ultimately on its ability (whether in the *Kirchliche Dogmatik* or elsewhere) to insightfully address the problems which are the object of theology and to fruitfully lead the way to application in Christian praxis.

ENDNOTES

[1]The most comprehensive work to date on the history of the doctrine remains the three volume work of F. C. Baur, *Die christliche Lehre von der Dreieinigkeit und Menschwerdung Gottes in ihrer geschichtlichen Entwicklung*, I–III (Tübingen: Osiander, 1843). The recent work by Edmund J. Fortman, *The Triune God: A Historical Study of the Doctrine of the Trinity* (Grand Rapids: Baker, 1972), offers a comprehensive overview of essential texts but suffers from a certain superficiality in its analysis. On the earliest development of the doctrine cf. also G. Kretschmar, *Studien zur frühchristlichen Trinitätstheologie*, Beiträge zur historischen Theologie 21, ed. G. Ebeling (Tübingen: Mohr, 1956); J. N. D. Kelly, *Early Christian Doctrines* (New York: Harper, [3]1965); Harry Austryn Wolfson, *Faith, Trinity, Incarnation*, The Philosophy of the Church Fathers, I (Cambridge, Mass.: Harvard, 1956); and A. M. Ritter, "Dogma und Lehre in der alten Kirche," in *Die Lehrentwicklung im Rahmen der Katholizität*, Handbuch der Dogmen- und Theologiegeschichte, I, ed. Carl Andresen (Göttingen: Vandenhoeck & Ruprecht, 1983), 99–283.

[2]Robert Jenson, "The Triune God," in *Christian Dogmatics*, I, ed. C. Braaten & R. Jenson (Philadelphia: Fortress, 1984), 140. Cf. C. M. LaCugna and K. McDonnell, "Returning from 'The Far Country': Theses for a Contemporary Trinitarian Theology," SJTh 41 (1988) 191–215. The authors defend the context of doxology and the source of salvation history as the decisive criteria for a contemporary doctrine of the Trinity.

[3]Jenson, "Triune God," 108f.

[4]A phrase with which E. Schlink wants to describe the theological root of the doctrine. E. Schlink, "Trinität, III," [3]RGG, VI, 1032.

[5]Gregory of Nyssa, *Against Eunomious*, in *Opera*, vols. 1–2, ed. W. Jaeger (Leiden: Brill, 1960), 3/7.53.13. Cited R. Jenson, *The Triune Identity* (Philadelphia: Fortress, 1982) 26.

[6]M. Luther, "The Three Symbols or Creeds of the Christian Faith," 1538, in *Luther's Works*, American Edition, vol. 34. 219. Tr. R. R. Heitner from WA 50, (255) 262–283. Cf. the well-known warning of Melanchthon: "Mysteria divinitatis rectius adoraverimus, quam vestigaverimus." In "Introductio," *Loci Communes*, 1521. Melanchthons Werke, vol. II (Gütersloh: C. Bertelsmann, 1952), 6.

[7]Schlink, 1033f.

[8]Ibid.

[9]Kelly, 234–42; 338–44. James P. Mackey has recently emphasized the polemical place of the early doctrine to the extent that its further usefulness for Christian faith is seriously questioned: "...most of the positions finally occupied by the orthodox are positions to which they are driven rather than positions they would otherwise have chosen. It would be foolish indeed to believe without question that the end results of the long and discreditable struggles of the fourth century would inevitably coincide with the theological results of peaceful reflection by these same Christian men (who on both sides behaved in the most unchristian manner) on the data of Scripture and on the actual experience of truly Christian living.... The more defensive a position is seen to be, the less claim it has to

permanence after the particular threat it was meant to meet has declined." *The Christian Experience of God as Trinity* (SCM: London, 1983), 170.

[10]C. Welch, *The Trinity in Contemporary Theology* (SCM: London, 1953), 3.

[11]Karl Rahner, "Der dreifaltige Gott als transzendenter Urgrund der Heilsgeschichte," *Mysterium Salutis*, Grundriss heilsgeschichtlicher Dogmatik, II (Einsiedeln: Benziger, 1967), 319. ET = *The Trinity*, tr. J. Donceel (New York: Herder & Herder, 1970), 10. The following observations are adapted from this essay. Welch notes a similar situation within contemporary fundamentalism, such that "while the Trinity is maintained as a necessary part of the faith, it is mostly accepted on authority and left aside as largely irrelevant to life." Welch, 41.

[12]Rahner, 319. ET, 10.

[13]Ibid., 322. ET, 14.

[14]Ibid., 323–27. ET, 15–21. Barth shares this point of critique with Rahner. He warns of the *schwerste Gefahr* of losing sight of the *Konkretheit* of God as it is manifest in *der trinitarischen Gestalt des christlichen Gottesbegriffs* when one begins inquiry in a place other than with the triune God. Further, it is when the doctrine loses its place of prominence, becoming an addition or supplement to the doctrine of God, that the real danger of speculation begins. KD I/1 316f.

[15]Rahner, 324f. ET, 17f.

[16](1) The Second Person of the Trinity is equated with finite existence, physical nature and finite spirit. The generation of the Son and the creation of the world are not essentially distinct. (2) The divine *oikonomia* assumes a new role distinct from its traditional relation to the revelation and redemption in Christ. It is now the general world historical process. Welch, 12f.

[17]Ibid., 15–17. Cf. Wolfhart Pannenberg, "Die Subjektivität Gottes," *Grundfragen systematischer Theologie*, II (Göttingen: Vandenhoeck & Ruprecht, 1980), 96–111. Pannenberg identifies Dorner as the key influence behind Barth's own doctrine of the Trinity (99). In Pannenberg's analysis, however, Barth actually stands closer to Hegel's speculative idealism than Dorner does (100). For Pannenberg, Barth's doctrine would easily assume the role we have designated here as philosophical trinitarianism, a view which we do not share for reasons that will become evident below.

[18]So the analysis of Welch, 15–17.

[19]Philosophical trinitarianism is of course hardly limited to the venerators of Hegelian Idealism. Charles Hartshorne's analogy of the Trinity which emerges from his anthropological metaphysics and Dorothy Sayers' derivation of the doctrine from an analysis of human artistic experience are but two examples from a vast field of contenders. Welch, 77f, 85–92.

[20]Friedrich Schleiermacher, *The Christian Faith*, ET, ed. H. R. Mackintosh & J. S. Stewart (Edinburgh: T. & T. Clark, 1902), §170. [= *Der christliche Glaube*, II, ed. Martin Redekker (Berlin: de Gruyter, 1960), 458.]

[21]Welch, 18f.

[22]Ibid., 19f.

[23]Ibid., 3f.

[24]Cf. the radical historical critique of the doctrine and in particular Barth's interpretation of it in Samuel Laeuchli, "Das 'Vierte Jahrhundert' in Karl Barths Prolegomena," in *Theologie zwischen Gestern und Morgen: Interpretationen und Anfragen zum Werk Karl Barths*, ed. W. Dantine and K. Lüthi (Munich: Kaiser, 1968), 217–34. The doctrine of the Trinity is a *kulturelles Phänomen*. "Mit dem Fallen dieser kulturellen Lage der Kirche fällt die Trinitätslehre." (229) "Die Trinitätslehre läßt sich nicht übersetzen, weil sie zum Imperium und zur Philosophie des 4. Jahrhunderts gehört." (229) Mackey applies the historical-critical critique with an equally sustained vigour, yet draws conclusions far less severe. "The need is long overdue to adopt a thoroughly historical approach to the whole issue." Mackey, 104. The dawning of historical consciousness and the realization that the doctrine of the Trinity and indeed all dogmas are human creations which are no less historically conditioned than the Old or New Testaments need not lead us to patent rejection. Rather, dogma "must be set in relation to the richer and more varied theologies of Scripture" and "to the foundational faith of Christians which comes to them from Jesus." (104) The discovery of the historical conditioning of the Trinity is an invitation to contemporary believers to imitate the Fathers, "who were themselves only too painfully aware of the risks and the courage required to advance their own creative reformulations of the faith," (103) and recover the doctrine of the Trinity in a way that points to the living faith of Jesus. On Laeuchli, see below, 158ff.

[25]Technically the distinction belongs to the predecessor to the KD, sc., *Die christliche Dogmatik* (CD), Barth's self-declared "false start" which like KD I/1 and I/2 was also designated "prolegomena." The doctrine of the Trinity already figures prominently in its place within the prolegomena of the CD.

[26]G. T. Thomson, "Note by the Translator," in *Church Dogmatics* I/1 (Edinburgh: T. & T. Clark, 1936), v.

[27]G. W. Bromiley and T. F. Torrance, "Editor's Preface," in *Church Dogmatics* I/1 (Edinburgh: T. & T. Clark, [2]1975), ix.

[28]The problem forms one of the major themes of the Barth - Harnack correspondence. "Die Aufgabe der Theologie ist eins mit der Aufgabe der Predigt. Sie besteht darin, das Wort des Christus aufzunehmen und weiterzugeben." TFA, 10.

[29]"Die Notwendigkeit der Dogmatik ist eine andere als die der kirchlichen Verkündigung." KD I/1, 84.

[30]KD I/2, 939.

[31]Cf. KD I/1, 323, 405f, 445f, 492.

[32] Following Kantian logic, Barth intends a process which explicates solely that which is contained in the object of inquiry, as opposed to a synthetic process in which different objects are brought together for the formulation of new knowledge. See below, 55.

[33]"Das Trinitätsdogma...will uns nicht über die Offenbarung und den Glauben hinaus, sondern in die Offenbarung und in den Glauben hinein, zu ihrem rechten Verständnis führen." KD I/1, 416f.

[34]Cf. Otto Weber, who defends the same point with some vigor in *Grundlagen der Dogmatik*, I (Neukirchen: Verlag der Buchhandlung des Erziehungsvereins, 1955), 419–30. ET = *Foundations of Dogmatics*, I (Grand Rapids: Eerdmans, 1981), 379–88.

[35]Cf. KD I/1, 393f, 415–19, 465, 497f. Barth affirms the definition employed by Thomas Aquinas: "Appropriation is nothing other than ascribing something which is common to an individual [Person]...not...such that it is more fitting for one Person than the others...but rather such that that which is common, has a greater similarity to that which is the property of the particular Person than to the properties of the others." *De veritate*, Qu. 7, Art. 3. Cited KD I/1, 394. (My translation).

[36]A more thorough discussion of the peculiar problems of language inherent in Barth's doctrine which urge themselves at this point follows in Chapter 5.

[37]KD I/1, 391.

[38]"Warum sollten uns jene *begreiflichen* Unterschiede in Gottes Offenbarung nicht in ihrer ganzen Vorläufigkeit vor das Problem seiner *unbegreiflichen* und ewigen Unterschiede stellen?" KD I/1, 393.

[39]Emil Brunner, *Dogmatik*, I (Zürich: Zwingli-Verlag, 1946), 251. ET = *Dogmatics*, I, tr. O. Wyon (Philadelphia: Westminster, 1949), 235. Cited by Welch, 164f.

[40]Brunner, 251. ET, 235.

[41]Robert Jenson, *God After God* (Indianapolis: Bobbs Merrill, 1969), 95f.

[42]Ibid., 95–122.

[43]Ibid., 97f.

[44]Ibid., 99.

[45]Ibid., 96.

[46]Title of §9.4, KD I/1, 395–404.

[47]The polemical place of the doctrine is perhaps most striking with Barth in his treatment and rejection of the doctrine of *vestigium trinitatis* (KD I/1, 352–67). See below §5.2.1.

[48]For Barth speculation is talk about God whose "Voraussetzung die sein müßte, daß wir Gott eben doch beizukommen vermöchten." (KD I/2, 255) That is, speculation is by definition talk about God which draws from a source other than God's own self-revelation. Revelation is the criterion. A definition of speculation as any talk of God which transcends our experience of God has for Barth already fallen into error by employing an arbitrarily chosen criterion (in this case an anthropological one) for theological language.

[49]"Wir kommen nicht auf einem anderen Weg zur Trinitätslehre als eben auf dem Weg einer Analyse des Offenbarungsbegriffs." KD I/1, 329. Cf. 352.

[50]"Der Trinitätslehre aber entnehmen wir in der Tat: wer der Gott ist, der sich offenbart." Ibid., 328.

[51]"Als ob nicht bei der Lehre von der Heiligen Schrift sowohl wie bei der Lehre von Gott die schwerste Gefahr bestünde, daß man sich in Erwägungen verliert und zu Festellungen veranlaßt sieht, die mit dem angeblichen konkreten Gegenstand beider Lehren gar nichts zu tun haben, wenn man dessen Konkretheit, wie sie eben in der trinitarischen Gestalt des christlichen Gottesbegriffs manifest ist, zunächst dahingestellt sein läßt." Ibid., 317.

[52]It is this aspect of Barth's doctrine in which Eberhard Jüngel recognizes a common intention between Barth's doctrine of the Trinity and Bultmann's program of demythologization. The function of Barth's doctrine to disallow the possibility of deriving, supporting, or confirming the event of revelation by means of a *logische Konstruktionsmöglichkeit* (KD I/1, 365) corresponds to the category of myth which for Bultmann means to talk about "the unworldly as worldly, the gods as human." R. Bultmann, "New Testament and Mythology," *New Testament & Mythology*, tr. S. Ogden (London: SCM, 1984), 10. The fundamental intention of each to protect language about God from inauthentic intrusions is the same. It is the criteria by which that language is tested which is at variance. Eberhard Jüngel, *Gottes Sein ist im Werden* (Tübingen: Mohr, 1965), 22f, 33, 71f. ET = *The Doctrine of the Trinity* (Grand Rapids: Eerdmans, 1976), 11f, 21f, 58–60.

[53]KD I/1, 391. See above, 46.

[54]"The 'economic' trinity is the 'immanent' trinity, and the 'immanent' trinity is the 'economic' trinity." Rahner, 328. ET, 21f.

[55]KD I/1, 392. The formal device of the "appropriations" as an "improper" mode of speaking allows Barth to place a certain distance between the *doctrine* of the Trinity and the inner divine life. (Ibid., 416f Cf. also KD II/1, 76f) Barth denies he is committing an "encroachment" (*Übergriff*) upon the divine life in his assertion of the possibility of knowledge of the inner life of God. The encroachment is the divine encroachment of revelation. Any human encroachment consists in resisting this revelation.

[56]Cf. Hans Schwarz, "Die Aktualität des Trinitarischen im christlichen Gottesglauben," TZ 44 (1988) 211–21. Schwarz argues that in precisely this function of the historical doctrine its decisive relevance for contemporary protestant theology is to be found.

[57]Gerhard Ebeling, *Dogmatik des christlichen Glaubens*, I (Tübingen: Mohr, [3]1987), 14. "Die Prolegomena selbst [nahmen] schon die Dogmatik in nuce in sich auf, indem hier sogar, was zuvor nie der Fall gewesen ist, die Trinitätslehre ihren Ort fand."

[58]Sally McFague, following Thomas Kuhn, defines a paradigm in this sense as "a basic set of assumptions, shared beliefs, key models, and accepted exemplars" within which a relatively homogenous scientific community conducts its work. Sally McFague, *Metaphorical Theology* (London: SCM, 1982), 79.

[59]KD I/1, 41.

[60]"[Evangelische Dogmatik] weiß, daß alle ihre Erkenntnis—auch und gerade die Erkenntnis von der Richtigkeit ihrer Erkenntnis—nur Ereignis sein, nicht aber von einem Ort abseits und oberhalb dieses Ereignisses als richtige Erkenntnis gesichert werden kann." KD I/1, 42.

[61]"Die dogmatische *Methode*, d.h. der Weg, den die dogmatische Arbeit, in Anspruch genommen durch ihren Gegenstand, gehen muß, muß wie die dogmatische Norm identisch sein mit der in der Schrift bezeugten Offenbarung als Gottes Wort, sofern diese eben nicht nur Norm, sondern auch Weg: bestimmter, in sich selbst gegliederter und geordneter Inhalt ist. In und mit diesem Inhalt ist, wie der kirchlichen Verkündigung, so auch der Dogmatik ihr Weg, ihre Methode grundsätzlich vorgegeben." KD I/2, 957.

[62]Thus Gogarten's criticism that "in diesem Fall de facto die ganze Dogmatik zu den Prolegomena [gehört]" which he registered with regard to the CD (in which Barth's conception of prolegomena is already fully stated) would appear to miss the point, or at least refuse to take it seriously. Friedrich Gogarten, "Karl Barth's Dogmatik," TR 1 (NF) (1929) 62.

[63]Richard Muller, *Dictionary of Latin and Greek Theological Terms* (Grand Rapids: Baker, 1985) 245f, 248.

[64]"Unser Grund, von dieser Gewohnheit abzuweichen, ist dieser: Es läßt sich schwer absehen, wie denn über die Heilige Schrift das für die Heiligkeit nun gerade dieser Schrift Bezeichnende gesagt werden kann, wenn nicht zuvor (natürlich aus der Heiligen Schrift selbst) klar gemacht ist, wer denn derjenige Gott ist, dessen Offenbarung die Schrift zur heiligen macht." KD I/1, 317.

[65]"Wir werden sehen, daß der Kardinalsatz der Lehre vom Worte Gottes, die wir im folgenden zu entwickeln versuchen, in der Tat sachlich kein anderer sein wird als der von der Autorität und Normativität der Heiligen Schrift als des Zeugnisses von Gottes Offenbarung und als Voraussetzung der kirchlichen Verkündigung." The form of the doctrine as "eine Lehre von Der Heiligen Schrift im Zusammenhang einer umfassenden Lehre vom Worte Gottes" Barth attributes to his dispute with Neo-Protestantism and Catholicism. Ibid., 43.

[66]"'Gottes Wort' heisst: Gott redet." Ibid., 137.

[67]"Die dogmatische Norm, d. h. die Norm, an die die Dogmatik die kirchliche Verkündigung und also zuerst sich selbst zu erinnern hat als an die objektive Möglichkeit reiner Lehre, kann keine andere sein als die in der Schrift bezeugte Offenbarung als Gottes Wort." KD I/2, 911.

[68]Linguistic character means for Barth that the Word is spiritual (KD I/1, 138–41), personal (141–44), and that it is intentional in the sense of address (an "uns gerichtetes, uns angehendes Wort") (144–47). In TT, a collection of transcriptions from Barth's colloquia from 1953–56, the linguistic/rational emphasis found in these passages is defended and even sharpened. "[Revelation] happens in the sphere of language—yes, in the literal sense—but it is the language of God. The language of God is nowhere without human language. You cannot divide the Word of God from human words. Think of the Prophets: 'Thus says the Lord:'—and then followed their Hebrew words! I do not think there is a Word of God alone—a Godly Word. Our praying is an attempt to speak to God. Our hearing is only an attempt. Our preaching is an attempt. But the attempt must be made. By means of this attempt God speaks!" (TT, 31). Even the "symbols" of Christianity must be understood in terms of their linguisticality: "The Cross is a Word of God and therefore a Word for us, but not apart from the witness of Holy Scripture and proclamation. The Word in the sacraments (I do not like this term 'sacrament'!) is not more than language, but another form of language. And the sacraments are not without words" Ibid., 31.

[69]On proclamation see KD I/1, 95–97; on Scripture, 111–13; on revelation, 119–24.

[70]"Gerade in seinem Wort ist Gott Person" (KD I/1, 143). The Word addresses us in an encounter which does not dissolve personal being. "Die Begegnung mit dem Worte Gottes ist echte, unaufhebbare, d.h. nicht in Gemeinschaft aufzulösende Begegnung" (146). Cf. Barth's definition of revelation as *Dei loquentis persona*, which he elaborates as follows: "Gottes Offenbarung ist nach der Schrift Gottes eigenes unmittelbares Reden, nicht zu unterscheiden von dem Akt dieses Reden, also nicht zu unterscheiden von Gott selbst, von dem göttlichen *ich*, das dem Menschen in diesem Akt, in dem es *du* zu ihm sagt, gegenübertritt" (320, emphasis mine). Barth speaks of the God who reveals himself as the "Subject" of revelation: "Das Subjekt der Offenbarung ist *das* Subjekt, das *unauflöslich* Subjekt bleibt.... Es kann nicht Objekt werden" (402, cf. 143). And "Gemeinschaft mit dem, der sich da offenbart, bedeutet für den Menschen auf alle Fälle und unter allen Umständen, dass jener ihm gegenübertritt wie ein Du einem Ich gegenübertritt und sich mit ihm verbindet, wie sich ein Du mit einem Ich verbindet. Nicht anders!" (402).

[71]This superiority is observed by Barth as a phenomenon in the life of the Church. "Die Unterschiedenheit des Hauptes vom Leibe und seine Überlegenheit über ihn drückt sich konkret darin aus, daß der Verkündigung in der Kirche eine ihr als Phänomen höchst ähnliche, wie sie selbst zeitliche und nun doch von ihr verschiedene und ihr ordnungsmäßig überlegene Grösse gegenübersteht. Diese Größe ist die *Heilige Schrift*." (Ibid., 103) The superiority of Scripture over proclamation consist in "die schlechthin konstitutive Bedeutung der ersteren für die letztere, die Bedingtheit der Wirklichkeit heutiger Verkündigung durch ihre Begründung auf die Heilige Schrift und durch ihre Bindung an sie—also die grundsätzliche Auszeichnung des geschriebenen Propheten- und Apsotelwortes vor allem in der Kirche später gesprochenen und heute zu sprechenden sonstigen Menschenwort." Ibid., 105.

[72]Revelation is the "superior", and the Bible the "subordinate" principle. (Ibid., 116) Revelation *erzeugt* the Scripture (117), which becomes a *Bezeugung* to revelation (114). Revelation is the source from which the other two forms are only derived: "Die Offenbarung ist nach allem Gesagten ursprünglich und unmittelbar, was die Bibel und die kirchliche Verkündigung abgeleitet und mittelbar sind: *Gottes Wort*" (120). Cf. 309f.

[73]Barth develops his notion of the ontic priority of revelation to all human understanding most thoroughly in FQI. Cf. FQI, 40–59, "Der Weg der Theologie". "Ontische Necessität geht auch noetischer Rationalität voran: Die *Vernunft* der Erkenntnis des Glaubensgegenstandes besteht auch in der Anerkennung des ihm eigenen *Grundes*" (50). In the KD this translates into the axiom of the priority of reality over possibility. Thus the reality of knowledge of God precedes any question regarding its possibility. (KD I/1, 194–8) A discussion of the incarnation begins with the "objective reality" of revelation (KD I/2, §13.2) and is only then followed with a discussion of the "objective possibility" (KD I/2, §13.2). Discussion of the reality and possibility of subjective revelation proceeds likewise. (KD I/2, §14) Similarly the *principium essendi* is given priority to the *principium cognoscendi*. (KD I/1 316f) The alternative in each case engenders the threat of abstraction, speculation, and a loss of the concreteness which is given with the object of theology.

[74]Cf. FQI, 40–59. "Die *Begründung* der Erkenntnis des Glaubensgegenstandes besteht in der Anerkennung des dem Glaubensgegenstand selbst eignen *Grundes*. Die ontische Necessität geht der noetischen voran" (50). "Das Faktum als solches, wie es etwa hinter dem Dogma von der Dreieinheit Gottes oder hinter dem von der Inkarnation sichtbar wird, ist unbegreiflich" (27).

[75]KD I/1, 311f, 323, 331f. With this formula we encounter the complex question which Barth designates the "root" of the doctrine. What follows is only a brief summary of Barth's understanding of the root. A more thorough analysis follows in the next chapter.

[76]Cf. Barth's concept of revelation as the proper object of theology, articulated in Barth's characteristic actualistic framework in the Barth—Harnack correspondence. "Ein Briefwechsel mit Adolf von Harnack," TFA, 167, 178–80. See also K. Barth, "Offenbarung, Kirche, Theologie," TFA, 158–166.

[77]Revelation is, as Barth is careful to indicate, the ground of *knowledge* of the Trinity. The three-in-oneness of God is grounded in an ultimate sense only in the being of God. Revelation does not determine the Trinity. The Trinity is an analysis not merely of revelation, but of the God who reveals Himself (who is identical with His revelation). KD I/1, 328f.

[78]Far from grounding the doctrine, the formula assumes it. Reacting to the negative critique of the similar formula employed in CD, 127, *Deus dixit*, and the Subject, Predicate, Object schema which formed the root of the doctrine in that discussion, Barth clarifies: "Ich dachte und denke natürlich nicht daran, die Wahrheit des Trinitätsdogmas aus der allgemeinen Wahrheit einer solchen Formel abzuleitien, sondern aus der Wahrheit des Trinitätsdogmas ist vielleicht die Wahrheit einer solchen Formel in diesem bestimmten Gebrauch, nämlich für das Trinitätsdogma abzuleiten." KD I/1, 312.

[79]KD I/1, 329. But Barth also relativizes this axiomatic status of the doctrine: "Aber das schliesst nicht aus sondern ein, dass die Dogmatik das Dogma zu *beweisen*, d.h. aber seinen Grund, seine Wurzel in der Offenbarung bzw. im biblischen Zeugnis von der Offenbarung nachzuweisen hat." 327.

[80]"Die Offenbarung muss, um richtig interpretiert zu werden, als Grund der Trinitätslehre interpretiert werden; man kann die für den Offenbarungsbegriff entscheidende Frage nach dem sich offenbarenden Gott nicht in Absehung von der in der Trinitätslehre gegebenen Antwort eben auf diese Frage beantworten, sondern gerade die Trinitätslehre ist die hier zu gebende Antwort." KD I/1, 329.

[81]See also KD I/1, 319; KD I/2, 1–3, 222f.

[82]Pannenberg, "Subjektivität," 101.

[83]See below, 193ff.

[84]On omnipotence, see KD II/1, 595; on eternity, 693f.

[85]Jüngel recognizes the significant interrelationship of these two doctrines in the KD and considers the consequent implications for the being of God. See Jüngel, *Gottes Sein*, 95. ET, 82f.

[86]The doctrine of election stands at the pinnacle of Barth's ontological concept of the trinitarian *Urbild* which grounds not only salvation history but the whole of the created order. See below, 192ff.

[87]The creation of man as male and female is interpreted from an explicit trinitarian perspective. The simultaneous otherness and togetherness which characterizes the male-female relationship is prefigured (following an *analogia relationis* and not the *analogia entis*) in the eternal otherness and togetherness of the triune God. "Wie sich das anrufende Ich in Gottes Wesen zu dem von ihm angerufenen göttlichen Du verhält, so verhält sich Gott zu dem von ihm geschaffenen Menschen, so verhält sich in der menschlichen Existenz selbst das Ich zum Du, der Mann zur Frau." KD III/1, 220. Cf. TT, 46.

[88]Cf. John Thompson, "On the Trinity," *Theology Beyond Christendom*, ed. John Thompson, Princeton Theological Monograph Series 6 (Allison Park, PA: Pickwick Publications, 1986). Thompson seeks to draw out the doctrine of the Trinity implicit in vol. IV of the KD in order to demonstrate its greater richness and profundity over the explicit doctrine in KD I/1 which in his view suffers from a certain formalism.

[89]On the problem of "theological systems" see Wilfried Joest, *Fundamentaltheologie* (Stuttgart: Kohlhammer, 1974), 237f; Weber, 65–79; ET, 50–62. G. Gloege, "Dogmatik," [3]RGG II, 228; G. Sauter, "Dogmatik I," TRE IX, 43–70; S. W. Sykes, "Systematic Theology," in *A New Dictionary of Christian Theology*, ed. A. Richardson & J. Bowden (London: SCM, 1983), 560–62. On the question of a system in the KD, compare the thorough discussions in Hans Geisser, "Die Trinitätslehre unter den Problemen und in den Prolegomena christlicher Theologie" (Unpubl. Diss., Tübingen, 1962), 385–456, and Isidro García-Tato, *Die Trinitätslehre Karl Barths als dogmatisches Strukturprinzip* (Bad Honnef: Bock & Herchen,

1983), esp. 604–73. Cf. also Hans Urs von Balthasar, *Karl Barth* (Einsiedeln: Johannes, 1976 [=1962]), 201–10, 230–5. ET = *The Theology of Karl Barth*, tr. J. Drury (New York: Holt, 1971), 164–70, 181–85; and G. Cornelius Berkouwer, *The Triumph of Grace*, trans. H. R. Boer (Grand Rapids: Eerdmans, 1956), 13–17.

[90]"Das organisierende und disponierende Zentrum der Dogmaitk ist darum doch nicht die Trinitätslehre, sondern befindet sich ausserhalb der Reihe der *Loci*, zu denen als Teil der Gotteslehre auch die Trinitätslehre gehört." KD I/2, 983.

[91]TT, 23f.

[92]Joest, *Fundamentaltheologie*, 237. A more common distinction is that between a formal and material system. Cf. Weber, 68–77; ET, 53–62. As Weber seems to recognize, however, the point at which a system in form becomes a system in material is in practice difficult to ascertain. Ibid., 77f; ET, 61.

[93]Joest, *Fundamentaltheologie*, 237. Cf. KD I/2, 963.

[94]Joest, *Fundamentaltheologie*, 237. (My translation)

[95]See quotation above, 69.

[96]As Joest points out, this infringement need not be understood in a purely negative way. For even the method of the *Loci* is not without its own fundamental perspectives. The classification system has the advantage of making explicit what in the *Loci* is only implicit. Further, "in der Gestalt des Zuordnungssystems kann eine Theologie ihre Aussagen und vor allem ihre Grundvoraussetzungen m.E. durchsichtiger vermitteln und besser Rechenschaft über Voraussetzungen, Zussammenhang und Begründung ihrer Aussagen geben, als wenn die (faktisch irgendwie doch wirksame) Perspektive unexpliziert (und vielleicht sogar unreflektiert) bliebe. Das ist für das Gespräch sowohl 'nach aussen' als innerhalb der Theologie selbst ein Vorteil." Joest, *Fundamentaltheologie*, 238.

[97]Cf. Weber's observation: "Barth's approach is unmistakably Trinitarian. Yet one gains the impression that at times the basic Christological conception, instead of being incorporated into this approach, actually replaces it." Weber,79. ET, 62.

[98]Jüngel, 15. ET, 4.

[99]Ibid., 15f. ET, 4f.

[100]Gerhard Ebeling, "Hermeneutische Theologie," *Wort und Glaube*, II (Tübingen: Mohr, 1969), 105.

[101]International Encyclopedia of Unified Science, II, 2 (Chicago: Univ. of Chicago Press, [2]1970).

[102]Ibid., 10.

[103]Ibid., 28.

[104]Ibid., 23f.

[105]TT, 48f, 54.

[106]For an instructive analysis of this profound though often misunderstood critique of Barth which originated with Bonhoeffer, see Regin Prenter, "Dietrich Bonhoeffer und Karl Barths Offenbarungspositivismus," *Die mündige Welt*, III (Munich: Kaiser, 1960), 11–41.

CHAPTER THREE

Philosophical Influences upon the Development of the Trinitarian Hermeneutic

In the previous chapter we observed the presence of a trinitarian paradigm throughout the *Kirchliche Dogmatik* whose hermeneutical function it is to provide the proper context for interpreting the subject-matter of theology and a systematic ordering of its subsequent content. In the present and following chapter the concern is to consider the derivation or construction of the trinitarian hermeneutic in light of the criteria which Barth himself establishes for a biblical hermeneutic. The present chapter is divided into four sections. The first offers a sketch of the relevant criteria which Barth would defend for a biblical hermeneutic. The second considers his development of a trinitarian hermeneutic in light of those criteria. This will carry us to a consideration of what Barth designates as the "root" of the doctrine of the Trinity. The third section considers the presence of philosophical influences at work in Barth's trinitarian construction and the problems which this poses for Barth's employment of the doctrine as a hermeneutical device. The fourth and final section offers a critical assessment of the harmful effects introduced into Barth's trinitarian hermeneutic via "unreflected" philosophical thought forms. Chapter four extends the present discussion with a consideration of the related problem of the influence and role of tradition upon Barth's trinitarian construction.

The intention behind this exercise is twofold. It should first of all allow a fresh insight into the tension between Barth's claim to derive the Trinity from the biblical concept of revelation and the presence of unacknowledged philosophical concepts in the derivation of the doctrine. This means clarity with regard to the correspondence between Barth's declared theological method and the hermeneutical function which he executes with the doctrine of the Trinity. Secondly, the perspective which the study gains should offer a platform from which Barth's antipathy toward a philosophically articulated hermeneutic may be addressed, a concern taken up at the conclusion of the work.

Barth's Biblical Hermeneutic

Barth's own contribution to the field of hermeneutics has been largely overshadowed in the contemporary discussion. This is true in part because of the impressive corpus of works dealing directly with the hermeneutical question which stem from the theological line associated with the names of Bultmann, Ebeling, and Fuchs. The theological orientation of this hermeneutical school is considered in many ways to be an alternative or competitor to the program of Barth. Barth's own declared aversion to an undue emphasis upon a hermeneutical formalism would appear to be another factor in the neglect of his contribution to the field.[1] Nevertheless, Barth does speak to the problem of a biblical hermeneutic, and his contribution has not gone wholly unrecognized by specialists in the field.[2]

Barth's biblical hermeneutic may be brought together under five general descriptive headings: (1) intrabiblical, (2) fiduciary, (3) content-oriented, (4) nonspecialized and (5) confessional.[3]

For Barth it is axiomatic that God has spoken, speaks, and will speak through his written Word, the Bible. The written Word forms the norm and criterion by which the proclaimed Word is measured (KD I/2, 505). Consequently, dogmatics, whose task it is to scrutinize the proclaimed Word, is itself "determined" by the revelation of God *as Scripture bears witness to it* (910). On an ultimate level it is the Word of God alone which informs and guides dogmatics. On the penultimate and human level this means that it is the collection of texts known as Holy Scripture to which dogmatics must orient itself, to which dogmatics must listen, and upon which dogmatics must draw for its task (917f). Theology for Barth is bound to give the biblical texts an elevated status above all other texts (557).

> Damit sind wir an diese Texte gebunden und können uns die Frage nach der Offenbarung nur stellen, indem wir uns der in diesen Texten bezeugten Erwartung und Erinnerung unsererseits hingeben. (545)

It is in this sense that Barth's hermeneutic may be spoken of as "intrabiblical"[4] or "intratextual."[5]

The intrabiblical hermeneutic excludes the possibility of grounding theological assertions in philosophical or non-biblical ideas (KD I/1, 86), which is to say in alternative "texts." An intrabiblical and intratextual hermeneutic stands over and against an extra-biblical or intertextual hermeneutic. The philosophical language and constructs of alternative "texts" may be allowed for articulating or illustrating theological reflection, but the theologian must constantly guard against allowing external concepts to usurp that place which belongs only to the Word of God as source and norm of dogmatics.[6]

A second crucial aspect of Barth's biblical hermeneutic is the self-vindicating character of the Bible's authority for the Church. It is in this sense that Barth represents a "fiduciary" hermeneutic.[7] It is the Bible which offers the answer to the question of the concept of revelation, an answer which points the way to the doctrine of the Trinity. It is this simple fact which for Barth grounds the authority of the Bible for theology.

> Der grundlegende Satz dieser Lehre, der Satz: dass die Bibel das Zeugnis von Gottes Offenbarung ist, ist selber schlicht darin begründet, dass die Bibel auf unsere Frage nach Gottes Offenbarung tatsächlich Antwort gegeben, dass sie uns die Herrschaft des dreieinigen Gottes vor Augen gestellt hat. (KD I/2, 511)

Acknowledgment of the Bible's function as normative witness to the divine revelation and a willingness to subject oneself to that witness is a happening with no ground outside itself. It is for Barth a "ganz wunderbares und ganz schlichtes, ganz anspruchsloses Geschehen" (506). Once the revelation of the triune God has occurred, there can be no going back, no searching for external

90   Philosophical Influences

or internal reasons and justifications for the authority of the Bible. Within the Church there is simply a memory that in this book the Word of God has been heard, and consequently there is an expectation that that Word will be heard there again (588f).

Barth is sharply critical of an historicist approach to the Scripture (545–48). While historical-critical work is prerequisite to an understanding of the text, it represents a danger to theology when the object of interpretation becomes the historical facts which lie behind the text and when the main concern becomes a reconstructed history. It is rather the content of the text itself which is the proper concern of the interpreter. Thus, a third hermeneutical axiom for Barth is that interpretation must be guided by the content or subject-matter of the text, which is of course identical with the Word of God.[8] If the Scripture is really read as the Word of God, which for theology is the only way that it may be read, then the subject-matter of the text will be allowed to "seize" the reader (520). The text will cease to be an object as such, controlled, analyzed and understood by the interpreter. Rather, Barth speaks of the "sovereign freedom of the subject-matter" which imposes an *epochē* upon the reader (520). The text masters the reader instead of the reverse. It is the weight of this conviction in Barth's approach to Scripture which perhaps more than any other is responsible for his aversion to theories of "understanding" and hermeneutical "methods" in the approach to the biblical texts. Understanding is an event which comes to the interpreter from the side of the text and not vice versa.[9]

Barth does not wish to understand these hermeneutical principles as a special biblical hermeneutic in distinction from general hermeneutics. A fourth principle of biblical hermeneutics is its character as a nonspecialized undertaking. What applies hermeneutically to biblical texts applies equally to other texts in general.

Wir haben mit dem, was über die Offenbarung als den Inhalt des biblischen Wortes und über die durch diesen Inhalt vorgeschriebene Hermeneutik gesagt wurde, keineswegs ein mysteriöses Separatvotum zugunsten der Bibel ausgesprochen. (523)

Barth does observe, however, at least one very serious difference existing between biblical and general hermeneutics in practice. Biblical hermeneutics is thoroughly consistent in allowing the subject-matter to determine the interpretation of the text in that it acknowledges the sovereign freedom of that subject-matter. General hermeneutics allows itself this course only within certain limits in that it proceeds according to its own preconceived assumptions as to what is possible and what is true and develops its interpretation accordingly (812f).[10] Biblical hermeneutics demands an openness to the text, such that the text informs as to what is true and appropriate with regard to itself. The difference is due simply to a failure on the part of general hermeneutics to remain true to its task. It is in this sense that Barth will allow the designation of biblical hermeneutics as a special hermeneutics.

> [Die biblische Hermeneutik] muss gerade darum diese besondere Hermeneutik sein, weil die allgemeine Hermeneutik so lange tot- krank ist, als sie sich nicht durch das allerdings höchst besondere Problem der biblischen Hermeneutik auf ihr eigenes Problem mindestens hat aufmerksam machen lassen. (523)

The consistency of biblical hermeneutics in this regard, however, could just as easily become the insight of a general hermeneutic (815). It does not represent a special case or an exception to the rule on the part of biblical hermeneutics. On the other hand, this does not mean that biblical hermeneutics derives its principles simply from general hermeneutics. Quite to the contrary, the hermeneutic which biblical hermeneutics must apply is one derived from the Bible itself. And this hermeneutic is for Barth the "true" general hermeneu- tic.[11]

A fifth hermeneutical rule for Barth is that the authentic interpretation of Scripture happens in a confessional context. Barth would want to subordi- nate this rule to the other four, but one can hardly overestimate its influence in shaping the whole of his theology. By confessional context we mean Barth's insistence that the Scripture is read within a particular horizon, the horizon determined by the Church Fathers and the formal confessions of the Church (729). We are not alone when we read the Scripture. We stand in continuity with a particular historical community which has also read the same texts and which from time to time has expressed itself regarding their correct understanding and application.[12]

The confessions and the Church Fathers, among whom Barth would include the Reformers, clearly occupy a place of authority for Barth in the hermeneutical process. He devotes considerable space to an explanation and clarification of their authority with regard to the theologian's efforts to appropriate Scripture for the contemporary needs of the Church (672–740, 919–38). The authority of the confessions and the writings of the Church Fathers is an authority subordinate to the Scripture which they seek to interpret. They represent a human and fallible creation not binding upon the interpreter (694f). They form a "commentary" upon Scripture. They are, however, the "first commentary" with which the interpreter has to deal (728). The confessions challenge and test later understandings of Scripture by their own understandings which occupy a place of respect in the Church.[13]

Interpretation of Scripture is for Barth then a "confessionally determined" undertaking in the sense that the space or direction within which one carries out his own encounter with the text is marked off by the confessional tradition (728). One could perhaps speak of a confessional "pre-understanding" as the appropriate "pre-understanding" for a biblical hermeneutic. Barth dismisses as comical the notion of a presuppositionless exegesis (520).[14] The confessional starting point does no more violence to the text than any other set of presuppositions. Nor will it determine in advance the results of an interpreter's encounter with the text in the sense of depriving him of responsibility for his own exegesis and application. But it does mean that the direction proclaimed by the confession or the Church Fathers will have been taken seriously by the interpreter as an authority of the first rank (728).

Deriving the Doctrine of the Trinity

Each of these five hermeneutical principles find a certain degree of illustration in the hermeneutical process which is at work in Barth's derivation and development of the doctrine of the Trinity. Three significant moments of that development are considered below: (1) the analysis of revelation, (2) the role of christology, and (3) the derivation of the trinitarian relations.

The Analysis of Revelation

An analysis of the fact of revelation yields according to Barth an identification of God with the subject, object, and predicate of revelation, which in turn yields the pattern of Revealer, Revelation, and Revealedness. How Barth arrives at this analysis was outlined in the discussion of Chapter Two. What was also noted in that context is that Barth does not intend with this analysis to actually derive the doctrine nor even to confirm it. The point of the subject-object-predicate schema is simply to provide an introduction to the question and to indicate "dass und inwiefern wir durch die Offenbarung selbst an das Problem der Dreieinigkeit herangeführt werden" (KD I/1, 331).

When Barth turns to the question of "The Root of the Doctrine of the Trinity" in §8.2, he leaves aside the analytical schema and returns to the fact of revelation itself represented in the summary thesis, "God reveals Himself as Lord." The decisive question for an understanding of the root of the doctrine is the degree to which the form and content of biblical revelation correspond to the doctrine of the Trinity. Or in Barth's words,

> Muss man diesen Satz [Gott offenbart sich als der Herr] ohne der Einheit seines Gehaltes zu nahe zu treten, in einem dreifachen Sinn verstehen und ohne seinem dreifachen Sinn zu nahe zu treten, als einheitlich in seinem Gehalt? (331)

The root may be established by enquiring after the context which existed and does exist between biblical revelation and the historically developed doctrine and by determining how the latter was and is able to proceed from the former (332).

It is a question which can only be resolved on the ground of exegetical observation. Barth is of course under no illusion as to the presence of the doctrine in the biblical texts. The doctrine of the Trinity is a creation of the Church (325). It is given full expression in neither the Old nor the New Testament (331). Barth, therefore, intentionally lays aside passages in which tradition has often claimed to find the doctrine pre-figured, such as the Matthean baptismal formula (330f). On the other hand, Barth is certain that Scripture bears witness to a God who in undisturbed unity is distinctly three and who in threeness is a single unity. Declares Barth, "Wir finden die Offenbarung selbst in der Heiligen Schrift so bezeugt, dass unser auf dieses Zeugnis sich beziehendes Verständnis der Offenbarung bzw. des sich offenbarenden Gottes eben die Trinitätslehre sein muss" (329). The doctrine gives explicit expression to what is implicitly true in the revelation to which Scripture bears witness. It functions as an "interpretation" or as an "explanation" of the text of Scripture (325). Indeed, for Barth, interpretation means "saying the same thing with different words" (364). But different words may well include different concepts and a different historical cultural context from which the words emerge. Such is the case with the doctrine of the Trinity as Barth himself is well aware. The question is once again the degree to which the "different words" are an appropriate and faithful interpretation of revelation and thus the degree to which both may be understood as the "same thing."

The result of the inquiry for Barth is the emergence of a set of triadic patterns from the biblical revelation which offer confirmation for the Church's traditional doctrine of the Trinity (332–52). Formally these triads emerge from an analysis of yet another summary thesis: "Revelation in the Bible means the self-unveiling imparted to persons by the God who according to his nature cannot be unveiled to persons."[15] In a series of three brief discussions the emphasis is shifted alternately from the "self-unveiling" (Revelation), to "the God who according to his nature cannot be unveiled" (Revealer), to "imparted to persons" (Revealedness).

Were that the extent of the exposition, the discussion would appear not to have progressed beyond the earlier schema of Subject-Object-Predicate. The real weight of the discussion, however, belongs not to the threefold analysis as such, but to the phrase at the beginning of the thesis: "In the Bible." Barth wants to demonstrate that the root of the doctrine lies within the actual narratives and themes of both the Old and New Testament.[16] The narratives of the Bible have a revelatory function. In these narratives God reveals Himself. But the God there unveiled also remains the God who by nature may not be unveiled, the God who remains absolutely distinct from his creation. In revelation the God who cannot be unveiled communicates Himself through his unveiling. The threefold pattern which emerges of "Veiling, Unveiling, and Communication" is paired with the analogous pattern of "Form, Freedom, and Historicity," both of which are interpreted through the narrative moments of Easter, Good Friday, and Pentecost and the biblical designations Son, Father, and Holy Spirit. The triads are hardly exhaustive in indicating the three-in-one character of the revelation event. Indeed others emerge throughout the *Kirchliche Dogmatik*.[17] Their function for Barth is to point toward the "threeness" which appears as a characteristic of the single event of revelation. With the triadic patterns he is able to speak of revelation with "a threefold meaning and yet a single content" (351). Barth finds here the sufficient justification for speaking of revelation as the root of the doctrine of the Trinity.[18]

The Heart of the Trinity

It is significant that in Barth's discussion of the root of the doctrine that the order of the triadic designations is altered from the initial order of Revealer, Revelation, and Revealedness. When Barth turns to the biblical witness, he notes that the three moments of revelation do not appear to carry the same weight (332). Rather, the second moment, the moment of the Revelation itself, the Self-unveiling, tends to dominate. Barth's christological emphasis in his development of the doctrine parallels in many respects the historical development of the trinitarian tradition. Christological questions provided the emphasis which led to trinitarian thinking.[19] The confession in the divinity of Christ required a clarification of the confession in the one God. The inclusion of Spirit language within this complex is generally recognized to represent a secondary expansion of a more fundamental theological development which occurred in the earliest years of Christian reflection. In the case of Barth, the dominant role of christology is consequent to the noetic interest which is a basic motif throughout his later work. Christology is so to speak the fulcrum upon which the Trinity doctrine rests. Christology forms not only the starting point, but represents the epistemological principle on the basis of which the whole doctrine is and must be developed. It is the Second Person of the Trinity who enables a knowledge of the First and the Third. Geisser has trenchantly summarized this relationship in the formula, "Alles das also, was die Christologie einbringt, ist in der Trinitätslehre ausgebreitet."[20] It is christology and specifically the *homoousios* which forms the necessary foundation for a knowledge of the divine Trinity.[21]

The *homoousios* is a basic axiom of the trinitarian paradigm. This is evident in his presentation of the summary thesis of revelation, "God reveals Himself as Lord" (323f). Barth's analysis of the thesis leads to the conclusion that, "The distinction between form and content *cannot be applied* to the biblical concept of revelation."[22] If Jesus Christ is the form of God's revelation, he must also be the content of that revelation; there can be no division. Revelation is the proclamation of the Lordship of God, else it is not revelation at all (323). It is proclamation of God's freedom and God's divinity. This revelation is concrete. It is no abstraction which is revealed, but God Himself.

> Indem Freiheit, Herrschaft, Gottheit wirklich und wahr sind in Gott selbst und nur in Gott selbst, unzugänglich und unbekannt also, wenn nicht Gott selbst, wenn nicht dieses Ich redet und mit Du anredet—so, in Gott selbst, sind sie der Sinn des Ereignisses, das die Bibel Offenbarung heisst. (324)

Only God can reveal Himself as Himself. When one has to do with God's self-revelation, then one has to do with God. These assertions have for Barth the character of axioms. They are given with the biblical concept of revelation and require no further justification.

That Jesus Christ is God is a basic datum of the biblical witness to revelation. It is not up to theology to derive this truth. It is rather a fundamental theological assumption (436). Its character as dogma does not relativize its significance for the dogmatic task.[23]

> Das Dogma [von der ewigen Gottheit Christi] als solches steht nicht in den biblischen Texten. Das Dogma ist eine Interpretation. Aber wir können uns überzeugen, dass es eine gute, sachgemässe Interpretation dieser Texte ist. (436)

It becomes apparent that the doctrine of the Trinity is already largely prefigured in Barth's christological assumptions which themselves form a key aspect of the concept of revelation. When the doctrine of the Trinity speaks of an identity of essence between the Father and the Son, what is offered is simply a trinitarian formulation of the statement that Jesus Christ is God's self-revelation. The concept of revelation already contains the element of self-differentiation—the communication which comes from God which itself is God.

Christology alone of course is not the doctrine of the Trinity. Their convergence for Barth is most evident in the context of the root of the trinitarian dogma. The doctrine of the Trinity represents an advance on christology (carried out on the basis of christology) in its careful delineations of the relations between the Son, the Father, and the Spirit. How Barth derives these trinitarian relations and thereby the doctrine of the Trinity proper is the question to which we must now turn.

Deriving the Trinitarian Relations

Barth's primary justification for the theological integrity of the doctrine of the Trinity is its root in the biblical witness to revelation. The analysis of the concept of revelation as Barth finds it in Scripture yields an unmistakable threefold pattern, a threefold repetition of moments which together constitute the single event of revelation. In the language of the dogmatic tradition, this justifies talk of a threefold distinction (*distinctio*), economy (*oeconomia*), or order in God (KD I/1, 374). This constitutes only a portion, however, of the Barthian dogma and remains only on the outer edge of what the dogmatic tradition regards as the doctrine of the Trinity proper.

The language of the three moments of revelation orients itself toward the redemptive event in Jesus Christ. It is reflection on the divine act but not yet on the divine being. In the tradition of Western trinitarianism, action is a category which may be predicated only of a unitary essence.[24] If any of the outward acts of God were to be ascribed to only one of the divine Persons and not to all three, then there would be grounds for a plurality of essences or natures in God, which would contradict Christianity's monotheistic confession. Thus, the Western doctrine from Augustine on has affirmed the rule *opera trinitatis ad extra sunt indivisa* as a barrier which insures that the language of the Trinity does not degenerate into tritheism. If God is one in essence, then there can be no question of the Son willing and acting in one way while the Father wills and acts in another. All of the outward acts of God are acts in his unity as opposed to particular acts of particular divine Persons.

Barth affirms the Augustinian rule. All talk of the historical acts of God is talk of the one and the same God.

> Denn Alles, was da zu sagen ist, kann und muss, ob es sich nun um den inneren Besitz oder um die äussere Gestalt des Wesens Gottes handle, letztlich von Vater, Sohn und Geist in gleicher Weise gesagt werden. (381)

What Barth is able to achieve, therefore, directly on the basis of the biblical concept of revelation is in essence an "economic" trinity with yet no clear guide as to its relationship to the eternal being of God. Revelation acts as a kind of pointer to the problem of threeness and oneness in God, but it falls short of an a clear identification of these distinctions with the "immanent" being of God (381f).

Barth, however, cannot simply stop here. Without grounding the doctrine of the Trinity unequivocally in the eternal being of God, trinitarian language is in danger of representing an arbitrary reality, and revelation becomes something alienated from God Himself, that is, it becomes something other than *self*-revelation. Barth offers a two phase discussion in which he suggests a way out of the apparent cul-de-sac by developing a more elaborate foundation for trinitarian language. The first phase takes up another time-honored trinitarian principle from the dogmatic tradition, namely the doctrine of God's internal relations. The doctrine of relations brings trinitarian language to the very heart of the classical doctrine as articulated by Augustine and the Scholastics after him. The center piece of the doctrine for Barth is to be found in the New Testament names Father, Son, and Holy Spirit. Following the principle of divine unity in revelation, each of the three names must refer to the one God in His wholeness. The names are, however, by no means arbitrary in Barth's reckoning. Nor may they be taken metaphorically. God has revealed Himself as Father because there is something akin to fatherhood in God. Likewise, He has revealed Himself as Son because there is something like Sonship in God (383). The significance which Barth attaches to the trinitarian names acts as a basis for the doctrine of relations which Barth affirms in its traditional (Augustinian) form.[25] Accordingly,

Das unterschiedliche Stattfinden der drei göttlichen Seinsweisen ist zu verstehen aus ihren eigentümlichen *Beziehungen*, und zwar aus ihren eigentümlichen *genetischen* Beziehungen zueinander. Vater, Sohn und Geist sind dadurch voneinander unterschieden, dass sie ohne Ungleichheit ihres Wesens und ihrer Würde, ohne Mehrung oder Minderung der Gottheit in ungleichen *Ursprungs-verhältnissen* zueinander stehen. (382)

The genetic relations between the trinitarian Persons implied by the trinitarian names of the revelation provide the ground for the three distinctions in God's being. According to the logic of the doctrine of internal relations the three realities in God are not separate substances or beings but rather "subsisting relations." The so-called "fundamental law of the Trinity" formulated by Anselm and codified by the Council of Florence in 1439 provides the logical criterion by which a real distinction in God might be determined: "*In Deo omnia sunt unum, ubi non obviat relationis oppositio.*"[26] A total of four real opposing relations may be determined to exist: *generare, generari, spirare,* and *spirari.* Three of these relations constitute actual hypostases or *relationes personificae:* The Father is the Father in the relation of begetting (*generare*) the Son; the Son is the Son in the relation of being begotten (*generari*) by the Father; the Spirit is the Spirit in the relation of procession or passive "spiration" (*processio, spiratio passiva*) from both the Father and the Son. Active spiration does not constitute a subsisting relation in God since the Spirator as such is not a single *hypostasis,* but rather the common work of both the Father and the Son and thus an "impersonal" reality.[27]

Barth deviates from the tradition in how he designates the trinitarian distinctions. It is not three "persons" which are discernable in the being of God.[28] The term "person" is objectionable in this context for Barth on two general grounds: (1) the general lack of clarity as to its precise meaning in the early phases of the development of the Church doctrine, and (2) an exacerbation of the confusion with the introduction of the modern notion of personality as self-consciousness, a concept relatively foreign to *persona* (374–79). It runs the ironically dual danger of leading either in the direction of tritheism (suggesting three separate substances or centers of consciousness) or toward Sabellianism (for which "person" designates God acting in the economy of salvation with no application to the divine being). Barth offers what he terms the "relatively better" designation "Mode of Being" (*Seinsweisen*) (379), a literal translation of *tropos hyparxeōs*, a term appearing as early as Basil of Caesarea as a synonym for *hypostasis*.[29] Barth wishes to express with "Mode of Being" what traditional theology has intended with *subsistentia* or subsistent relation. God subsists as the one God in three Modes of Being. "Person" and "personality" are appropriate predicates of God when applied only of the one God who is revealed in the three Modes of Being.

> Der eine Gott, d. h. aber der eine Herr, also der eine persönliche Gott ist, was er ist nicht nur in einer Weise, sondern—wir berufen uns dafür schlicht auf das Ergebnis unserer Analyse des biblischen Offenbarungsbegriffes—in der Weise des Vaters, in der Weise des Sohnes, in der Weise des Heiligen Geistes. (379)

On the basis of the revelation, then, one is led to the trinitarian names, or what Barth refers to as the "formal characteristics" of God's eternal Modes of Being (383). These "formal characteristics" are themselves a set of relationships between the Modes of Being of God in His revelation. The doctrine of relations provides the logic for carrying the revelational relations into the eternal being of God.

This, however, is only the first phase of the discussion. The second phase, which methodologically is intimately bound to the first, takes up the linguistic basis (i.e., the names of God in His Revelation) which underlies Barth's adoption of the traditional doctrine of relations. It is in this phase of the discussion that Barth begins to elaborate a linguistically oriented foundation for talk of God's trinitarian being which is far more significant for the remainder of the *Kirchliche Dogmatik* than the doctrine of internal relations. The second phase rests upon another of the axioms of the trinitarian paradigm, namely, the assertion of identity between God's action and God's essence.

Wesen und Wirken Gottes sind ja nicht zweierlei sondern eins. Das
Wirken Gottes ist das Wesen Gottes in seinem Verhältnis zu der
von ihm unterschiedenen, zu schaffenden oder geschaffenen Wirklichkeit. (391)

Barth would understood the assertion as a logical extension of the concept of

revelation itself, whereby revelation is not a mere effect of God, but God

Himself.[30] Consequently, knowledge of the revelation is simultaneously

knowledge of the God who reveals Himself in the event of revelation. The

distinction between God's action and God's essence can be no more than a

formal distinction which serves as an indication or reminder that God's works

arise from a free divine decision, grounded in the divine nature, but not

required by it (391). The identity which Barth asserts, however, does not intend

to disallow the notion of God "in and for Himself." It is not to be understood

as a conflation of the eternal being of God with His historical revelation or of

the immanent Trinity with the economic. The copula in the equation may not

be taken in an absolute sense. God is not exploited in His revelation. That

theology distinguishes the immanent from the economic Trinity follows from

the confession of the Lordship of God, the sovereign *freedom* in which God has

acted. The economic Trinity is not a necessary extension of God's eternal

being. It is free act and free expression of the divine nature. The freedom in

which God enacts His revelation is thus the category by which Barth would

preserve the divine transcendence, or stated in the epistemological context in

which the problem arises for Barth, the "inconceivability" of God.

Gott gibt sich dem Menschen ganz in seiner Offenbarung. Aber
nicht so, dass er sich dem Menschen gefangen gäbe. Er bleibt *frei*,
indem er wirkt, indem er sich gibt.... In dieser Freiheit gründet die
Unbegreiflichkeit Gottes, die Unangemessenheit aller Erkenntnis
des offenbarten Gottes. (391)

Indeed, says Barth, the conceivability in which God exists in and for Himself

is not relatively, but absolutely divorced from whatever human conceptuality

we might have (391).

The chasm which Barth sought to bridge with the doctrine of internal relations would appear to have been reopened, only this time more radically than before. There is for Barth no doctrine, no philosophy, nor any turn of logic which would enable humanity to bridge the chasm. If there is a bridge it must come from the side of God. It is thus by virtue of divine grace that the absolute distinction between human knowledge and its object in this case is "nevertheless not without truth" (391). Barth asserts the presence of an analogy between the names Father, Son, and Holy Spirit as given in revelation and the three Modes of Being comprised by the genetic relations in the eternal being of God (393). Thus, for Barth, the economic Trinity *corresponds* to the immanent Trinity. The *doctrine* of the Trinity corresponds to the God who is triune in and for Himself and this by virtue of an act of divine grace, by virtue of the *analogia fidei*. This principle of correspondence lies at the very foundation of all of Barth's assertions regarding the God who is Father, Son, and Holy Spirit both in His revelation and antecedently in Himself (*zuvor und in sich selber*).

The Doctrine of the Trinity and the Hermeneutical Criteria

On the basis of the foregoing it becomes clearer to what degree Barth's declared criteria for a biblical hermeneutic correspond to the methodological principles with which he develops the doctrine of the Trinity. Intrabiblical fidelity undergirds the concept of a threefold pattern of revelation with which he would ground the doctrine. Its fiduciary character surfaces repeatedly. Particularly with the affirmation of the homoousios and the principle of correspondence between God's works and God's essence, one is faced with self-vindicating theses, assertions with no warrant other than the biblical concept of revelation in which Barth would find them present. Barth is faithful to his rule of content-orientation both in the exegesis as well as in the appropriation of the tradition. The biblical names Father, Son, and Holy Spirit are taken up in an analogical interpretation, as given analogs to a real and corresponding subject-matter, virtually ignoring the historico-cultural milieu which gave rise to them. The historical doctrine of the Trinity is appropriated on the basis of its insights into the subject-matter of revelation, particularly for its capacity to analyze the event of revelation such that within each of its critical moments the object remains God, that is, God in threefold repetition. The traditional element is of course present throughout. The very absence of the word "Trinity" from the pages of Scripture serves as a reminder of the form already given to the discussion via the dogmatic tradition. The Church Fathers and the confessions offer the linguistic and conceptual tools which bring the doctrine to expression. A constant process of dogmatic retrieval is underway seeking after those thought-forms which can help bring the subject-matter to expression and opposing those which appear to lead into error.

Finally, that it is a dogma or perhaps a series of dogmas which perform the hermeneutical function for Barth is an evidence of what we have called the non-specialized character of hermeneutics which his criteria would prescribe. The capacity of the Trinity dogma and indeed any dogma to function hermeneutically for Barth resides solely in the degree to which they faithfully give expression to the subject-matter of the texts. The appropriateness of the doctrine for this task may be tested ultimately by no other criterion. In this sense Barth would deny having developed any sort of "special" hermeneutic for the understanding of the biblical texts.

To summarize, we have illustrated the convergence of a dominant motif both from within Barth's reflections toward a biblical hermeneutic and from his development of the doctrine of the Trinity. In the biblical hermeneutic it takes the form of a fiduciary, content-oriented loyalty to the biblical text. In the Trinity doctrine it takes the form of an exclusive status for the revelation in Christ as set forth in the biblical witness as the ground of the doctrine. It is within the context of this convergence that the real strength of Barth's trinitarian hermeneutic becomes visible. The trinitarian hermeneutic embodies a series of interpretive moments quite circular in their movement. It begins with a willingness to take seriously the claim of the text to address the reader with the Word of God; and it begins with a willingness to allow oneself to be informed and transformed by this claim. It looks to Jesus Christ as the focal point of the event of divine address and thus as the heart of the subject-matter of the text. This event of address in Jesus Christ is the event of revelation, the analysis of which yields the triadic pattern: God as the speaking subject; God as the spoken Word; and God as the event of understanding in which the human being knows himself addressed. The hermeneutic conceptualizes the threefold repetition of God in the revelation event with the doctrine of the Trinity. Subsequently, the doctrine offers an interpretation of the text, a way of listening to the text which allows the subject-matter to come to expression and which presumably would insulate the text against efforts to impose an interpretive scheme which would locate the subject-matter of the text elsewhere.

Philosophical Influences Upon the Trinitarian Hermeneutic

The discussion thus far has focused upon a portrayal of Barth's derivation of the doctrine of the Trinity largely in terms of his own claims of loyalty to the biblical concept of revelation as the sole ground of the doctrine. Accordingly, Barth's hermeneutical employment of the doctrine would appear to function quite in accordance with his overall theological program. Yet, it is precisely Barth's claim to ground the doctrine of the Trinity exclusively in the biblical concept of revelation which has become the source of some of the most significant challenges to his formulation of the doctrine. For if it can be shown that at the root of Barth's doctrine of the Trinity is something other than a concept of revelation warranted by Scripture, or if it can be shown that the basis of the doctrine actually lies outside of the Bible altogether, then the claim of hermeneutical fidelity to the text is significantly jeopardized. The doctrine of the Trinity as Barth conceives it and employs it throughout the *Kirchliche Dogmatik* would become simply another instance of a method which imposes itself between the Bible and the reader. Rather than allowing the text to come to its own, it would actually hinder the process. Likewise, if the derivation of the doctrine may be seen to draw from external sources, it could be understood as an instance of an anthropologically determined model operative at the very foundation of Barth's theological construction, a possibility very much opposed to Barth's own stated intentions.

The question is often put to Barth whether the biblical record of divine revelation genuinely warrants a fully developed doctrine of the Trinity. Hans Geisser poses the critical question of whether Barth's logic of the correspondence between revelation and the immanent Trinity is really an application of the logic of the self-interpretation of God or whether it is not much more an application of a human interpretation to the revelation.[31] Barth, argues Geisser, would appear to have erred in identifying the language of the Trinity too closely with the revelation itself. The doctrine of the Trinity is the product of various linguistic traditions and must not therefore be simply explained as an original, self-evident ideogramm of the revelation.[32] In a similar way, R. D. Williams disputes Barth's claim to be exegeting the simple fact of revelation. The finely defined character of the model of revelation employed is sufficient in itself to put the claim in doubt.[33] Barth simply fails to do justice to the complexity and pluriformity of the biblical witness to revelation. "In spite of all, Barth is, it seems, determining in advance what can and what cannot be admitted under the heading of 'revelatory events.'"[34]

Even more threatening to the Barthian claim than the denial that Barth has simply analyzed the fact of revelation are the commentaries which identify extra-biblical and thus competing influences operative in Barth's development of the doctrine. Timothy Bradshaw is representative of a number of critics who have noted the presence and influence of particular philosophical conceptualities in the development of the doctrine, notably existentialism and German idealism. The existentialist character is rooted in the categories of actualism.[35] One thinks of the "event" of revelation in its threefold repetition. One thinks of the postulated identity of divine works and divine essence. Bradshaw summarizes this conception of God grounded in actualistic thinking:

> Just as divine being and act are inseparable *ad extra*, so *in se*. The triune life is utterly complete and concretely real. God's being is eternal yet ever new in the miraculous history of the Father, Son and Spirit. God is God, therefore, in repetition.[36]

Likewise, the use of "historicity" (*Geschichtlichkeit*) (KD I/1, 350) to describe the function of the Spirit in the revelational triad "Form, Freedom, and Historicity" has distinctly existential overtones.

> It signifies that God's self-revelation is imparted to specific men in specific circumstances: in God *in se* this historicity is the genuine meeting of Father and Son in pure authenticity. This is the historicity of the inner participation of the freedom of God and the *forma servi*.[37]

Bradshaw also notes the complementary influence of German idealism in Barth's trinitarian construction. The formal structure of Barth's trinitarian logic bears remarkable similarities to the Hegelian principle of the logic of relation. "This entails the free positing of the other, and the overcoming, without destroying, the distinction. For Hegel, the subject posits itself as an Other, knows itself in that Other, and then negates the otherness of that Other, in a return to itself."[38]

This Hegelian influence upon Barth's trinitarian development has received increased attention in recent years.[39] Jenson would interpret Barth's doctrine as a "christological inversion" of Hegel's speculative trinity. "Only put Jesus in the place of Hegel's 'world' [i.e., the object of the Divine Mind], and you have the doctrine of Barth's *Church Dogmatics* volume I/1."[40] The same reflective structure of differentiation binds both the Barthian and Hegelian doctrines. This is also the ground for Jürgen Moltmann's critique of Barth's doctrine. He notes the employment of the reflective structure to secure the subjectivity, sovereignty, and personality of the one God.[41] Particularly problematic is the use of a speculatively derived principle in exposition of the concrete and specific revelation of God in Jesus Christ.

> A reflection of subjectivity like this has not necessarily anything whatsoever to do with the biblical testimony to the history of God. The notion of God's reflexively differentiated subjectivity and self-revelation can be conceived even without any biblical reference at all.[42]

Not only does the Hegelian reflexive logic represent a speculative intrusion into Barth's doctrine, but it leads to a conception of the Trinity decidedly modalistic in character. The consequence of interpreting God in his unity as sovereign subject is the necessary denial of subjectivity for each of the three Persons of the Trinity. This is objectionable to Moltmann whose social doctrine of the Trinity wants to place God's subjectivity at each of the trinitarian revelatory moments.

One of the most articulate expositions of this Hegelian borrowing by Barth has come from Wolfhart Pannenberg.[43] Pannenberg notes Barth's express indebtedness to the work of the nineteenth century theologian I. A. Dorner.[44] Dorner, who developed his theology out of a Hegelian framework, strove toward a retrieval of the doctrine of the Trinity to a central place in Christian doctrine. Pannenberg notes the striking similarities between the trinitarian doctrines of Barth and Dorner. Dorner wanted to interpret the unity of God in terms of "absolute personality" which meant consequently that the three trinitarian Persons could not be thought of as persons in the same sense.[45] Dorner, consequently, preferred not to speak of Trinitarian "Persons" at all, but rather of the three "Modes of Being" (*Seinsweisen*) of God which together yield the "personality" of the one God. Pannenberg makes the reasonable suggestion of a line of influence from Dorner to Barth even though Barth nowhere cites Dorner in reference to the thesis of the singular personality of God. The significant difference between Barth's and Dorner's conceptions, according to

Pannenberg, lies in their logical development. Dorner would establish the absolute personality of God on the basis of the three Modes of God's Being. For Barth the direction of the logic is reversed—the doctrine of the Trinity develops logically from the thesis of God's lordship in his revelation, (a thesis which Pannenberg equates with the subjectivity of God in his revelation) and not vice versa. The difference is one which places Barth actually closer to the speculative idealism of Hegel than Dorner himself.[46] For Hegel developed the trinitarian structure of the divine life on the basis of a conception of God as spirit and God as subject. It is the structure of this argumentation which for Pannenberg is virtually identical for Hegel and Barth.

> Auch Barth entwickelt nämlich seine Trinitätslehre nicht primär von exegetischen Befunden her, also etwa aus dem historischen Verhältnis Jesu zum Vater, sondern argumentiert mit der inneren Logik des Offenbarungsbegriffs, in welchem Subjekt, Prädikat und Objekt oder der Offenbarer, die Offenbarung und das Offenbarsein zu unterscheiden seien. Dabei handelt es sich auch für Barth um die Selbstobjektivation Gottes in seiner Offenbarung, dergemäss er schon von Ewigkeit her "nicht ohne den Andern sein" will, sondern "sich selbst nur haben" will, "indem er sich mit dem Andern, ja in dem Andern hat" (KD I/1, 507). Ist das nicht der Sache nach dieselbe Struktur der Subjektivität, die Hegel in seiner Ableitung der Trinität aus dem Begriff des Geistes oder Selbstbewusstseins entwickelt hat?[47]

Platonic or Neo-Platonic thought forms, also play a2 significant role in the structure of Barth's Trinity doctrine.[48] Regin Prenter has ventured to classify the platonic tendency in Barth's thought as an influence which is actually stronger than the patristic-Reformation tendency which Barth would prefer to emphasize.[49] A Platonic line of thought is suggested in the scheme of correspondence between the immanent and economic Trinities and in the related concept of the trinitarian *Urbild* or *Urgeschichte*. Prenter elaborates the Platonic character by developing the intimate relationship between Barth's actualism and a pre-existent immanent Trinity.[50] The immanent Trinity which stands outside of time in eternity relates to the historical revelation in its actualistic conception in a way which is remarkably similar to the relationship between Plato's forms and their sensuous perception in the temporal order. The historical manifestation is the epistemological medium for human knowledge of the trans-historical reality. For both Plato and Barth each pole is the necessary dialectical counter-part of the other. In Barth, this dialectical relation is visible in the movement from God's eternal election of Himself to its temporal revelation in the incarnation. The dialectic remains genuine in that neither pole may be emphasized at the expense of the other. The immanent Trinity does not become metaphysical speculation since its epistemological medium is restricted to historical revelation. But neither is Barth interested in a history of revelation in a strict historical sense as is often alleged. History is never revelation in and of itself but is always a witness to an eternal divine reality.[51] Consequent to this conception, however, is an inescapable relativizing of history. This relativizing tendency is for Prenter as true for Barth as it is for Plato. Historical reality is an analogous reality which reflects the eternal in parabolic fashion. It is this aspect of Barth's revelational theology that Prenter would designate as Barth's "evangelical Platonism."[52] Whether the Platonic influences in Barth's Trinity doctrine are as intensive as Prenter suggests, and whether they have entered Barth's thought via a conscious encounter with Platonic philosophy or whether they reflect a subconscious archetypal characteristic of all Western and particularly German idealistic thought forms which have simply found unconscious expression in Barth's doctrine are questions which escape any final conclusion. What is quite clear from the analysis of Prenter and others, however, is the indisputable presence of Platonic analogies in Barth's trinitarian scheme. The question of origin does not figure in significantly when one wants to ask regarding the consequence and influence of a particular thought form upon a given content.

The evidence in favor of a substantial philosophical influence in Barth's trinitarian development would appear to be conclusive. Barth utilizes (although without acknowledging the sources) not only concepts and categories of particular philosophical lines of thought in order to give expression to the doctrine of the Trinity, but he also utilizes a philosophically developed scheme of logic, the idealistic doctrine of reflective differentiation, in the derivation of the doctrine. The presence and influence of philosophically derived conceptualities create a set of tensions within Barth's doctrine of the Trinity, particularly with regard to its hermeneutical function. These may be delineated in the following way: (1) There is a tension between the philosophical concepts and the rule of textuality. One must ask if philosophy, whether in the thought-forms of actualism, absolute subjectivity, reflective logic, etc., have usurped the place which Barth's hermeneutic would allow only to the biblical text. (2) There is a tension between the philosophical concepts and the rule of content-orientation. One must ask if the philosophy is genuinely aiding in the process of allowing the biblical witness to revelation to come to its own and if the "sovereign freedom of the subject-matter" can be given adequate regard, or if indeed the philosophical conceptualities do not import their own content and their own agenda for thought, consequently binding the text to a particular set of anthropologically determined structures. (3) There is a tension between Barth's thesis for the root of the doctrine and the origin in a speculative philosophy of certain concepts which he uses. Barth identifies the exclusive root of the doctrine with God's concrete and historical revelation. It is revelation which acts as a reference to the triads; it is revelation which names God three times—Father, Son, and Spirit—thus justifying the doctrine of internal relations; and it is revelation which bears witness to God *in se* since God's works in his revelation may be identified with His eternal being. Particular aspects of Barth's understanding of God and revelation expressed in this thesis, however, are demonstrably derivative of a particular speculative philosophy. In the remainder of the discussion we will seek to assess the significance of these tensions for the integrity of Barth's trinitarian hermeneutic.

"Unreflected" Thought-Forms and the Apotheosis of Dogma

Our conclusions with regard to the relationship between philosophical influences at work in Barth's derivation of the doctrine of the Trinity and the integrity and consistency with which the trinitarian hermeneutic is applied throughout the *Kirchliche Dogmatik* may be summarized by way of two theses: (1) The philosophical dimension of Barth's trinity doctrine is consistent with his own theological method and axioms and with his principles for a biblical hermeneutic. (2) The refusal, however, to explicitly recognize the philosophical elements operative in the doctrine tends toward an unwarranted identification of the doctrine of the Trinity with the divine self-revelation it seeks to interpret.

In consideration of the first thesis it must of course be acknowledged that philosophical analysis is not in and of itself disallowed by the theological method which Barth proposes. Barth's repudiation of existentialism in the "Vorwort" of *Kirchliche Dogmatik* I/1 is a repudiation of the "Begründung, Stützung oder auch nur Rechtfertigung der Theologie" with existential philosophy and not an absolute ban on its use or that of any other philosophical scheme of thought within theological discourse (KD I/1, vii). Barth recognizes the inevitable presence of philosophical categories within theological discourse. His anecdotal phrase, "Wenn wir den Mund auftun, so befinden wir uns im Bereich der Philosophie,"[53] is one which must be taken quite literally. The science of dogmatics makes use of philosophical conceptualities just as every science must. Barth's relative mistrust of philosophy must not be misinterpreted so that it is transformed into an opposition to its use. Barth lays great stress on the recognition of both conscious and unconscious philosophical and ideological prejudices which every theologian and which every Bible reader brings with him when he encounters the text.

> Wie könnten wir den Text objektiv verstehen, ohne subjektiv, d.h. aber mit unserem Denken, dabei zu sein? Wie könnten wir ihn zu uns reden lassen, ohne mindestens die Lippen bewegend (wie es

ja die Leser der Antike auch äusserlich sichtbar und hörbar taten), selber auch mitzureden. Der Erklärer kann gar nicht anders: schon in dem, was er als Beobachter und Darsteller sagt, wird er auf Schritt und Tritt verraten, dass er—bewusst oder unbewusst, in ausgebildeter oder in primitiver, in konsequenter oder in unkonsequenter Weise—von einer bestimmten Erkenntnistheorie, Logik und Ethik, von bestimmten Vorstellungen und Idealen hinsichtlich des Verhältnisses von Gott, Welt und Mensch her an den Text herangekommen ist und dass er diese auch als Leser und Erklärer des Textes nicht einfach verleugnen kann. Irgendeine *Philosophie* d.h. irgendeine selbstgeformte Konzeption hinsichtlich dessen, wie Alles im Grunde sei und sich verhalten möchte...hat jeder. (KD I/2, 816)

Consequently, it is a meaningless theological critique which merely points to the philosophical underpinnings of a particular theological stance. For even the critic must ultimately confess that he likewise is bound in the end to a particular conceptuality, philosophy, or culturally formed perspective with which he expresses himself (818).

It is evident that Barth operates on the basis of a distinction between the very human and frail instruments of theological expression and the transcendent truth of the theological content which these instruments seek to bring to expression.[54] One cannot approach the subject-matter of theology other than as a sinful human being whose mode of thinking is in and of itself unfit for the task. Whatever intellectual tools the theologian employs, philosophical or otherwise, remain inadequate. Adequacy, which is bestowed only by the grace of God, is not contingent on thought-forms or philosophical tools. Thus Barth can designate it in principle as a matter of indifference which philosophy one chooses to employ in order to aid theological expression. There is no intrinsic advantage of one over the other (822f).

Von Balthasar seems to echo Barth's own understanding of the philosophy-theology relationship in his defense of Barth against the charge of philosophism.[55] Philosophy provides the conceptual tools for articulating a particular theological content. The theological content remains the determinative factor in the relationship. The question for Barth is not the adequacy of a particular philosophical framework, but rather, "ob dieser Systempunkt inhalt-lich richtig ausgefüllt und beschrieben wird."[56]

Barth's clarification of the role of philosophy as well as von Balthasar's defense would seem to correspond in large measure to what one actually finds when the philosophical concepts operative within Barth's doctrine of the Trinity are examined as to their function. Barth adapts the Hegelian categories, for instance, which he employs to articulate the Trinity doctrine for his own purposes so that what emerges resembles far more the traditional Western doctrine of the Trinity than Hegel's own speculative doctrine.[57] If the form of Barth's derivation of the doctrine resembles that of Hegel's, the starting point is significantly different. The root of the doctrine for Barth, the summary thesis that "God reveals Himself as Lord," is presented as a summary of the biblical witness, and cannot be construed as a general ontological principle.

If one accepts the distinction between philosophical form and theological content assumed by Barth, then the tensions outlined above would appear to dissolve easily in favor of the trinitarian hermeneutic. Yet, the distinction is one which may not easily be taken over without qualification. Barth himself gives recognition to the danger,

> dass die Begriffe, die man sozusagen nur als Formen verwendet, schon einen bestimmten Inhalt haben, der mitschwingt und der u. U. den Theologen auf eine Gedankenbahn weist, die mit dem, was er als Theologe zu sagen hat, nichts zu tun hat.[58]

Thus, when Barth speaks of God as "absolute subject" here and as an "I" addressing a "you" there, there can be no simple division between the concept and the content it brings to expression. The concept brings its own content with it. The question which one must ask is whether Barth does not at certain points fall victim to this very danger against which he warns. With this question we come to the second thesis: the refusal of Barth to explicitly recognize the philosophical elements operative in the doctrine tends toward an unwarranted identification of the doctrine of the Trinity with the divine self-revelation it seeks to interpret.

In §21.2 of the *Kirchliche Dogmatik*, entitled "Die Freiheit unter dem Wort," Barth offers a number of methodological principles which should govern the use of philosophical schemes of thought in the hermeneutical process. The first of these principles requires that the application of a particular scheme of thought be a principally conscious process, lest the scheme of thought become identified with the object of interpretation (818f). Implicit is the obligation that the theologian reflect upon the cognitive tools of his trade. "Unreflected" tools represent a risk in that their capacity to shape the content of the material to which they give form goes unrecognized. The second principle dictates that no scheme of thought may have more than hypothetical character. Its application to Scripture takes the form of an experiment which may or may not serve the Word of God (819f). These basic principles of interpretation represent fundamental insights into the hermeneutical event which no one would dispute. What is significant is that in the case of the trinitarian hermeneutic which Barth brings with him to the text, and which forms a paradigm within which he develops his theology, these rules would appear to have no effect.

Barth does indeed set a distance between the doctrine of the Trinity and the revelation it seeks to interpret. It is the human and fallible exercise of the Church which seeks to "exegete" or "translate" the event of revelation as portrayed in Scripture (KD I/1, 325). Barth does not allow language about the Trinity of God to claim an identity with the revelation of God. Barth would have done better in this case, however, to have left off the dialectical counter-statement in which the language of the Trinity claims an "indirect identity" with the revelation (326). The language of the Trinity is inseparable from the thought-forms which structure that language. Talk of its "indirect identity" with revelation can only mean an "indirect" apotheosis of the philosophical categories which Barth employs to develop the doctrine. The danger is compounded by Barth's tendency to avoid expressly identifying and explicitly reflecting upon the philosophical tools with which he works, a danger against which his own hermeneutical rule clearly warns.

Thus the narrow association between Barth's trinitarian formulation and revelation threatens to imply an absolute claim for the hermeneutical paradigm which Barth employs throughout the *Kirchliche Dogmatik*. It threatens the reality of human reflection upon revelation by dictating the pattern for that reflection from the side of the revelation. It is forgetful of its own anthropological roots, of its own *Sitz im Leben*, and of its own hypothetical character. It threatens to abandon its hermeneutical function in favor of a "revelational positivism."

Fortunately, the tendency toward absolutizing the trinitarian perspective in the *Kirchliche Dogmatik* is not inherent to the perspective itself, nor does it jeopardize the integrity and appropriateness of the doctrine in its hermeneutical function. Its philosophical underpinnings need not bind the text—they may just as well serve the text. Philosophical concepts need not annul the principle of textuality. Rather, they offer the possibility of creative reinterpretation essential if the text is to continue to speak again and again to each new age.

Barth's trinitarian hermeneutic remains an attempt to take seriously the concept of revelation. Revelation remains the object of its reflection, even though it brings its object to expression by means of certain philosophical categories and concepts. Barth's trinitarian hermeneutic approaches the biblical text in utter seriousness and seeks to allow the God to whom the text bears witness to speak as God. It is an attempt to focus upon the concrete characters active in the salvation narrative and thus to guard against unwarranted speculations leading away from the text rather than to it. But as such, it is an attempt, a human attempt, subject to the relativities and risks of any such human endeavor. It is a hermeneutical way of thinking which the theologian must test and critique just as other hermeneutical ways of thinking must be tested.

It is precisely hermeneutical criticism, as we saw in Chapter One, which Barth is quite reluctant to allow into the realm of theological discussion, whether material or formal. Barth fears with some justification a derailment of urgent theological concerns and a preoccupation with purely epistemological questions. He defends the view,

> dass Hermeneutik kein selbständiger Gesprächsgegenstand sein, dass ihr Problem nur in unzähligen hermeneutischen Akten—alle sich gegenseitig korrigierend und ergänzend, aber vor Allem: alle auf den Inhalt der Texte bezogen—angegriffen und beantwortet werden kann.[59]

Yet, the price which Barth must pay for the refusal to allow the hermeneutical dimension of his own theologizing to become an independent object of discussion is a certain confusion in the hermeneutical process, a confusion which we have seen to take the form of a dangerous blurring of the lines between a hermeneutical construction and the transcendent truth of the texts which Barth wishes to interpret. Hermeneutical reflection is able to uncover what for Barth remained hidden, to make conscious what previously was only unconscious. It is thus Barth's own hermeneutical rules which seem to demand the type of overt hermeneutical reflection which he finds so threatening.

ENDNOTES

[1]See above, 21ff. Cf. Anthony Thiselton, *The Two Horizons* (Exeter: Pater Noster, 1980), esp. 88–90, 315–18, for a hermeneutical study which considers only Barth's critical stance toward hermeneutical theology.

[2]Most discussions of Barth's contribution to the field of hermeneutics focus upon his critique of the historical-critical method (particularly in the *Römerbrief*) and his principles of "theological exegesis". Cf. Georg Eichholz, "Der Ansatz Karl Barths in der Hermeneutik," in *Antwort* (Zollikon-Zürich: Evangelischer Verlag, 1956), 52–68. On the relationship of Barth's work to the broader themes of theological hermeneutics, cf. Mark Wallace, "The World of the Text: Theological Hermeneutics in the Thought of Karl Barth and Paul Ricouer," USQR 41 (1986) 1–15; George A. Lindbeck, "Barth and Textuality," ThT 43 (1986) 361–376; Thomas E. Provence, "The Sovereign Subject-matter: Hermeneutics in the Church Dogmatics," in *A Guide to Contemporary Hermeneutics*, ed. D. McKim (Grand Rapids: Eerdmans, 1986), 241–62; and Ernst Fuchs, *Hermeneutik* (Tübingen: Mohr, [4]1970), 3–12.

[3]For the first of the three descriptive headings I am indebted to the analysis of Mark Wallace. Wallace, 2–4.

[4]Wallace, 3.

[5]Lindbeck, 366.

[6]"Als Theologe habe ich meine Sprache, wie immer sie auch sei, und trete mit ihr einem Gegenstand entgegen, der mir im Zeugnis der Heiligen Schrift begegnet. Indem ich mir dieses Zeugnis aneigne, bin ich nicht frei von aller Philosophie, aber auch nicht gebunden an eine bestimmte Philosophie. Es ist mir alles erlaubt, es soll mich aber nichts gefangen nehmen." Credo, 158f. See also KD I/2, 825f.

[7]Wallace, 3.

[8]"Gilt die allgemeine hermeneutische Regel, dass ein Text nur in Wissen um seinen Gegenstand und von diesem Gegenstand her recht gelesen, verstanden und ausgelegt werden kann, dann musste von diesem Gegenstand her—gar nicht apriorisch, sondern aus diesem Text selbst—die Beziehung zwischen Gegenstand und Text als eine wesensmässige und unauflösliche erkannt, dann durfte also jene Trennung von Form und Inhlat nicht vollzogen, es durfte nicht unter Absehen von der Form nach dem Inhalt gefragt werden." KD I/2, 546.

[9]The priority of the text is not exclusively a Barthian theme in the hermeneutical discussion but has recently been championed by the representatives of the "New Hermeneutic" by way of emphases in the work of Georg Gadamer. See below, 255, note 18.

[10]Whether this is a fair complaint against general hermeneutics is of course another question. Cf. R. Palmer, *Hermeneutics*, Northwestern University Studies in Phenomenology & Existential Philosophy, ed. J. Wild (Evanston: Northwestern Univ., 1969), 244, for a defense of the priority of the text to the interpreter on purely hermeneutical grounds.

[11]"Aber gerade die allgemein und allein gültige Hermeneutik müsste an Hand der Bibel als Offenbarungszeugnis gelernt werden." KD I/2, 515.

[12]"Man wird sich, um hier das Grundsätzliche zu verstehen, vor allem folgendes klar machen müssen: Wie die heilige Schrift in ihrer göttlichen Autorität zu jeder Generation in der Kirche in der Gestalt des bestimmt umschriebenen Kanons und insofern auch mit menschlicher Autorität, mit der Autorität der vorangehenden Kirche redet, so redet sie auch zu keiner Generation und zu keinem Einzelnen in der Kirche allein, nie bloss als das nackte, geschriebene Wort von damals. Sie redet vielmehr zu uns als zu solchen, die der kirchlichen Gemeinschaft angehören und in ihrer Geschichte stehen." KD I/2 677. Cf. 725.

[13]"Ist es echtes Bekenntnis, dann ruft es ja zur Entscheidung auf, das heisst: es fordert die Anderen auf, sein Zeugnis von einem bestimmten Schriftverständnis zu hören und damit auch ihr eigenes Schriftverständnis auf seine Rechtmässigkeit zu prüfen." Ibid., 719.

[14]"Nur mit seinen eigenen Augen hat noch niemand die Bibel gelesen und soll sie auch niemand lesen." Ibid., 728.

[15]KD I/1, 332, 338, 342.

[16]This relationship between biblical narrative and Barth's theology has been explored in an insightful way by D. F. Ford, "Barth's Interpretation of the Bible," in *Karl Barth: Studies of his Theological Method*, ed. S. W. Sykes (Oxford: Clarendon Press, 1979), 55–87. Ford speaks of a "metaphysics of the Gospel story" which he understands as "a thoroughgoing attempt to understand the eternal God through a temporal history" (63). The doctrine of the Trinity is a case in point since for Barth it represents "an order in God expressed in the interrelation of crucifixion, resurrection, and Pentecost" (60).

[17]God as "Reconciler," "Creator," and "Redeemer" form the primary "appropriations" used by Barth to identify Son, Father, and Holy Spirit (KD I/1, 419, 404, 470). Cf. also the designations "Word," "Speaker," and "Meaning"; "Middle," "Beginning," and "End" (384); and "Mercifulness," "Holiness," and "Kindness" (392).

[18]"Die biblische Lehre von der Offenbarung ist implizit und an einigen Stellen auch explizit *Hinweis* auf die Trinitätslehre. Sie muss in ihrem Grundriss als Grundriss auch der Trinitätslehre interpretiert werden." KD I/1, 352.

[19]Cf. Georg Kretschmar, *Studien zur frühchristlichen Trinitätstheologie*, Beiträge zur historischen Theologie, 21, ed. G. Ebeling (Tübingen: J. C. B. Mohr, 1956), 219f, who demonstrates that it was the Easter event which made trinitarian thinking necessary.

[20]Hans Geisser, "Die Trinitätslehre unter den Problemen und in den Prolegomena christlicher Theologie: Beobachtungen am Schicksal des Dogmas in der evangelischen theologischen Tradition des 19. Jahrhunderts bis zur Rezeption durch Karl Barth" (Unpubl. diss., Tübingen, 1962), 425.

[21]Cf. Thomas F. Torrance, "The Legacy of Karl Barth," SJTh 39 (1986) 289-308. Torrance offers an interpretation of Barth's entire theological program from the perspective of the *homoousios* doctrine.

[22]KD I/1, 323. Translation and emphasis mine.

[23]That the assertion has axiomatic status does not, however, justify the allegation of "revelational positivism." As an axiom, the divinity of Christ represents a key aspect of the trinitarian paradigm whose function is hermeneutical and heuristic but not positivistic. See above, 72ff.

[24]Cf. the Roman Catholic exposition of the doctrine of Joseph Pohle, *The Divine Trinity*, adapted and edited Arthur Preuss (St. Louis: Herder, 1950), (= Pohle-Preuss). "Philosophy teaches that '*Operari sequitur esse, i. e., naturam.*' If the nature of a thing is its 'principle of operation,' it follows that the number of principles of operation, and their specific manifestations (e.g., intellect and freewill in spiritual natures), depend on the number of active essences and natures." (279).

[25]On the doctrine of relations as articulated in traditional Catholic dogma, cf. Pohle-Preuss, 228–235. For Barth's discussion, see KD I/1, 384–86.

[26]Ibid., 230–2.

[27]Ibid., 234f.

[28]The issues raised by Barth's decision in this regard are considerable as the continually growing literature on the subject of "persons" in the Trinity would seem to indicate. See Karl Rahner, "Der dreifaltige Gott als transzendenter Urgrund der Heilsgeschichte," in *Mysterium Salutis*, II (Einsiedeln: Benziger, 1967), 342–44, 353f, 385–92; (ET= 42–45, 56f, 103–115); (cf. the earlier version in *Schriften zur Theologie*, IV [Einsiedeln: Benzinger, 1960], 103–33; ET = *Theological Investigations*, IV [London: Dartman, Longman & Todd, 1966] 77–102); Wolfhart Pannenberg, "Person und Subjekt," in *Grundfragen systematischer Theologie*, II (Göttingen: Vandenhoeck & Ruprecht, 1980), 80–95; "Die Subjektivität Gottes und die Trinitätslehre," *Grundfragen*, II, 96–111; Lawrence B. Porter, "On Keeping 'Persons' in the Trinity: A Linguistic Approach to Trinitarian Thought," ThS 41 (1980) 530–48. A summary of contemporary alternatives is offered by Ted Peters, "Trinity Talk," Dia 26 (1987) 44–8, 133–8. Jenson offers the designation "Identity" as a contemporary improvement over the term "person." Robert Jenson, *The Triune Identity* (Philadelphia: Fortress, 1982), 1–20; 118–30.

[29]*de Spiritu Sancto*, 43f. Cited Welch, 190.

[30]"Wollen wir die Offenbarung wirklich von ihrem Subjekt, von Gott her verstehen, dann müssen wir vor allem verstehen, dass dieses ihr Subjekt, Gott, der Offenbarer, identisch ist mit seinem Tun in der Offenbarung, identisch auch mit dessen Wirkung." KD I/1, 312.

[31]Hans Geisser, "Der Beitrag der Trinitätslehre zur Problematik des Redens von Gott," ZThK NF 65 (1968) 247f.

[32]Ibid., 248.

[33]R. D. Williams, "Barth on the Triune God," *Karl Barth: Studies of his Theological Method*, ed., S. W. Sykes (Oxford: Clarendon Press, 1979), 153f.

[34]Ibid., 157.

[35]Timothy Bradshaw, "Karl Barth on the Trinity: A Family Resemblance," SJTh 39 (1986) 159–61. See also Robert S. Franks, *The Doctrine of the Trinity* (London: Gerald Duckworth, 1953), 178–80. Cf. Hans Urs von Balthasar, *Karl Barth* (Einsiedeln: Johannes Verlag, [4]1976), 230–5; ET = *The Theology of Karl Barth* (New York: Holt, Rinehart, & Winston, 1971), 181–85, on the role of existential categories within Barth's theology as a whole. One of the most detailed explications of the actualistic character of Barth's thought is Horst Georg Pöhlmann's *Analogia entis oder Analogia fidei?* Forschungen zur systematischen und ökumenischen Theologie, XVI, ed. E. Schlink (Göttingen: Vandenhoeck & Ruprecht, 1965); see esp 116–19.

[36]Bradshaw, 160.

[37]Ibid., 161.

[38]Ibid., 159.

[39]The idealistic color of Barth's theologizing has of course long been noted. Cf. v. Balthasar, 210–29, 244f (ET = 170–81, 192f); Franks, 181–84.

[40]Robert Jenson, *The Triune Identity* (Philadelphia: Fortress Press, 1982), 136.

[41]Jürgen Moltmann, *Trinität und Reich Gottes* (Munich: Kaiser, 1980), 154–61; ET = *The Trinity and the Kingdom of God* (London: SCM, 1981), 139–44.

[42]Ibid., 158f. ET, 142.

[43]Pannenberg, "Subjektivität," 96–111. Bradshaw, Moltmann and Jenson all draw from Pannenberg's analysis. Pannenberg has reaffirmed the Hegelian comparison in his recently published *Systematische Theologie*, I (Göttingen: Vandenhoeck & Ruprecht, 1988), 322f, 325f.

[44]Barth lists Dorner among his theological mentors in the Foreword to CD, page VI. Dorner is named in the text of the book as one of the few modern theologians who had recognized the dangers inherent in the neglect of the doctrine of the Trinity (CD, 198). Cited Pannenberg, "Subjektivität," 99. Cf. parallel reference in ProtTh, 526.

[45]Pannenberg, "Subjektivität," 99.

[46]Ibid., 100f.

[47]Ibid., 101f. Pannenberg notes other points of contact between Barth and Hegel as well. (1) The philosophy of speculative idealism and particularly its Hegelian articulation are responsible for having reclaimed a central place for the trinity doctrine in human reflection about God. (2) For both Hegel and Barth the doctrine is linked with a particular understanding of revelation, namely that of the divine self-revelation grounded in God's trinitarian manifestation. (3) Barth shared with Hegel an appreciation for Anselm's ontological proof for God, which Barth employed as a description of the self-evidence of God in His revelation. Ibid., 98.

[48]Platonic influences are particularly characteristic of the dialectical phase of Barth's work, due at least in part to the work of Barth's brother Heinrich in platonic studies. See Eberhard Busch, *Karl Barths Lebenslauf* (Munich: Kaiser, 1975), 129; ET = *Karl Barth*, tr. J. Bowden (London: SCM, 1976), 116. See also on the early Barth, v. Balthasar, 71–73, 75–78, 79f; ET, 48–51, 53–56, 58f; Henri Bouillard, *Karl Barth: Genèse et évolution de la théologie dialectique* (Paris: Aubier, 1957), 104f, 109f, 114, 116, 139, 179–82; and Jean-Louis Leuba, "Platonisme et Barthisme: Quelques Perspectives Théologiques," *Archivio di Filosofia* 53 (1985) 153–72. Leuba is interested primarily in the early Barth, although not without reference to the *Kirchliche Dogmatik*. On Platonic influences in Barth's later work, see Regin Prenter, "Karl Barths Umbildung der traditionellen Zweinaturenlehre in lutherischer Beleuchtung. Einige vorläufige Beobachtungen zu Karl Barths neuester Darstellung der Christologie," StTh 11 (1957) 75–78.

[49]Prenter, "Umbildung," 76.

[50]"Ich bezeichne als den Barthschen 'Platonismus' die im Interesse eines universalistischen Christomonismus oder christomonistischen Universalismus vorgenommene Verbindung des Präexistentialismus und Aktualismus, die ich hier als die wesentliche Eigentümlichkeit im Denken Barths aufgezeigt habe. Es ist eine Konstanz, die ohne *wesentliche* Abänderungen das Denken Barths vom 'Römerbrief' bis KD, IV bestimmt." Ibid.

[51]Ibid., 77f.

[52]Ibid., 78. While Prenter's analysis of the relationship between the historical and the eternal in Barth's trinitarian conception of reality is formally correct, the implicit critique that the consequent relativizing of history signifies a diminution of historical reality or historical self-understanding need not follow. See below, 245ff.

[53]Credo, 158.

[54]Cf. the recent analysis of Barth's thought by Ingolf Dalferth, "Theologischer Realismus und realistische Theologie," EvTh 46 (1986) 402–22. "Kritische Selbstbescheidung im Blick auf sich selbst und emphatischer Wahrheitsanspruch im Blick auf ihren Gegenstand kennzeichen Barths Theologie somit gleichermassen. Insofern sie Theologie als Produkt fallibler Subjekte begreift, die in der Sprache der Welt und unter den Konstitutionsbedingungen unserer Erfahrungswirklichkeit die Wirklichkeit des Wortes Gottes zur Sprache zu bringen suchen, ist sie neuzeitlich. Sie ist aber nicht nur neuzeitlich, insofern sie darauf insistiert, dass so gegen unsere gängige Wirklichkeitsauffassung tatsächlich *Wirklichkeit* zur Sprache gebracht wird und dass diese und nicht jene Massstab der Sachgemässheit theologischer Rede zu sein hat." (403f).

[55]V. Balthasar, 228f, 229–51. ET, 180f, 181–96.

[56]Ibid., 235. ET, 186.

[57]Even Pannenberg must concede the significant difference between the Hegelian understanding of the ontologically necessary process of God's self-manifestation in creation and Barth's own emphasis upon the free decision and act in which God reveals Himself. (Pannenberg, "Subjektivität," 102.) Cf. Walter Kreck, "Zum Trinitätsproblem bei Hegel und

Barth," in *Grundfragen der Dogmatik* (Munich: Kaiser, 1970), 282f. Kreck portrays Hegel's knowledge of the Trinity as "a logical and ontological principle, which in spite of its analogies to the Christian doctrine leads to an apotheosis of reason" (283, my translation). For Barth, this knowledge is dependent exclusively upon God's free and sovereign decision to reveal Himself in Jesus Christ. Cf. Barth's own critical analysis of Hegel in ProtTh, 342–78, esp. 366–78. See also Isidro García-Tato, *Die Trinitätslehre Karl Barths als dogmatisches Strukturprinzip* (Bad Honnef: Bock & Herchen, 1983), 598–604, for an elaboration of the argument that the christological foundation of Barth's trinitarianism represents a material distinction between Barth and Hegel which significantly conditions any claim to formal similarity.

[58]Credo, 158.

[59]Karl Barth, Letter to Hermann Diem, 27.11.49. Cited Busch, 362. ET, 349.

CHAPTER FOUR
The Role of the Tradition
in the Trinitarian
Hermeneutic

The previous chapter has offered an analysis of Barth's development of the doctrine of the Trinity in the *Kirchliche Dogmatik* in light of the claim to find the root of the doctrine in a biblical, christologically-centered conception of revelation. Barth's use of various philosophical categories in his development of the doctrine, which on first inspection would appear to stand in tension with the claim for a biblical root, were shown not to threaten Barth's fundamental theological aim, although his reticence to expressly articulate the philosophical tools he employs represents an unfortunate danger which risks a mistaken identification of the trinitarian hermeneutic with biblical revelation itself.

The present chapter is likewise concerned with Barth's trinitarian construction. Here, however, the focus will be directed toward the role which Barth allows the dogmatic tradition in his development of the doctrine. Bringing the hermeneutical issues to light requires the consideration of two broad concerns: (1) the function of the tradition in relation to Barth's claim to find the root of the doctrine in the biblical concept of revelation, and (2) a clarification of the status which Barth's trinitarian hermeneutic affords the tradition as such. As in the case of philosophical influences, Barth's reliance on certain strands of the tradition may be seen to stand in tension with the claim for a biblical root to the doctrine, insofar as certain traditional statements within the doctrine would appear to have no grounding within the biblical texts themselves. The first concern then must raise the same question raised in the previous chapter, although here in light of the tradition: to what extent does the hermeneutical force of the doctrine represent a foreign intrusion upon the biblical text as opposed to an attempt to understand the text in light of its own theme and subject-matter?

Unlike the former case, Barth is quite explicit in the traditional elements which he adopts and quite intentional in the use he makes of them. The careful consideration and delimitation of the role and function of the tradition which he undertakes in *Kirchliche Dogmatik* I/2 was already mentioned in Chapter Three and will be given more detailed consideration below. We shall assume that the model developed there for relating Scripture and tradition forms Barth's own conceptual interpretation for the way in which he actually handles the tradition in his presentation of the Trinity doctrine. Using the conceptual model as a backdrop, we shall attempt to measure the significance and influence of traditional trinitarian theology upon the doctrine as it appears in *Kirchliche Dogmatik* I/1. Conclusions in this regard will hopefully offer some insights into the hermeneutical significance which Barth assigns the theological tradition, particularly within the Trinity doctrine.

The chapter is divided into three sections. The first sets forth Barth's conceptually developed model for relating tradition to Scripture and dogmatic theology. The second considers the extent to which this model corresponds to actual practice in Barth's trinitarian construction. The third will bring together the conclusions and results of the study.

Barth's Model for Relating Scripture and Tradition
The "Event" of the Church

One of the hermeneutical rules referred to in Chapter Three which for Barth is incumbent upon the systematic theologian is that of the "confessional attitude."[1] Barth's model for relating Scripture to the confessions of the Church (or the dogmatic tradition as a whole) is one rooted in a particular conception of the being of the Church, a model which stresses the event-character of the Church in history.

[Die Kirche] hat also nicht nur eine Geschichte, sondern sie
ist...indem eine bestimmte *Geschichte* geschieht: indem sie nämlich
von dem lebendigen Jesus Christus durch den Heiligen Geist versammelt wird, sich versammeln lässt, sich selbst versammelt. (KD
IV/1, 726f)

The Church is a dynamic reality which Barth prefers to describe in many of the
same actualistic categories characteristic of his concept of revelation.[2] It is on
the one hand a historical phenomenon which may be observed in the same way
that other historical phenomena are observed. It may be described according
to its psychological, social, historical, and cultural characteristics (728). What
happens within this historical phenomenon, however, is a spiritual event
perceptible only to faith. It is a work of the Holy Spirit in which believers are
gathered together, a divine work happening in the form of human activity
(726). The recurring event of the Church always assumes concrete and visible
form as a historical happening, as the gathering of men and women at different
times and places. The character of this historical event as a "living congregation
of the living Lord Jesus Christ" is a spiritual reality happening in and through
the concrete form (733). To a certain degree the actualistic conception may be
seen in contrast to a historical or linear conception whereby the Church is
conceived principally in terms of a series of temporally connected moments,
each of which must be understood in light of the conditions prevailing at that
particular time. Barth, of course, does not wish to obscure the historically
conditioned character of the Church. But he clearly wishes to subjugate it to
the Spirit-oriented actualistic concept.

Barth's actualistic concept of the Church also bears an important
relationship to his *doctrine of time*. In *Kirchliche Dogmatik* I/2 Barth develops
a threefold differentiation of time rooted in his concept of biblical revelation
(KD I/2, 50–52). "Our time," the time of the present, is a "fallen" time, an
inauthentic time. "Our time" is set over and against time as God created it.
"Our time" is a perversion and distortion of God's created time. Between these
two concepts of time comes a third, the time of revelation or "fulfilled time."

Indeed for Barth the statement, "God reveals Himself," is equivalent to the statement, "God has time for us" (50). The time which God has for us is the time of His revelation, which is the time of Jesus Christ. It is also the time of God's presence. Declares Barth, "Die Zeit, die Gott für uns hat, wird dadurch konstituiert, dass er uns in Jesus Christus gegenwärtig wird: *Deus prasens*." (55)

God's fulfilled time is a particular historical time such that one may venture the statement, "The fulfilled time is the time of the years 1–30" (64). More precisely, it is the forty days of the risen Christ which stand as the historical point, so to speak, around which the New Testament witness to God's historical revelation revolves.[3] The forty days of the Easter event, "in der Mitte der Zeiten," stand as a unique self-enclosed history of God with humanity. It was the time of *direct* revelation, and *direct* encounter between God and his Apostles (604f). In the forty days, the eternal significance of the history of Jesus culminating in his death on the cross was revealed in utter clarity. Not only was the fulfillment of the divine plan revealed, but time itself was fulfilled in the event of unveiling. It was a time qualitatively different from the times preceding and following it. The significance of revelation is such that all other time can run only relative to God's fulfilled time. "Our time" is "die durch die erfüllte Zeit *begrenzte* und *bestimmte* Zeit" (72). The time of God's revelation impinges upon the remainder of time as a dynamic presence within history whether before or even long after the time of those who walked and spoke with Jesus of Nazareth. In a passage of profound depth Barth speaks of fallen time standing in the light of and under the sign of "another time," a time which because of its fulfilled character forms the horizon of the remainder of human time and defines its boundaries, no matter how distant the past or the future of that fallen time may be (72f).

The Church is an event in a particular time, in the time between the resurrection and the second coming of Christ. As a concrete and historical event, the Church happens within the fallenness of "our time." Fulfilled time however imposes itself upon "our time" (73). Genuine and authentic time takes the place of time which is false and inauthentic. Revelation becomes contemporaneous with our time. In this sense the simultaneity of the time of revelation to every moment of the Church's history and the subjugation of an historical interpretation of the Church to an actualistic interpretation tend to create a kind of historical compression in the reality of the Church in Barth's theology.[4] The essence of the Church is not to be found in the vicissitudes of its history, but in the same event of obedience repeated again and again across time.

This understanding of the reality of the Church which emphasizes its event-character from the side of God is significant for Barth's interpretation of the tradition, a term used here to designate the collective texts which include the biblical canon, time-honored writings of the Church's theologians, and the creeds and confessions, all of which have grown out of the life of the Church through the ages. His understanding gives rise to a model of the Church which, while not denying the historicity of the Church, emphasizes the dynamic of communion which the Church enjoys with itself in all ages. The Church is a reality in communion and dialogue with itself, united in the event in which God confronts the Church with His Word, His self-revelation in Jesus Christ. This event of confrontation is the same in all ages. The Church responds to this confrontation in the form of its confessions. The Church makes its confession in the face of particular issues and problems which press upon its existence so that its confession is always a culturally and historically conditioned expression. The object of the confession, however, is always the unchanging Word of God. Consequent to this understanding is Barth's willingness to stress the continuity of the traditions of the Church throughout its historical life. The concept of "continuity" is of course one which allows for considerable ambiguity. It is worthwhile to inquire after the precise sense in which Barth wishes to use the term.

Barth affirms an "uninterrupted continuity" and an "uninterrupted context" between the Church of the present and the Church of the past when he writes,

> Es gibt neben aller gegenseitigen Fremdheit und neben aller Zer-spaltung in der Kirche, wo immer wirkliche Kirche ist, auch ununterbrochene Kontinuität zwischen der Kirche einst und jetzt und ununterbrochenen Zusammenhang zwischen der Kirche dort und hier. Da wäre bestimmt nicht Kirche, wo die Gemeinschaft auch nur in einer von diesen beiden Dimensionen ganz fehlte, wo man in einem kirchlichen Gebilde wirklich gar keine Väter hinter sich oder gar keine Brüder neben sich hätte. (KD I/2, 725)

The element of continuity in the tradition stands for Barth upon the one and same Word of God spoken to the Church throughout its history and upon the one and same faith with which the Church responds. For authentic tradition functions solely in its explanatory and interpretive relation to Scripture (715). Scripture is the criterion which confirms or rejects the validity of any particular moment of the tradition. The texts of tradition are admittedly human and historically conditioned works, but each represents an event in the life of the Church happening in the context of the faith called forth by God, a faith which is unchanging through the ages.[5] This double-sided moment of God's confrontation of the Church with His Word and the response of the Church in faith forms the primary reality of the tradition. Differences in culture, history, world-views, and patterns of thought are indeed present and real for moments in the history of the Church separated by long periods of time, but these differences are a secondary concern and do not in and of themselves deny the more fundamental continuity and common context which transcends the whole of the time of the Church.[6] In spite of the distance of the ages, in spite of the "hermeneutical gap" which separates different historical horizons, Barth assumes at least the possibility that the tradition can address the Church and be heard in a meaningful and relevant way.

The authority of the tradition is rooted for Barth in the human authority of the Church. It is a derived authority which stands not alongside revelation, but rather subject to it. In actualistic terms, the authority of the Church happens only in the event of obedience of the Church to the Word of God (638–40). This authority extends not merely throughout the Church of a particular time or period but speaks across the ages as well. Barth illustrates the trans-historical authority of the tradition with the fifth commandment, "Honor thy Father and thy Mother."[7] As the voices of those who have gone before, the tradition demands at least a "privileged hearing" from the Church of the present as it seeks to carry out its own appropriation of Scripture. The refusal to hear and consider the voices of the past is above all the error of "biblicism." "Biblicism" is employed by Barth to depict the attempt to make direct contact with Scripture by by-passing the Church of both past and present.[8] Barth's critique stresses the irony that a theology which tries to proceed along the radical *sola scriptura* path of the biblicists (which was not the path of the Reformers), is far more likely to fall victim to the particular spirit of its age than a theology which begins with an attentive listening to the voices from the Church's past. Thus the tradition, far from being hopelessly time-bound, is for Barth one of the means available to the theologian for overcoming his own time-bound limitations.

The tradition is the collective reality of the Church in conversation with itself. It is through the texts which the Church produces that the Church of later years knows its earlier self. The tradition then is what actually forms the boundaries of what we call the Church, and not merely the Church as it exists at any particular moment. It is in this sense then that Barth can speak of the confession of the Church as forming the "Horizont unseres eigenen Denkens und Redens" (729). It is in this sense that one should interpret Barth's choice of words in the title of the *Kirchliche Dogmatik*.[9] The task of theology is a careful listening to the Word of God to which Scripture bears witness. But it is a listening which occurs in a particular "space," the "space" of the Church. The boundaries of this space are marked off by the tradition (730).[10]

With his concept of the continuity of tradition, Barth is able to avoid the dangers of an historicist approach which in its particular brand of reductionism tends to overlook the faith character of the Church's historical confessions and is thus unable to appropriate their insights. An interpretation of the tradition solely in terms of the world-views, political influences, philosophies and thought forms which contributed to its formation is historically interesting but poorly suited as an aid to the Church in its efforts to hear the Word of God for the particular situations facing it at a given time.

One might well object at this point that Barth runs a serious risk in his identification of the essence of the tradition with the divine-human encounter which occasions it. It is one thing to argue for the transcendence of the event of divine address and human obedience and quite another to elevate the particularities of a concrete instance of that event to normative status. The continuity of the tradition, a phenomenon which Barth concedes can be understood in no other way than as a historically conditioned human act (699–704), cannot be secured simply on the grounds of the act of faith which calls it into being. The appropriation of the tradition is a hermeneutical problem which requires a careful scrutinizing of the texts in question if form is not to be confused with content or letter with spirit. The degree to which this objection is justified in Barth's appropriation of the tradition will become clearer as we consider the actual use he makes of traditional elements in his development of the doctrine of the Trinity.

Tradition and the Hermeneutical Spiral

For Barth, the Church is not cut off from its past but stands in dialogue with itself. The tradition of an earlier moment in the life of the Church addresses later moments. It may be heard, understood, and bears authority. But if the tradition is to become a functional part of his theological method, Barth must bring the authority of the tradition into relation with the other authorities in the Church, namely, the authority of God's revelation and the indirect authority of the Scripture which bears witness to revelation. The problem of hermeneutics presses itself at each moment of the methodological construction necessary for establishing the proper relationship. The texts of the tradition are themselves in large part an attempt to interpret the texts of Scripture in light of particular situations. These same texts stand in need of interpretation if they are to be heard and understood by a later time. Assuming they may be understood, the further question arises as to their proper role for informing a careful listening to the Scripture which stands at the basis of theological construction.

It has already been shown how Barth seeks to deal with the problem of interpreting the tradition by an identification of its fundamental character with the two-sided event of divine address and faith response. The further problem of relating this tradition to the dogmatic task involves the combination of two hermeneutical patterns: a linear or hierarchial hermeneutic, and the hermeneutical circle.[11]

Barth, standing securely within the evangelical *sola scriptura* tradition, identifies a straightforward hierarchy of authorities which stand as guide and measure for the proclamation of the Church. The texts of Scripture stand as an indirect authority subject only to the event of revelation to which it points. Scripture is the Word of God insofar as it bears witness to the event of revelation (KD I/1, 114-16). But as witness, the Scripture is the "concrete means" through which the Church remembers the revelation event and through which she is called to an expectation of future revelation (114). The Bible represents the sole avenue which the Church has to hearing the Word of God and is thus the indirect norm of dogmatics (KD I/2, 911). Subordinate to Scripture, but nevertheless essential to dogmatics, is the tradition. This subordination is illustrated by Barth's criteria for determining the relative authority of the writings of the Fathers, the foremost of which is the faithfulness of their scriptural exegesis, which for Barth is equivalent to the question, "ob er dem Wort Gottes gedient hat" (685). In a corresponding way the genuine confessions of the Church are those which speak not on the basis of some immediate or otherwise derived revelation, but solely on the basis of the revelation attested in Scripture (695). Barth employs the metaphor of "commentary" to describe the function of the tradition with regard to Scripture, as the following passage illustrates:

> Die kirchliche Konfession erklärt die Schrift, sie legt sie aus, sie wendet sie an. Sie ist also *Kommentar*.... Sie kann aber...auch *nicht mehr* als Kommentar der Schrift sein, sie kann sich also jener nicht in der gleichen Würde an die Seite stellen wollen.[12]

The tradition bears authority only insofar as it fulfills this function. It may offer no new truth, no new "article of faith" (694).

The tradition of the Church is a human work which claims an authority far more relative than that of Scripture. It is always a restricted and preliminary authority (660f). The possibility is always open that its instruction is poor and imperfect.[13] Each confession of the Church can be no more than a step along the way of the Church's journey with the Scripture. The responsibility for advance or improvement is incumbent upon every new age (739).

Operative in Barth's method then is a traditional protestant hierarchial system of authorities whose order is determinative for the work of dogmatics. Were we to extend the hierarchy further, we could easily add the concrete situation of the Church as a fourth link in the hierarchial chain which forms the comprehensive norm and guide for dogmatics.[14] According to such a scheme the movement of interpretation moves always in a single direction, from revelation to the situation, with each interpretive moment along the way bearing less authority than its predecessor. The danger of such a framework is its tendency toward a hermeneutical process characterized by reduction to a single interpretive principle and a rigidity in its application.[15] The linear idea is one that binds the concept of revelation, so that far from being the "event" of which Barth speaks, it becomes a stultified concept calcified in this or that particular historical form. Fortunately, Barth's procedure does not move toward this extreme, nor may it be characterized solely in terms of a linear hermeneutic. A second movement supplements the first, a hermeneutical pattern widely identified as the "hermeneutical circle."[16]

The hermeneutical circle is generally used to describe the character of encounter with a text as an event which is preceded by certain preconceptions or a pre-understanding regarding its content. This pre-understanding exerts an influence on one's encounter with the text through the expectations and prior judgments which it forms. The text in turn exerts an influence on the understanding of the reader. Understanding arises on the basis of a dialogue or circular movement between reader and text. In an extended sense, this same process may be seen at work in Barth's efforts to relate the tradition to Scripture. Scripture forms the concrete source and norm of theological statements. Its interpretation is always in light of a prior understanding rooted in the theological tradition. The theological tradition, a relative authority subject to Scripture, must be scrutinized on the basis of its fidelity to Scripture. But the understanding of Scripture has already been formed through an encounter with the tradition.

The circular movement in Barth's method is neither vicious nor *ad absurdum*. Its strength is to be found in the dialectical appropriation of the tradition to which it gives way, thus avoiding the dangers of a rigid confessionalism. The dialectic is manifest, on the one hand, in the tradition as a relative authority within the Church. It demands a hearing from the theologian as the "first commentary" on Scripture and as an interpretation of the "first rank" (728). The tradition assumes a place above other theological documents which may address the same concerns. This relative authority of the tradition forms one pole of the dialectic. The individual responsibility of the theologian forms the other. The tradition is not simply an authority to be appropriated, as Barth adds:

> Nach dieser sozusagen privilegierten Anhörung der kirchlichen Konfession werden wir unseren Weg im Verständnis, in der Auslegung und Anwendung der heiligen Schrift nun freilich als unseren eigenen Weg antreten und gehen müssen. (728)

Barth concedes that it may well happen that theological insight leads in a direction other than that of the tradition. But the dialogue with the tradition may never cease. It remains over and against every theological undertaking and as such forms the horizon of theological thought and speech.

The problem of the competing authority of Scripture and tradition recedes in light of the circular model. Scripture and tradition are not competing entities. The tradition is more than a mere repetition or exegesis of Scripture (698). The tradition is rather the historical space in which the Scripture has been heard and particular decisions regarding its significance have been reached. This is its function in relation to Scripture, a function unlike that of Scripture itself. The tradition informs theology in a way subordinate to Scripture, but also unlike Scripture.

Together the two hermeneutical patterns may be depicted in their interrelation as a spiral movement—a circularity of dialogue complemented by the development and advance which are characteristic of teaching and learning. The tradition guides the hermeneutical task of theology but does not bind its particular decisions. It clarifies the subject-matter and themes of theology but does not depict its particular statements regarding the subject-matter. Plainly here however difficulties arise for Barth. One may not accuse Barth of rigid confessionalism nor of a repristination of scholastic orthodoxy. The failure, however, to sufficiently distinguish the response of faith from the particular historical form, philosophy, or pattern of thought in which it is expressed, the decision to lay the boundaries of theological thought and speech congruent with the boundaries of the tradition, and the preeminent place which Barth would give to a hearing of the tradition do imply a constraint upon theological work. It is a constraint which actually underestimates the word of address which has been heard and experienced by those who have encountered the Scripture in the past and those who will be addressed in the future. It underestimates the freedom of God's Word to break the boundaries of prior understanding and to speak to the situations of a rapidly changing world which are markedly different from those that have gone before. The Church may indeed form the horizon of theological thought and speech, but it is a horizon which extends in two directions. It is a dynamic horizon, not only with a past, but ever expanding into the future as the Church creates new tradition to meet the rapidly changing situations which it faces. At this point, however, such an observation remains no more than a vague generalization. It remains to be shown the shape of the hermeneutic which emerges in practice when Barth draws from the tradition for a reinterpretation of the doctrine of the Trinity.

The Criteria for Authentic Tradition

Before concluding this overview of Barth's conceptual model for relating Scripture and tradition, it is worthwhile to give at least brief attention to the criteria he develops for establishing the authentic tradition to which the Church is compelled to give a hearing. These may be classified under four headings: exegetical character, publicness, existential claim, and restricted context.

The foregoing discussion has already pointed to Barth's designation of the tradition as "commentary" on Scripture. Theological assertions whether of the Fathers or of the confessions may stand on no other authority than that of exegesis of the Bible (685, 694f). Rejection of the authority of a Father or a confession is a serious undertaking which is only possible in light of the conviction that the Scripture demands to be heard in a way differently than it was before (739f). That within the Christian world there are conflicting confessions, each of which claims to stand upon a common understanding and interpretation of Scripture does not appear to disturb Barth. The tradition is a human work which is fallible at every point of its development. The claim of a confession is always a claim which accepts the risk that it may be in error (696f). This does not however excuse the Church from venturing that risk. The genuine confession arises out of a compulsion in the Church that it cannot speak in any other way.

A second criterion asks regarding the publicness out of which the tradition arises. The authority of a confession or the decision upon the recognition of a Church Father is not a matter of individual decision. Barth speaks of the "choir of voices" or the "choirs" which must bear witness in agreement (659f). Confessions in particular must stand as a decision of the Church, and indeed a decision of its majority (713). Pressing the point, Barth contends, "Fehlt der *consensus ecclesiae,* dann fehlt auch die *ecclesia* selbst, dann handelt es sich auch nicht um eine *confessio ecclesiastica*" (714). Related to the requirement for consensus, is the necessity for the universality of the claim of a confession. For the Church confession means, "den Inhalt proklamieren, veröffentlichen, bekannt-, und zwar möglichst allgemein bekannt-machen" (716). For a confession is by nature "Wort der ganzen Kirche an die ganze Kirche" (716). A genuine confession speaks not for a portion of the Church only, nor does it merely seek the recognition of a particular point of view as being at least as valid as another. Rather it speaks for the whole Church in that it presumes to proclaim a right understanding of the Word of God, the deviation from which signals error. This is the sense for Barth of a confession's claim for ecumenicity.[17]

A third criterion stresses the existential claim which must characterize the tradition which is recognized as a relatively binding authority in the Church. A genuine confession, just as the texts of an authentic Church Father, intends not only to address the whole Church, but its content lays a claim for decision upon the whole Church. It calls for a decision of fundamental significance, as Barth stresses in the following passage:

> Ist es echtes Bekenntnis, dann ruft es ja zur Entscheidung auf, das heisst: es fordert die Anderen auf, sein Zeugnis von einem bestimmten Schriftverständnis zu hören und damit auch ihr eigenes Schriftverständnis auf seine Rechtmässigkeit zu prüfen, bzw. neu zu prüfen, vielleicht erst wieder sich darüber klar zu werden, dass Lehre und Leben der Kirche an der Schrift geprüft werden muss, ja dass es überhaupt eine heilige Schrift gibt, deren Zeugnis das Gericht über das Denken, Reden und Leben der ganzen Welt bedeutet. (719)

The decision called forth by a confession is existential in character. That is, it is a decision which calls into question the existence of the Church as such. It calls for a "Yes" or "No" on a question of such decisive significance in the life of the Church, that it simply cannot be ignored. The existential claim of the tradition must furthermore extend beyond the time of origin. If it is to be regarded as authentic and valid for the Church of today, the decision called for by the tradition must be relevant.[18] The authority of the tradition is thus not a constant, but depends on the needs and experiences of the Church in its concrete situation (688f). The relevant tradition of today might not speak a meaningful word to the Church in years to come. By the same token, tradition which has been swept aside for generations may suddenly make a new and profound claim on the life of the Church.

The tradition's character of existential claim has the further effect for Barth of justifying the struggle and debate which typically characterize its origin. Such struggles do not in and of themselves imply a scandal for the Church (although Barth acknowledges the scandal which often surrounds them).[19] Theology must interpret such struggles principally in terms of the struggle for a right understanding of God's Word and for the unity of the Church (702f). Because of the significance of the issues at stake, the struggle and conflict surrounding the origin of a confession or dogma (and its

endurance in spite of every counter-pressure marshalled against it) are not only
to be expected, but must be thought of as characteristic features (718–20).[20]

A fourth and final criterion of the authentic tradition is the restricted
context out of which it arises and to which it initially speaks. Barth wishes to
affirm the conditioned and relative character of the tradition not as a
contradiction to its universality, but rather as the particular concrete form of
the tradition's universal significance.[21] Barth observes and acknowledges the
extension of a confession's or dogma's authority within the limits of a particular
geography as well as that of a particular time. Again, it is the existential
character of the tradition which finds emphasis here, as the following passage
would illustrate:

> Der Antrieb und der Mut, Bekenntnis abzulegen, die Zuversicht,
> die Verantwortlichkeit für den damit erhobenen Anspruch auf sich
> zu nehmen und mit diesem Anspruch durchzuhalten, die Fähigkeit
> zu einer strengen, keine Konsequenzen scheuenden theologischen
> Haltung, die Freudigkeit, die das Geheimnis der Kraft einer kirch-
> lichen Konfession ist—das alles wurzelt geradezu darin, dass sie die
> Festlegung und Aussprache der der Kirche in *bestimmten Umkreis*
> gegebenen Einsicht [ist]. (699f)

It is in the recognition of the limited context out which the tradition
arises that Barth calls for close attention to the "No" of the tradition as well as
the "Yes." Because confessions and dogma tend to arise out of situations of
conflict and antithesis, it is the "No," the polemical character, which is
determinative in their formation (706). And because the stimulus for their
formation is confusion and polemic, the response is one carried out in what
Barth concedes to be a "very incompetent way" (709). All of the limitations of
the tradition in this regard simply point again to its human character, a
character which Barth seems at pains to emphasize. But the limitations and the
human character cannot be the sole point of reference for an interpretation
and appropriation of the tradition for a later time. Indeed, a decision as to its
authority cannot even be reached from this point of view. The decisive
perspective for Barth is the perspective of faith, which he describes as seeing

the documents of the tradition "im Lichte der über und in der Kirche wirk-
samen Herrschaft des Wortes Gottes durch das Instrument der heiligen Schrift"
(712). From this second perspective it is possible to see the tradition as an act
of obedience and even as a perception of truth which exercises authority
throughout the Church. For Barth the second perspective does not conceal the
restricted character of the tradition. It rather claims to see and hear something
spoken from historically conditioned texts which grants it an authority which
transcends the historical context out of which it arises. Here again, however,
Barth steers a dangerous course.[22] The second perspective tends to subsume
the first so far as theological analysis is concerned. The particularity of the
tradition is acknowledged for its limitedness. Yet, in failing to preserve the
necessity of the first perspective throughout the process of theological
appropriation of the tradition, it is quite possible to exalt not only a "perception
of truth" but simultaneously a particular mode of thinking, a particular
philosophy, a particular ideology, etc., to a place of unwarranted hermeneutical
significance.[23] It is of course a danger which is not unavoidable. How Barth
actually fares in this regard is one of the questions which must be considered
in light of his inclusion of traditional elements within his systematic presentation of the Trinity doctrine. It is to Barth's doctrine of the Trinity proper to
which we now turn.

Role of the Tradition

Barth's conceptual model for relating Scripture and tradition, as we have
seen above, emphasizes the subordinate, interpretive role of tradition as
commentary upon Scripture. We must now ask regarding the hermeneutics of
dogma effective in specific instances of appropriation of traditional materials.
In other words, we shall consider concrete instances in which Barth uses the
tradition with a view to his interpretation of it as well as his reinterpretation
of it to fulfill his own theological objectives. The implications of these findings

for the hermeneutical significance of the doctrine of the Trinity is explored in the final section of the chapter.

The analysis of the tradition is carried out here only with reference to a selection from the most overt instances of use of the dogmatic tradition and thus can make no claim beyond that of an abstraction drawn from a state of affairs far more complex than what the present analysis may indicate. The illusion of the abstraction suggests that the theologian, standing somehow outside the stream of the history and tradition of theology, dips into the stream as a source of his own independent thought and his own encounter with the Bible. In reality the theologian stands and can stand nowhere else except in the midst of the stream itself and is in some degree at least tossed about by currents over which he has no control. Standing on a heritage as rich and varied as that of the history of Christian thought, theological language defies any simple or absolute analysis into the contribution of its author, the contribution of the tradition, and the contribution from the texts of Scripture. What this means for the present case is that one could well extend the discussion of the place of traditional elements in Barth's trinitarian formulation to a deeper and more comprehensive level than what is done here. For instance, it might be worthwhile to consider the degree to which the theological use of the word "Trinity," a term which entered the tradition with Tertullian,[24] already predisposes theological language to a particular set of emphases, concerns and problems which have recurred throughout the history of Christian thought. Any of a number of other of theology's linguistic conventions could be considered with a view to the same determinative influence. Such an undertaking, however, would present us with a set of problems hardly peculiar to Barth, but rather the common burden of all Christian theological language. We must therefore content ourselves here with the more or less intentional and conscious ways in which Barth makes explicit use of traditional elements in order to carry forward his own trinitarian thesis as we seek to distinguish the hermeneutical character of the dogma as he reinterpreted it.

Recent Protestant Critique of the Received Trinitarian Tradition

Recent years have seen a flurry of attention directed toward a retrieval of the doctrine of the Trinity to a place of prominence for contemporary protestant Christianity.[25] Most of these exhibit a common desire to take seriously the struggles of the early Church to come to terms with the implications of its faith in Jesus Christ. The tradition is taken up as the raw material from which a contemporary doctrine is constructed. These works are likewise united by the common view that a mere repristination of the doctrine is of little benefit to the Church and faith. The traditional doctrine alone is, for whatever reason, an inadequate expression of biblical faith in Christ. The doctrine must be retrieved or "remade"[26] if it is to be meaningful for Christianity today.

Two works in particular which aim toward a renewal of the doctrine by means of thorough engagement with the historical tradition are those of Robert W. Jenson and James P. Mackey.[27] Jenson's critique of the traditional doctrine of the Trinity is particularly concerned with the Augustinian phase of the doctrine's development. In Jenson's analysis, the development of the doctrine from the second century until the time of the Cappadocians was relatively promising and fruitful for the attempt of faith to talk about the God which was its object. All this came to an end with Augustine. Until Augustine it is possible to interpret trinitarian theology as an attempt to understand the eternal God on the basis of His temporal works. The emerging Christian concept of God, in spite of the Hellenistic thought world which housed its language, had burst apart the Hellenistic notion of a timeless and impassible divinity.[28] The Nicene Creed, for example, with its affirmation "out of the being of the Father," affirms a differentiation within God and thus an internal relation within the deity.

"Begotten and not created" bespeaks an origination within God, a beginning which is proper to deity. Each assertion constitutes a profound contradiction to the "simple" deity of Hellenistic philosophy.

Augustine, however, represents a setback for trinitarian theology in that he allows the Hellenistic understanding of God to regain its lost ground in Christian thought. He begins with an understanding of God as timeless and changeless being.[29] The ultimate ramification of this decision is a doctrine of the Trinity which separates the triune character of God Himself from the history of salvation. Augustine's Hellenistic metaphysics required him to deny the possibility of accidents for God. Whatever might appear to be accidents are in fact substance. God *is* what he *has*.[30] All of God's attributes *are* his substance. Consequently, no attribute "can be predicated of one of the identities in any special sense without 'confusing' the substance and the identities."[31] But the original point of trinitarianism, at least for Jenson, was to make the relations between the trinitarian identities, and thus the structure of salvation history, constitutive for God. With Augustine this is no longer possible.

The final consequence for Augustine's doctrine of the Trinity was a metaphysical distinction and separation of the divine "processions" and divine "missions."[32] The processions happen eternally in the divine being without violating the divine simplicity. The missions are the "sendings" which constitute salvation history and may be predicated only temporally. The economic and immanent trinities thus become two separate sets of relations. The original intention of trinitarianism to identify God on the basis of the experience of the divine in salvation history is finally denied.[33]2

Mackey shares Jenson's criticism that the traditional doctrine reduces the life of God to a series of static abstractions which are ultimately severed from the events of salvation history which provided the initial impetus for the doctrine. Mackey's very thorough analysis of Hellenistic influences on the early doctrine highlights a resilient tendency toward subordinationism in most pre-Nicene theology. Early trinitarianism was fit into a Neo-Platonic framework which depended upon a doctrine of emanations to explain distinctions in the deity.[34] As long as this model prevailed, the subordination of whatever was generated by deity to the deity itself was inevitable. It was an advantage of the *homoousios* slogan that it functioned as a correction of subordinationism. But the more the *homoousios* was pressed to emphasize the numerical identity of the divine substance, the more difficult it became to maintain the distinctions between the *hypostaseis* or *personae*, and the more monarchian the orthodox doctrine became. Nor was the process helped by the rule *opera trinitatis ad extra sunt indivisa* which only blurred the distinctions between the divine Persons even further. The doctrine of relations affirmed an inner distinction in God, but not without allowing a subtle re-entry of subordinationist tendencies, a tendency held off only by the denial of the trinitarian theologians.[35] Finally, the Hellenistic notion of an immutable God seemed to grow in approval rather than diminish, such that the Christian experience of Jesus and the Spirit became further and further alienated from the trinitarian doctrine of God.[36]

Neither Mackey nor Jenson interpret their criticisms as fatal to trinitarianism. Both scholars wish to understand the critique of the tradition as the necessary prerequisite to a meaningful retrieval of the doctrine of the Trinity, a task to which both commit themselves, (albeit for Mackey, the end result is a far more radical revision of the tradition than that of Jenson).

The similar analyses of Mackey and Jenson point up two failings of traditional trinitarianism which would be acknowledged by a relatively widespread consensus: the developing dichotomy in trinitarian thought between the trinitarian doctrine of God and the events of salvation history, and the tendency to dissolve trinitarian distinctions into a Hellenisticly influenced concept of deity with decidedly monarchian results. Barth undertakes no such thorough analysis of the linguistic and philosophical elements which played such a significant role in the development of the doctrine. He is nevertheless sensitive to the snares inherent in the historical formulations of the doctrine, and frames his own doctrine with the intention of escaping the age old dilemmas as we shall see below.

Una Substantia

We have described above the sense in which Barth wants to understand the theological task as a "confessionally determined" undertaking, such that the theologian is bound to do theology from his own backyard, so to speak. As a servant of the Church the theologian works within the confessionally determined boundaries which constitute the Church of which he is a participant, and from that relatively restricted place develops theology with an ecumenical claim. It must then indeed be no surprise to find Barth's presentation of the doctrine of the Trinity to be decidedly Western in character.

The most pronounced feature of this Western character in Barth's doctrine is the priority of the unity of God over the triune distinctions. The doctrine of the Trinity is accordingly "die letzte und entscheidende Bestätigung der Einsicht: Gott ist *Einer*" (KD I/1, 368). Tradition provides ample precedent for what in the Western tradition is a well-established if not self-evident truth. The "one" is to be applied to the basic reality (*Wesen*) of God (369). Without engaging the linguistic subtleties of the received terminology, Barth brings together *ousia, essentia, natura,* and *substantia* as attempts to point to the single idea of God's basic reality, His Being as divine Being.[37] Barth offers "Lordship," the same comprehensive term with which he designates the biblical conception of revelation, as the theological equivalent of what each of these terms seek to bring to expression when applied to divine Being. The oneness of God's basic reality is not violated by the threeness, but rather the oneness consists precisely in the threeness of the "Persons" (369).[38]

Because God's reality is identical with his action, there can be no question of partitioning His acts to this or that divine Person. Barth affirms the rule *opera trinitatis ad extra sunt indivisa* (382, 395, 415f, 465). The event of revelation is always an event in which God in his full reality acts and is present. The threeness of the divine Being may not simply be derived from the pattern of threeness in revelation, that is, the pattern of Revealer, Revelation, and Revealedness which Barth observes as a consistent repetition in the revelation event (382f). When one speaks of the activity of God in the world as the act of any one divine Person, one speaks *per appropriationem* (393f, 415f, 465, 497). The doctrine of appropriations functions as a set of rules for ascribing a property or act to one of the divine Persons which properly belongs to all three, that is, to the triune God in His unity. It functions as the counterpart to the rule *opera ad extra*, by not only allowing, but commending certain theological patterns of speech, whereby one Person is spoken of in the knowledge that effectively all three are included. The rule functions for both Barth and the tradition as far more than a mere convention of speech, however. The knowledge which an appropriation conveys is a "true" knowledge, even if "non-actual" (*uneigentlich*). What may appear to be a not so subtle linguistic dodge Barth explains as follows:

> 'Uneigentlich' kann hier nur heissen: es ist an sich kein erschöp-
> fendes, sondern ein einseitiges, der Ergänzung bedürftiges Ver-
> ständnis, ein Verständnis, dem man sich nicht exklusiv hingeben,
> das man nicht exklusiv geltend machen kann und darf, ein Ver-
> ständnis, bei dem mitgemeint sein muss, was in ihm selber als
> solchen nicht enthalten ist. (416)

Barth's use then of the doctrine of appropriations, then, is not such that the temporal distinctions of revelation are dissolved into the unity of a "simple" deity. It rather acts as a reminder that whatever is ascribed to a divine Person is not ascribed to that Person exclusively, that it is not a mere part or department of God which is being spoken of, but rather God who in His basic reality is one.

The objection could well be lodged at this point that Barth does nothing which the traditional Western doctrine does not do. His emphasis upon the unity of God overpowers the triune distinctions. He is well on the road to monarchianism along with the rest of the Western tradition.[39] Barth's doctrine, however, is not easily subject to this line of critique. Barth borrows from Anselm an understanding of the triune God as a plurality of eternities.[40] Accordingly, the divine Persons may be thought of as *repetitio aeternitatis in aeternitate*. In Anselm's thinking a repetition of eternities offered an impressive image of the triune God, since logically any plurality of eternities could never exist outside of a single eternity. For Barth, it is more the *repetitio* which offers a powerful complement to his own actualistic conception of God and revelation. God is a happening in eternity; in the event of God, God always happens as one of his three Modes of Being, that is, as one of the divine Persons. In an impressive formulation, Barth explains,

> Der Name des Vaters, des Sohnes und des Geistes besagt, dass Gott in dreimaliger Wiederholung der eine Gott ist, und das so, dass diese Wiederholung selbst in seiner Gottheit begründet ist, also so, dass sie keine Alteration seiner Gottheit bedeutet, aber auch so, dass er nur in dieser Wiederholung der eine Gott ist, so, dass seine eine Gottheit damit steht und fällt, dass er in dieser Wiederholung Gott ist, aber eben darum so, dass er in jeder Wiederholung der eine Gott ist. (369)

Unfortunately, the concept of a threefold repetition in God is not developed further by Barth—unfortunate, because of its potential as a preferable alternative to the doctrine of genetic relations which tends inherently toward subordinationism. Indeed the doctrine of a divine repetition of eternities would seem to stand in a close relation to Barth's actualistic understanding of the event of revelation. Just as revelation is always an event in which God reveals Himself in a word of address, so God in Himself is the eternal threefold repetition to which the revelation corresponds. In addition, the threefold repetition of God stands as a rejection of any substantial or simple notion of deity.[41]

Barth's actualistic conception of the divine unity is supplemented by another doctrine from the tradition, the doctrine of *perichōrēsis* or *circumincessio* (390f, 417, 509). With the divine *perichōrēsis* he affirms that the divine Persons are not only one among themselves (*unter sich*) but within one another (*ineinander*) as well. Each of the three Persons condition and permeate one another so mutually and perfectly that "one occurs as invariably in the other two as the other two in the one."[42] As an affirmation of unity, the *perichōrēsis* does not allow a dissolution of the distinctions, but rather acts to confirm the three distinctions which actually constitute the unity.

Tres Personae

Barth brings the unity of the triune God to expression by means of a subtle reinterpretation of an eclectic selection of materials from the Western trinitarian tradition. In the case of the triune distinctions, however, we find Barth in confrontation with the tradition. This confrontation takes the form of a rejection of the traditional term "Person" as a designation for the trinitarian distinctions. The linguistic confusion which surrounded the term in the early development of the doctrine is well documented in a variety of places and need not be repeated here.[43] We already noted in the previous chapter Barth's unhappiness with the term, in part because of the confusion and imprecision surrounding its interpretation in the tradition, and in part because of the inevitable tendency of the modern notion of personality as self-consciousness to impose itself on the meaning of the word.[44] But the alternative formulation which Barth offers as relatively better, namely "Mode of Being" (*Seinsweise*), does not simply fall from heaven. Rather, it occurs as Barth confronts the tradition with the tradition itself. Barth contends,

> Es handelt sich also nicht um die Einführung eines neuen Begriffs, sondern darum, einen bei der Analyse des Personbegriffs von jeher und zwar mit höchstem Nachdruck gebrauchten Hilfsbegriff in den Mittelpunkt zu rücken. (379)

Barth defends the designation "Mode of Being" as a translation of the formula *tropos hyparxeōs*, appearing as early as the Cappadocians,[45] and its Latin equivalent *modus entis* (379). He argues moreover that "Mode of Being" captures the sense of *hypostasis* in the sense in which the West finally took it over from the East, that is, in the sense of *subsistentia* rather than *substantia*. Indeed, Barth contends to have captured the intention of the Western tradition while avoiding the linguistic traps hidden within the term "Person."

Barth perceives two potential dangers inherent to the term "Person" as a trinitarian designation: either a dissolution of the unity of God in the directon of tritheism, an ever-present danger once a plurality of centers of self-consciousness is ascribed to God, or the opposite danger of a retreat into Sabellian modalism as a reaction against seminal tritheism (377f). Consequently, it is no surprise that Barth's alternative should tend to stress unity—three Modes of Being of one divine reality. The stress on unity is not, however, without its own counter-balance as Barth's critics often seem to overlook.[46] Barth wishes to suggest with the term "Modes of Being" real and eternal distinctions within God, as the following passage would emphasize:

> Wohl ist Gott in allen drei Seinsweisen in sich selbst und der Welt
> und den Menschen gegenüber der eine Gott. Dieser eine Gott ist
> aber dreimal anders Gott, so anders, dass er eben nur in dieser
> dreimaligen Andersheit Gott ist, so anders, dass diese Andersheit,
> sein Sein in diesen drei Seinsweisen ihm schlechterdings wesentlich,
> von seiner Gottheit unabtrennbar ist, so anders also, dass diese
> Andersheit *unaufhebbar* ist. (380)

It is thus quite fair to maintain the correctness of Barth's assertion that in challenging the tradition he is in effect championing the tradition. It is by no means surprising that at least one Roman Catholic historian has bestowed a substantially positive evaluation upon Barth's presentation of the Trinity doctrine.[47]

The question remains regarding the extent to which Barth's doctrine of Modes of Being entails a breech between revelation and the doctrine of God,

or a division and separation between the economic Trinity and the immanent
as much of the Western tradition would threaten to do. The answer is to be
found in the principle of correspondence with which Barth would relate the
activity of God in the economy of salvation to the eternal divine Being. What
God is in His revelation, he is antecedently in Himself; what God is in Himself,
he is in His revelation. This is the principle of God's self-revelation which
stands at the basis of Barth's concept of biblical revelation, the analysis of
which is yields his doctrine of the Trinity. The economic Trinity happens in
human history because God is Himself triune in the same way. This does not
constitute for Barth a necessity in revelation—the very distinction between
God's working and God's being is a suggestion of the sovereign freedom in
which God wills to reveal Himself in His working as He already is eternally in
Himself (391). The trinitarian missions correspond to the trinitarian processions
as a temporal event grounded in an eternal reality. This is the trinitarian
principle of correspondence which forms the key to Barth's understanding of
the possibility of talk of God, a theme which shall be taken up in greater detail
in the following chapter.

That there are distinctions in God Himself which correspond to the
triune distinctions of the event of revelation, namely the threefold pattern of
Revealer, Revelation, and Revealedness, is thus a thesis drawn from the
concept of revelation itself. The economic Trinity implies the immanent. It
cannot be the variety of revelatory works ascribed to God, however, which
establish these distinctions. The creative work of the Father, the reconciling
work of the Son, and the redemptive work of the Holy Spirit, do not in
themselves justify talk of an immanent Trinity. For the whole Western
trinitarian tradition within which Barth works declares that these outward
works of the Trinity are not the exclusive work of any one Person but are
properly works of the whole divine perichoretic fellowship. It is thus necessary
for Barth to distinguish form and content in revelation, so that while the

content bears witness to the unity of God, the form bears witness to the three distinctions (382f). This of course is nothing other than an appropriation of the tradition's doctrine of relations which serves to identify distinctions within the divine Being on the basis of the identifiable genetic relations of revelation (i.e., the *paternitas, filiatio,* and *processio*).[48] The fundamental aim of the traditional doctrine, however, was not to offer a confirmation of an eternal immanent Trinity over a mere economic Trinity, but rather to smooth over difficulties which arose in the tension between unity and threeness in God. Augustine gave the doctrine its definitive form over and against Arian critics who contended that distinctions in God implied either on the one hand a plurality of substances or natures within the Godhead or else the predication of accidents to the divine Being. In the former case orthodoxy would be affirming three gods. In the latter, the coherency of the doctrine was threatened, since the Aristotelian categories in which the debate was carried out excluded the predication of accidents to the divine being by definition.[49] Augustine rejected both alternatives and proffered a third, namely that the distinctions be understood as relations in God. The doctrine of relations offered a means of affirming the trinitarian assertion of divine Persons without threatening the divine unity. Its original context thus was that of the question, *"Quid tres?"*.

Barth is of course well aware of the original aim of the doctrine and in fact uses it to support his own thesis regarding the inadequacy of the term "Person" in reference to the eternal Modes of Being (KD I/1, 385f). Far more significant than this use however is his employment of the doctrine as a justification for an immanent Trinity. For the divine relations of paternity, filiality and spiration refer not solely to the divine inner life, but must also be understood as an attempt to describe the economy of salvation presented in the New Testament. Because God reveals Himself truly, then the patterns of origination which appear repeatedly in the biblical account must correspond to

something similar within God (383). Barth's articulation of this conception
bears the same formal if not rigid character of the traditional doctrine itself:

> In diesen Verhältnissen gründet die Dreiheit in der Einheit Gottes.
> Darin besteht diese Dreiheit, dass in dem Wesen oder Akte, in
> welchem Gott Gott ist, einmal ein reiner Ursprung und sodann
> zwei verschiedene Ausgänge stattfinden, von denen der erste allein
> auf den Ursprung, der zweite andersartige auf den Ursprung und
> zugleich auf den ersten Ausgang zurückzuführen sind. (384)

Barth offers no thorough exegetical grounding for the doctrine of relations. It
is preeminently the triune names themselves, Father, Son, and Holy Spirit
which justify the genetic pattern which Barth also identifies with the alternative
revelational triads: Holiness, Mercy, and Love; Good Friday, Easter, and
Pentecost; Creator, Reconciler, Redeemer (381).

The energy with which Barth takes up and asserts this bit of the tradition
is matched, however, by an equal reserve toward the meaningfulness of the
language. Here we are using "meaningfulness" in the technical sense of the
ability of a word or statement to refer to an object or idea which can be
comprehended on the basis of human reason or experience. With regard to the
divine processions which compose the doctrine of relations Barth concedes that
language at this point can only point or indicate (*bezeichnen*) (498). In fact,
theology cannot in any real sense distinguish between the *generatio* of the Son
and the *spiratio* of the Spirit, "Denn wie unterscheidet sich Hauchung von
Zeugung, wenn doch mit beiden in gleicher Unbedingtheit die ewige Genesis
einer ewigen Seinsweise Gottes bezeichnet sein soll?" (498). This should not be
interpreted as a mere flight into mystery or an uncritical acceptance of
traditional theses. Rather, it is an illustration of one of Barth's most consistent
theological themes of the *Kirchliche Dogmatik*, namely, the bi-polar view of
theological language which remains simultaneously critical toward its own
fragile linguistic character and emphatically dogmatic toward the truth claim of
its object.[50] It is incidently a thesis conditioned far more by the contemporary

thought world and modern epistemology than the ancient world of the tradition.

Filioque

The *filioque* question offers a further illustration of the innovative way in which Barth takes up the tradition into his own dogmatic formulation. The tradition determines the theme for Barth. He acknowledges at the beginning of his first discussion of the *filioque* in the *Kirchliche Dogmatik* that the only reason for taking up the question at all is that the separation of the Latin and Greek Churches stands under the sign of this particular dogmatic controversy (502). Consistent with his confessionally determined starting point, Barth pursues the defense of the *filioque* by placing himself firmly on the Western side of the debate and using many of the same arguments which have become part of the standard Western defense for the inclusion of the *filioque* within the creed.

Barth contends that the emendation of the Nicaeno-Constantinopolitan creed by the Latin West to read *qui ex Patre Filioque procedit*, while imposed in a high-handed and loveless manner, was nevertheless a theologically legitimate addition.[51] Much of his defense for its inclusion amounts to a repetition of classical arguments. The Eastern defense has always been able to claim biblical evidence for its position in that the procession of the Spirit is expressly found in only one passage (John 15:26) and is there a procession from the Father only. Barth counters with what has become the standard Western reply, namely, that the Eastern contention represents the isolation of one passage over against the wealth of New Testament references which describe the Spirit as the Spirit of the Son.[52] While the Holy Spirit may not be simply equated with the Son, the subjective side of the redemptive event (*Belehrung, Erleuchtung und Bewegung des Menschen*) is always a work of the

Spirit bearing witness to Christ (475). The *filioque* brings this relationship of the Holy Spirit to the Son to expression.

The East, however, does not deny that the Spirit proceeds from both the Father and the Son in the economy of Salvation. It is only when the procession in revelation is read back into the divine essence as such that the Eastern theologians take objection. It is within this frame of reference, the relationship of revelation to the eternal Being of God, that Barth's concern for the *filioque* must be understood, just as it is at this point that the *filioque* clause becomes crucial for his own trinitarian construction.

Barth's argument is this: the third moment in the threefold pattern of revelation is the moment of Revealedness. It is the moment of encounter in which the person becomes a genuine recipient of the revelation of God in Jesus Christ (470–72). This particular moment is ascribed to the Holy Spirit *per appropriationem*, and in Barth's scheme is nothing less than the primary appropriation of the Spirit.[53] The moment of Revealedness is the moment in which the human being enters into communion with God. Prerequisite to this fellowship is the second moment of revelation, the moment of Unveiling, which is the reconciliatory work of Jesus Christ the Son. The moment of Revealedness does not happen independent of the Revelation in Jesus Christ. The work of the Holy Spirit assumes the work of the Son.[54] Barth's trinitarian principle of correspondence requires that what God is in His revelation correspond to what He is eternally in Himself. The community which the Holy Spirit establishes between humanity and God corresponds to the community which happens in the divine life between Father and Son.[55]

> In der *innergöttlichen*, zweiseitigen, vom Vater und vom Sohn ausgehenden Gemeinschaft des Geistes ist es begründet, dass es in der *Offenbarung* eine Gemeinschaft gibt, in der nicht nur Gott für den Menschen, sondern wirklich—das ist doch das *Donum Spiritus sancti*—auch der Mensch für Gott da ist (504).

If the inner-divine foundation for the divine-human fellowship of revelation is denied as it is in the Eastern rejection of the *filioque*, then the legitimacy of revelation itself is put into question.

> Ist der Geist nur in der Offenbarung und für den Glauben auch der Geist des Sohnes, ist er in Ewigkeit, und das heisst doch wohl: in seiner eigentlichen und ursprünglichen Wirklichkeit, nur der Geist des Vaters, dann ist die Gemeinschaft des Geistes zwischen Gott und Mensch ohne objektiven Gehalt und Grund. Sie steht, mag sie immer offenbart und geglaubt sein, als bloss zeitliche Wahrheit ohne ewigen Grund sozusagen auf sich selber. (504)[56]

The *filioque* also brings to expression for Barth the powerful christological focus of his trinitarian thought. It underscores what was called in the last chapter the christological heart of the Trinity. Thus there can be no question for Christian faith of a new or different leading of the Spirit beyond Christ. The Holy Spirit is not only the event of God's presence here and now, and not only God's *pro nobis*,[57] but is now and in eternity the Spirit of the Father and the Son (KD I/2, 273). When one separates the Holy Spirit from the Son with the result of this or that type of spiritualism, then it is some other spirit besides the Spirit of God which leads. The *filioque* establishes the objectivity of faith from which the subjective side, the side of the Spirit cannot depart.

Barth and the Fourth Century

At the conclusion of Barth's exposition of the Church doctrine of the Trinity in *Kirchliche Dogmatik* I/1, he pauses for a reflection upon the fourth century Church which gave the doctrine its initial form. The argumentation in his brief discussion provides a summary of many of the aspects and emphases of Barth's regard for the dogmatic tradition which we have considered in the present chapter. Within this essay which Barth entitles "Der Sinn der Trinitäts-lehre" (KD I/1, §9.4), two major theses are to be observed: (1) The decision which the fourth century Church made regarding the doctrine of the Trinity, given formal expression in the Nicaean and Nicaeno-Constantinopolitan

Creeds, far from being the artifact of a bygone era, is a decision which, in spite of its historically and culturally conditioned form, expresses a content *understandable and relevant* for the Church of every age. (2) The question with which the fourth century struggled is not simply a product of its time, but an urgent question implicit in the texts of Scripture, which *necessarily demands an answer* from the Church of every age. Each of these assertions warrants consideration.

In the discussion above of Barth's conceptual model for relating the tradition to the interpretation, we spoke of the historical compression effected by Barth's faith perspective for reading the tradition, a perspective which sets aside the historical differences between then and now and brings to focus an essential decision of faith which is trans-historical in character. This is particularly in evidence in the first thesis which he sets forth in the essay on the fourth century Church. It is significant that within the context of this discussion Barth offers no historical excursus on the events surrounding the Councils of Nicaea and Constantinople. That Church and state politics played a role in the outcome of the Councils, and that Neo-Platonic Logos speculation provided the conceptual structures through which trinitarian statements were formulated, are not challenged by Barth (396f, 400). But it is characteristic of Barth's method in this regard to insist on the necessity that the systematic theologian get beyond the vast array of non-theological factors and give heed to what is essentially a theological decision. From the perspective of faith, or rather from the perspective that it is the same Word of God which addressed the Church then as addresses the Church now, Barth is able to describe the Church of the fourth century and the Church of today as "one and the same" (397). Consequently, it is a meaningful undertaking for the Church today to inquire after the theological intentions (and not merely the historical, philosophical, and cultural influences) behind the initial formulation of the doctrine of the Trinity.

The most obvious objection which one could raise against Barth's trans-
historical theological approach to the tradition is that it represents an
unrealistic appreciation of the seriousness of the historical gap between the
Church of then and now. Samuel Laeuchli has registered what is perhaps the
sharpest objection to Barth in this regard.[58] Laeuchli charges Barth with the
construction of a "doketische Geschichte, eine Abstraktion eines Sektors,"
which has relatively little to do with the fourth century.[59] Barth's response to
historical research into the background of the theological texts of the time is
no more than "emotional, defensive polemic."[60]

Much of Laeuchli's critique is overstated to the point of the grotesque.
He portrays Barth as a defensive theologian who must affirm the Trinity
doctrine if he is to proceed further with the orthodox direction of his thought.
In order to do so he attempts, with a "bad conscience,"[61] to justify fourth
century trinitarian theology, a task which he can only accomplish by holding in
contempt historical research into the era and constructing his own imaginary
history to protect against the incriminating evidence of the history of the era
as historians know it. Laeuchli's own alternative is nothing short of an
unreserved leap into historicism, as the following passage illustrates well:

> Das 4. Jahrhundert ist konkrete Geschichte, Konzilien, politische
> Entscheidungen, wirtschaftlich-soziale Entwicklung; das 4. Jahr-
> hundert ist politischer Umbruch der römischen Welt zugunsten
> einer neuen religiösen Weltmacht, der katholischen Kirche, einer
> Weltmacht, die auf der einen Seite brutal politisch und auf der
> andern weltflüchtigen-asketisch lebt; das 4. Jahrhundert ist ein
> faszinierendes Kapitel des christlichen Dramas, und das heisst:
> eines Dramas mit menschlichen Entscheidungen, mit den Absurdi-
> täten zweideutiger Sprache und der Freiheit von Spekulation und
> Phantasie. Die Bischöfe, die unter politischem Druck und dem
> Pomp eines scheinbar bekehrten Kaisers zum Symbol von Nizäa Ja
> sagten, hatten zugleich ihre eigene Stellung als machtvolle
> Herrscher (Pantokrator-Christus als neuverstandenes Symbol der
> Kirche) und die grossartige Stärke und Arroganz der Ecclesia
> Catholica vertreten. Das 4. Jahrhundert war menschliche Freiheit
> und zugleich sozial und wirtschaftliche Gesetzmässigkeit innerhalb

des von Diokletian umgeformten Reiches und der aggressiven kirchlichen Institution, eben des politischen Katholizismus.

Die Entscheidungen der Kirche sind politisch, psychologisch, wirtschaftlich, sie sind künstlerisch und sozial, durch Zufall geworden und doch auch merkwürdige Gesetzmässigkeiten unterworfen.[62]

Laeuchli's critique strikes rather wide of the mark. It is true that Barth's regard for the theological integrity of the confessional decisions of the fourth century Church does indeed constitute a historical abstraction. It is far from obvious, however, how this observation alone should invalidate his methodological path, particularly since the process of abstraction is a wholly conscious and intentional undertaking which acknowledges the vast array of non-theological factors at work upon the object of observation. Barth does not create an imaginary fourth century as Laeuchli suggests. What he does do is to isolate a carefully selected portion of it and view it from a highly specialized perspective. The outcome is in no sense an account of the history of the era, nor even a history of dogma for that time. Barth is interested in neither recounting the history of the fourth century Church nor of refuting it. It is not to say, "This is what happened," but rather, "This also happened." And the historicism which Laeuchli offers as the alternative represents not only a refusal to take seriously the theological language of another era because of its conditioned character but means inevitably the refusal to take seriously the theological language of our own era for the same reason.

Laeuchli's objections are not however wholly without merit. At the heart of his critique lies the offense of a theological effort to *retrieve* the tradition which lapses into mere *repetition*. That Barth is not engaged in a mere repetition of tradition is one of the theses that this chapter has sought to advance. Nevertheless, it remains clear that Barth could do more than he has done to formulate the doctrine without clinging so faithfully to its Augustinian

and scholastic form. One of the criticisms which Laeuchli makes against Barth
is the historical abstraction which his theological interpretation constitutes. But
the real problem with the use which Barth makes of the trinitarian decision of
the early Church is not his historical abstraction, but rather that the abstraction
is not sufficiently refined. That is, theology must abstract more and not less
than Barth. Barth's account of the fourth century is one which seeks to reckon
with the kernel of truth in a theological struggle over a pressing problem posed
by Scripture. In providing an account of that kernel, however, Barth allows
much that is distinctively the contribution of fourth century life and thought to
shape his language. The kernel is not entirely freed from the shell which
encloses it. This observation is one which we shall develop further in the
conclusions which follow.

The second thesis asserted by Barth in the discussion of §9.4 posits the
"necessity" of the trinitarian decision. The question to which the doctrine of the
Trinity is the answer is one which imposes itself upon the Church of every era
which takes seriously the witness of Scripture.[63] Barth raises the rhetorical
question,

> ob das Dogma nicht etwa, bei und in aller nicht zu leugnenden und
> nicht zu verwischenden Bedingtheit seiner Entstehung, eine Ein-
> sicht ausspricht, zu der eine auf die Heilige Schrift hörende Kirche
> nicht nur kommen *konnte*, sondern zu bestimmter Zeit kommen
> *musste*? Ob man sich, indem man die Schrift und das Dogma für
> sich selbst reden lässt, der Überzeugung entziehen kann, dass hier
> die göttliche Wahrheit in einer Weise menschlich formuliert
> worden ist, in der sie einmal formuliert werden musste und so, dass
> diese Formulierung, nachdem sie einmal geschehen ist, nicht
> wieder verloren gehen oder vergessen werden darf? (399)

The inescapable question which the Church took upon itself was the question
of the identity of Jesus Christ and the Holy Spirit, or in Barth's phraseology,
the "Subjekt der Offenbarung" (440f). The necessity of which Barth speaks in
this context is a necessity for human reflection, or more specifically, the
reflection of faith. That God's revelation in Jesus Christ claims Lordship is the

clear testimony of Scripture. That this Lordship must be somehow related to the one Lord and God is an inevitable demand upon human reflection.

Barth ascertains a circular logic at work in the doctrine of the Trinity which he wishes to raise to the level of a hermeneutical principle for the whole of theology. The doctrine of the Trinity answers the question as to the subject of revelation. It is an assertion of the fact that God is the one who reveals Himself in Jesus Christ. In answering this question however it immediately adds the complementary thesis that God is no other than He who reveals Himself in Jesus Christ.[64] The doctrine identifies God in the event of revelation and then declares the revelation to be the definitive identification of God. Barth expresses this interpretation in more concrete terms as the double content of the doctrine of the Trinity: (1) the identity of essence of the Father, Son, and Holy Spirit, and (2) that God is God only as Father, Son, and Holy Spirit (401). It is this double content of the doctrine which carries its assertions beyond that of the Bible.

The double content of the doctrine is directed against two possible but erroneous understandings of revelation. It is directed first of all against the heresy of subordinationism, which Barth describes simply as the denial that the Father, Son or Holy Spirit in their particular Modes of Being are in equal measure God (401f). In subordinationism Barth recognizes a significant threat against the sharp distinction between God and creation which the doctrine of the Trinity serves to preserve. This is the heart of the error of the subordinationist heresy—a drawing of the divine into the realm of the creaturely, with the ultimate consequence that revelation itself must be denied, since the divine-human encounter is transformed into a dialogue of humankind with itself. It is directed secondly against the heresy of modalism which Barth describes as the denial that the three moments of revelation are constitutive of the divine nature as such (402f). Modalism is the attempt to understand revelation as something foreign to the actual nature of God. The Trinity belongs to the divine economy so that the actual reality of God lies ultimately behind the Father, Son and Holy Spirit. The consequence is a dissolution of the Trinity in favor of a fourth reality hidden in mystery. But the modalistic attempt to get behind the Trinity means in the end an effort to get behind God, which for Barth is equivalent to making the divine Subject into an object so that consequently God Himself is denied. Subordinationism and modalism are for Barth not merely historical but perennial possibilities which threaten the Church's knowledge and understanding of revelation. The doctrine of the Trinity is the vanguard against the threat, and this, quite simply, was the theological intention of the fourth century Church's initial formulation of the dogma.

For Barth then trinitarian thinking follows "necessarily" upon the Church's efforts to take the biblical witness to the Lordship of Christ and the presence of God in His Holy Spirit seriously. And this we can affirm. But what must be questioned is Barth's apparent insistence that trinitarian thinking means "necessarily" thought and speech within the framework of the Church's traditional *doctrine* of the Trinity. For Barth there is a necessity to the very form which the doctrine assumes, a form characterized by a rigidity of language which bears the marks of its linguistic inheritance from the thought world of Neo-Platonic emanationist theology. This is ever so striking in light of Barth's clear acknowledgements of the conditioned character of the language. And further, because the effective power of language to communicate truth is exercised only by means of the *analogia fidei*, and thus resides ultimately in God's grace, the particular linguistic form in which a truth content is conveyed becomes relatively incidental. Here Barth stands in need of a corrective which rises out of his own theological reflection. For if the task of theology is to be a reflection upon the proclamation of the Church today in light of Scripture, as Barth wills it to be, then it is incumbent upon the theologian to strive toward a meaningful expression of that reflection in the thought forms and language of his or her own day.

Strengths and Dangers of the Tradition-Retrieval Function

The foregoing discussion has sought to provide an overview of the role which traditional trinitarian dogma plays in Barth's own doctrine of the Trinity as presented in *Kirchliche Dogmatik* I/1. We began with a presentation of the conceptual model which Barth developed in I/2 for the authority of theological tradition, giving particular attention to the relationship envisioned there between the tradition and the ongoing life of the Church and the proposed hermeneutical relationship between Scripture and tradition. In the second part of the discussion we considered selected, overt instances of appropriation of the tradition in Barth's own trinitarian construction drawn from certain critical moments of traditional trinitarian thinking: the problem of unity and diversity, the problem of relating economic and immanent trinities, and the problem of the *filioque*. We concluded the section with an overview of Barth's interpretation of the origin of the doctrine of the Trinity in the early Church. The task remains to draw conclusions regarding the significance of this discussion for the trinitarian hermeneutic which we have observed to be at work throughout the *Kirchliche Dogmatik*. These conclusions may be brought together under three general headings. The first focuses upon the positive role of the tradition under the rubric of the ecclesiological significance of the trinitarian hermeneutic. The second and third point up deficiencies and dangers in the model under the general headings of the doctrine's "necessity" and the difficulty of the "commentary" metaphor in Barth's relating of Scripture and tradition.

(1) Barth's strong reliance on the language and conceptualities of Western trinitarian development for his own systematic statement of the doctrine signifies the construction of a hermeneutical frame of reference for which a dominant feature is an invitation to read the texts of Scripture within

the historical fellowship of the Church, that is, within that "place" in which the Scriptures have become the living Word of God. The doctrine of the Trinity is neither revelation nor Scripture, but rather a human interpretation of revelation and Scripture. But as such it is not just any interpretation. It is the interpretation which grew out of the struggles of a particular community, the Church, with its own special texts, the Bible. In referring again and again to the traditional formulations of the creeds and major texts of the Fathers Barth seeks to remind us that it is this particular interpretation of creation, redemptive history and God which has characterized the way in which the Church has read Scripture throughout most of its history. And if one wishes to read Scripture in that "place" in which it has life and in that "place" in which it has been known to speak a word of profound address to those who listen, then one will at least want to begin by reading it in this way. Taking seriously the confession of the triune God means taking seriously the choirs of voices of those who have gone before who bear testimony to the identity of the God whom Scripture reveals. The doctrine of the Trinity represents an understand-ing of Scripture and revelation which for Barth binds the Church together throughout history under the confession of the Lordship of the one and same God. Barth's willingness to grant a preeminent position to the doctrine in the *Kirchliche Dogmatik* must be taken as a rejection of theological individualism, and the theological communalism which he would confess extends not only throughout the contemporary Church but throughout history as well.

The high regard which this reveals for the Church's creeds and revered writings does not however signal a subtle form of authoritarianism. It is not orthodoxy for orthodoxy's sake. What has been demonstrated in each of the concrete instances of utilization of traditional materials is a creative appropria-tion of traditional formulations. Barth is selective in those materials which he adopts and often plays one position off another. The "hermeneutical spiral" which characterizes his method of appropriation allows for a creative interplay of tradition with Scripture without losing the Protestant principle of Scriptural priority. He seeks for the fundamental aim in any particular doctrinal formulation and readily acknowledges the limits within which it may be applied. Ancient formulations take on new life as Barth supplements traditional conceptualities with his own conceptual tools, the most obvious example of which is his replacement of a formal trinitarian structure steeped in substance categories with his own actualistic conception. For Barth the tradition takes on the role of sign-post. The tradition guides and directs but does not itself constitute the journey, that is, the process of encounter which the Church always undertakes anew with its Scripture.

(2) While Barth is neither rigid nor authoritarian in his estimation of the role and meaningfulness of the traditional Trinity doctrine, an ambiguity remains with his assertion of the necessity of the doctrine. Barth contends that the traditional doctrine brings to expression an insight which is inevitable wherever the Church takes seriously the biblical witness to God's self-revelation. But when Barth states what this insight is, it is already *in nuce* the Church doctrine of the Trinity: the double assertion of the identity of essence of Father, Son, and Holy Spirit, and God's eternal triune nature. It is helpful here to call upon a distinction suggested by Joest. The confession in the triune God precedes the doctrine of the Trinity. The doctrine is an attempt to give conceptual content to the confession.[65] Barth is correct in characterizing the confession in the triune God as an inevitability or necessity of Christian interpretation of Scripture. If God really reveals Himself in Jesus Christ and if God is really present in the Holy Spirit, then Christian talk of God will necessarily be trinitarian talk. We may even grant a necessity to the Church's rejection of subordinationism and modalism by means of trinitarian formulations. To grant necessity, however, to the positive formulation of the dogma amounts to a virtual denial of the historically relative and human character of the dogma which elsewhere Barth so staunchly defends.

Barth's intention in asserting the necessity of the early Church's formulation of the doctrine is to bind it as closely as possible to Scripture and revelation. The doctrine of the Trinity is indeed a human, fallible work, a creation of the Church. But the object which the doctrine seeks to express in language is already rooted in Scripture as the subject of God's self-revelation. The doctrine is necessary for Barth in the sense that the doctrine unfolds a content seminally present in the texts of Scripture. This characterization, however, is not a fair representation of the process of thought at work in the development of trinitarian dogma. The dogma did not simply lie hidden in the pages of Scripture waiting for the Church to develop the proper exegesis, a point which brings us to our final conclusion.

(3) One of the ways in which Barth seeks to secure the close bond between the doctrine of the Trinity and Scripture is his often repeated "commentary" metaphor for relating tradition and Scripture. The tradition is a commentary which exegetes and interprets the Scripture but which may add no new "article of faith" not already found in Scripture. With regard to the trinitarian tradition appropriated by Barth, however, the metaphor is stretched beyond recognition. A commentary is normally thought of as an aid to understanding a text which enlightens the reader by offering a thorough explication of the text. It is not usually the task of a commentary to pursue that which the text leaves unresolved. The trinitarian tradition in theology can certainly be understood as an attempt to explain and interpret Scripture. But the tradition begins precisely where the Scripture leaves off, precisely at those points where the Scripture leaves itself open and unresolved. "Reflection" is the far more appropriate term to depict the process at work in the history of the early Church, as the Church thought to make sense of its own trinitarian confession. "Reflection," too, is a far more appropriate designation for the trinitarian hermeneutic proffered by Barth. The doctrine of the Trinity which Barth takes over from the tradition is more than an "exegesis" and more than

a "translation" of the biblical account of revelation. It is rather a reflective expansion of that account which is necessary if the trinitarian confession is to become a meaningful part of the Church's talk of God.

The deficiencies noted here are not intended as a rejection of Barth's trinitarian formulation nor a discrediting of the process of appropriating traditional materials which constitutes a significant portion of that development. Far more significant than these particular overstatements is the process of doctrinal retrieval itself, the "remaking" of the doctrine of the Trinity which Barth undertakes. In so doing, Barth has rediscovered for the Protestant tradition of the modern era a creative resource for the Church's reading of Scripture, namely, its own past. This is of course but one aspect of Barth's doctrine, and it is a feature characteristic not only of the Trinity doctrine but of the whole *Kirchliche Dogmatik*. Nevertheless, it should not be underestimated when assessing the hermeneutical significance of the doctrine as Barth wishes to formulate it.

ENDNOTES

[1]See above, 91. Meckenstock traces the development of Barth's use of traditional and ecclesiastical themes as an element of increasing significance in the early phases of his work. See Günter Meckenstock, "Karl Barth's Prolegomena zur Dogmatik: Entwicklungslinien vom 'Unterricht in der christlicher Religion' bis zur 'Kirchlichen Dogmatik,'" NZThR 28 (1986) 296-310.

[2]"Wir müssen, um ihr Sein zu beschreiben, die üblichen Unterscheidungen von Sein und Akt, Statik und Dynamik, Essenz und Existenz hinter uns lassen. Gerade ihr Akt ist ihr wahrhaftes Sein, gerade ihre Dynamik ihre Statik, gerade ihre Existenz ihre Essenz" (KD IV/1, 727). Cf. "Die Kirche," 22–27. "Es geschieht in dieser Zeit vom Himmel herunter und hinunter auf die Erde, von Gottes ewigen Throne her hinein in die ihrem Ende entgegen-laufende Weltgeschichte, aus dem Geheimnis des dreieinigen Gottes hinein in der Geschöpfwelt, dass diese Gemeinde versammelt wird. Die Kirche ist, indem das *geschieht*. Die Kirche ist das *Ereignis* dieser *Versammlung*" (22).

[3]On Barth's peculiar fascination with the forty days, see KD I/2, 126–30, 455, 468, 604f; III/2, 529f, 538–555; IV/1, 332–4, 352–9, 373–8, 820.

[4]This is confirmed by Barth's thesis on the proper relationship of the categories "revelation and history": "Offenbarung ist nicht ein Prädikat der Geschichte, sondern Geschichte ist ein Prädikat der Offenbarung." KD I/2, 64. The intention is to deny any attempt to derive revelation from a general notion of history. This need not suggest an infringement upon the reality status of human history as such, as suggested in the critical essay of R. H. Roberts, "Karl Barth's Doctrine of Time: Its Nature and Implications," in S. W. Sykes, ed., *Karl Barth: Studies of his Theological Method* (Oxford: Clarendon Press, 1979), 88–146, esp. 102–8. The telescoping of history which is often evident with Barth results from the perspective of revelation which addresses all of human history from the vantage point of a particular historical moment, the revelation of God in Jesus Christ. The ontological grounding of revelation and indeed of time and creation in a free eternal decision of God does not violate the dignity of human history; the self-understanding of the world of human experience is neither denied nor contested. Rather, it is interpreted in light of what the Church confesses to be final (i.e., eschatological) reality, the reality of God's self-revelation in Jesus Christ. See Ingolf Dalferth, "Theologischer Realismus und realistische Theologie bei Karl Barth," EvTh 46 (1986) 402–22, who describes Barth's view of temporal worldly reality as "enhypostatic reality" (411), a concept which represents a distinctive advance in the efforts of theology throughout history to think God and the world together (414f).

[5]"Ist aus der Gegenwart einer solchen Konfession Vergangenheit geworden, so kann nämlich gerade das *Alter*, das sie damit bekommt, für ihre Würde sprechen; die Kirche späterer Zeit kann dann besonderes Gewicht darauf legen, sich dieser Konfession gerade darum anzuschliessen, weil sie sich damit zu dem einen unveränderlichen Glauben aller Zeiten bekennt." KD I/2, 701.

[6]Barth's view should be understood in distinction to those who would simply posit an optimistic appraisal of the continuity between past and present and the ability of the historian to reproduce an "accurate" and "objective" picture of the past. Richard P. C. Hanson would represent basically the same affirmation of relative continuity between the tradition of the Church and its recipients but offers a defense based more on anthropological and historical-cultural observations than theological analysis. See *The Continuity of Christian*

Doctrine (New York, Seabury, 1981), esp. Ch. 1, "Are We Cut Off from the Past?" 1–19. Cf. also Richard J. Bauckham, "Tradition in Relation to Scripture and Reason," in *Scripture, Tradition and Reason: Essays in Honour of Richard P. C. Hanson* (Edinburgh: T & T Clark, 1988), 117–145. Bauckham proposes a model which interprets tradition in terms of its context. Retrieval remains at all times a relatively possible undertaking contingent upon the degree of contextual overlap between one time or culture and another.

[7]KD I/2, 655f. Cf. *Credo*, 156.

[8]Cf. Barth's critique of the biblicism of Gottfried Menken in ProtTh, 469–83. See also KD I/2, 678–80 and Credo, 155–58.

[9]Barth declares in the foreword to KD I/1, "Wenn im Titel des Buches an die Stelle des Wortes 'christlich' das Wort 'kirchlich' getreten ist, so bedeutet das, ...dass ich zum vornherein darauf hinweisen möchte: Dogmatik ist keine 'freie' sondern eine an den Raum der Kirche gebundene, da und nur da mögliche und sinnvolle Wissenschaft" (viii).

[10]It is in characterizing this confessional horizon as a *sine qua non* of the theological task that Barth denies the possibility of "dogmatic tolerance" in authentic theology, a less than fortunate choice of words which states, or perhaps overstates, a nevertheless valid characteristic of Christian theology (KD I/2, 920). Cf. the observation of Ernst Kinder: "Zumindest in ihrem Ansatz ist Dogmatik nicht anders möglich als aus dem Stehen in einer bestimmten, kirchlich vorgegebenen Bekenntnisrelation zu der christlichen Botschaft heraus, und faktisch wird auch keine dogmatische Arbeit anders getrieben." "Dogmatik und Dogma," *Dogma und Denkstrukturen*, ed. W. Joest & W. Pannenberg (Göttingen: Vandenhoeck & Ruprecht, 1963), 23.

[11]The nomenclature is taken from a model developed by Randall Bush, in "The Hermeneutical Spiral and the Revelation of God as Trinity," PRSt 14 (1987) 11–27.

[12]KD I/2, 694f. Cf. also K. Barth, "Das Bekenntnis der Reformation und unser Bekennen," in TFA, 264.

[13]By emphasizing the relative and restricted authority of the tradition which is subordinate to the concrete norm of Scripture, Barth wishes to set himself apart from what he saw as two dominant streams of Christian theology: from Neo-Protestantism's virtual break with Christian tradition, and from Roman Catholic theology, for whom "Dogma...ist Offenbarungszeugnis wie die heilige Schrift selber." KD I/2, 737. Barth's relativizing of the tradition's authority is of course directed against the latter. Cf. Barth's critique of the historical development of the Roman Catholic concept of revelation, Church, and tradition (609–37). The case for Barth's criticism of Catholic theology's elevation of the tradition to a second source of knowledge of revelation is sufficient as long as the 1940 date of publication is kept in mind. The contemporary situation in Catholic theology is (fortunately) not quite so simple. Yves Congar has argued persuasively on behalf of a dynamic understanding of the "Church's Tradition, conceived not just as a material object but as the active presence of revelation in a living subject, by power of the Holy Spirit."* He seeks to interpret the tradition in light of an ecclesiology which identifies the Church as the *locus* of God's continuing revelation. Congar like Barth stresses the interpretive function of the tradition relative to Scripture. See Yves Congar, O. P., *Tradition and Traditions*, tr. M.

Naseby & T. Rainborough (London: Burns & Oates, rpt. 1966 [=1960]), esp. Pt. 2, Ch. 5, "Scripture and Tradition in Relation to Revelation and to the Church," 376–424. *Citation from Congar, 401.

[14]"Die Dogmatik hat sich bei ihrer Prüfung der kirchlichen Verkündigung zu orientieren an der konkreten Situation, in der die kirchliche Verkündigung heute ausgerichtet werden muss, an ihrer Stellung und Aufgabe gegenüber ihrer besonderen Zeitgenossenschaft, d.h. an dem Worte Gottes, wie es in der Gegenwart von Gott gesprochen und von der Kirche zu verkündigen ist.... Sie muss sich in den Problemen, Sorgen, Verlegenheiten und Hoffnungen, die das Kirchenregiment (im weitesten Sinn dieses Begriffs) dieser jeweiligen Gegenwart so oder so in Anspruch nehmen und beschäftigen, mit diesem unbedingt solidarisch wissen und aus dieser unbedingten Solidarität heraus wird sie zu denken und zu reden haben" (KD I/2, 939).

[15]Cf. the analysis of the "linear hermeneutic" of Bush, 19–23.

[16]See Lewis S. Mudge, "Hermeneutical Circle," *A New Dictionary of Christian Theology*, ed. A. Richardson and J. Bowden (London: SCM, 1983). For a summary of the significance of the concept for the hermeneutics of Schleiermacher and Heidegger, see Anthony Thiselton, *The Two Horizons* (Exeter: Pater Noster, 1980), 104–10, 163–68, 194–97.

[17]Cf. Barth on the ecumenical character of dogmatics (KD I/2, 919–938).

[18]With regard to the determination of the Fathers of the Church this means, "Ein Lehrer der Kirche ist derjenige, der uns in Auslegung der heiligen Schrift heute etwas uns Angehendes zu sagen hat" (KD I/2, 688).

[19]Cf. Barth's comment on profane motives in the history of dogma. KD I/1, 398.

[20]Cf. the alternative view of Mackey, for whom "the more defensive a position is seen to be, the less claim it has to permanence after the particular threat it was meant to meet has declined." James Mackey, *The Christian Experience of God as Trinity* (London: SCM, 1983), 170.

[21]"Gerade in dieser Einschränkung hat es kirchliche Universalität, ist es kirchliches Dogma, hat es also kirchliche Autorität" (KD I/2, 699).

[22]Cf. remarks above, 136.

[23]It is precisely this danger, a danger which threatens all theological language rooted in the tradition, which is the foremost justification for an intentional and explicit hermeneutics of dogma, such as that outlined by William R. Crockett, "The Hermeneutics of Doctrine," in *The Future of Anglican Theology*, ed. M. D. Bryant, Toronto Studies in Theology, 17 (New York: Edwin Mellen Press, 1984), 59–71. Cf. also the chapter of Avery Dulles, "The Hermeneutics of Dogmatic Statements," *The Survival of Dogma* (Garden City: Image Books, 1973 rpt. [=1971]), 176–91.

[24]J. N. D. Kelly, *Early Christian Doctrines* (New York: Harper & Bros., 1958), 113.

[25] In addition to the works of Mackey and Jenson discussed below the following should also be noted: David Brown, *The Divine Trinity* (London: Duckworth, 1985); Joseph Bracken, *The Triune Symbol* (Lanham: Univ. Press of America, 1985); William Hill, *The Three-personed God* (Washington D.C.: Catholic University of America, 1982); Walter Kasper, *Der Gott Jesu Christi* (Mainz: Matthias Grünewald, 1982); ET = *The God of Jesus Christ*, tr. M. J. O'Connell (London: SCM, 1983); Jürgen Moltmann, *Trinität und Reich Gottes* (Munich: Kaiser, 1980); ET = *The Trinity and the Kingdom of God*, tr. M. Kohl (London: SCM, 1981). Wolfhart Pannenberg has given considerable space to a treatment of the doctrine in *Systematische Theologie*, I (Göttingen: Vandenhoeck & Ruprecht, 1988), 283–364.

[26] "Remaking" is the very appropriate term employed by Wiles to depict the process of development which is necessary for Christian doctrine to thrive. See Maurice Wiles, *The Remaking of Christian Doctrine* (London: SCM, 1974), esp. 1–19.

[27] James P. Mackey, *The Christian Experience of God as Trinity* (London: SCM, 1983). Robert Jenson, *The Triune Identity* (Philadelphia: Fortress, 1982).

[28] Jenson, *Triune,* 84–6.

[29] Ibid., 117f.

[30] Ibid., 118.

[31] Ibid.

[32] Ibid., 125.

[33] The criticism is also one shared by Pannenberg. See *Theologie*, 332–4, 360f. While Pannenberg acknowledges that an immanent Trinity is the necessary implication of a revelational Trinity, so that principally the historical development of the dogma represents a correct theological intention, he wishes to emphasize the concomitant danger that as soon as the concept of an immanent Trinity is allowed place, it begins to take on an independence which loses relevance for temporal revelation (360f). Pannenberg applies himself to a revision of the immanent-economic schema on the basis of a new understanding of the unity of the divine Persons which is genuinely rooted in an exegetical consideration of the history of Jesus. Pannenberg's impressive alternative to the traditional doctrine of relations is an analysis of the biblical relationships which obtain between Jesus, God the Father, and the Holy Spirit. It is here that he finds the "Beginnings of the Doctrine of the Trinity," with which he initiates the discussion (283–305).

[34] Mackey, 126–29, 165.

[35] Ibid., 170f. Cf. Pannenberg, *Theologie*, 303f.

[36] Ibid., 171f.

[37] Following a definition of Quenstedt, Barth defines the basic reality of God as, "Das, was den Jahve-Kyrios zu dem macht, oder das, worin der Jahve-Kyrios der ist, als der er sich in diesem Namen, dem Herrennamen bezeichnet." KD I/1, 369.

[38]The emphasis which Barth gives to the one over the three is the critical point in Pannenberg's dispute with Barth (and indeed the whole Western tradition). Pannenberg's basic thesis is as follows: "Jede Ableitung der Pluralität der trinitarischen Personen aus einem Wesensbegriff des einen Gottes, sei es als Geist oder als Liebe, führt also in die Schwierigkeiten hier des Modalismus, dort des Subordinationismus." Pannenberg, *Theologie*, 325. Such a derivation of the three Persons from a previously established concept of divine singularity is precisely what Barth undertakes in his (Hegelian) trinitarian construction which proceeds on the basis of a notion of God as Absolute Subject (322f). While Pannenberg reasons that the flaw in this procedure is its inability to give full account of the mutual relatedness of the divine Persons which is constitutive not only for their mutual distinction but for their divinity as well, the real error seems to be simply the priority of unity which is the result. Pannenberg's conception of the triune Persons as "Lebensvollzüge selbständiger Aktzentren" (347) and his subsequent social Trinity must be viewed as the criterion by which he judges the tradition. The difficulty which this criterion brings to light is one endemic to the problem of the Trinity itself and not the result of a particular methodological decision. In this light one must ask Pannenberg if every derivation of the unity of the triune God out of a concept of three distinct Persons, such as his own of "independent centers of action," does not in fact lead into the difficulty of tritheism?

[39]Monarchianism of the Sabellian type is in fact precisely the complaint which Moltmann brings against Barth. That the complaint is unjustified will become clearer below. Moltmann, 154–61. ET, 139–44. Cf. Pannenberg, *Theologie*, 322–26.

[40]Anselm, *Epistola de Incarnatione Verbi* 15. Cited KD I/1 370.

[41]Moltmann, however, is unconvinced. He complains, "In der Trinitätslehre kann es sich nicht um das dreimalige Setzen desselben handeln." Moltmann, 158. ET, 141. The criticism is painfully imprecise and hardly helpful. Indeed, the doctrine of the Trinity does have to do with the "same thing" three times, inasmuch that whenever we have to do with a trinitarian Person we have to do with God. This is as true for Moltmann's social trinity as it is for Barth's doctrine. Moreover, in the Barthian formulation it is not only the "same thing" three times, but the "same thing" always in one of three distinct, non-interchangeable, eternal "Modes of Being."

[42]KD I/1, 390 (my translation).

[43]Barth offers a brief history of the term and its problems in KD I/1, 375–78. See also "Persona" in R. A. Muller, ed., *Dictionary of Latin and Greek Theological Terms* (Grand Rapids: Baker, 1985); Jenson, *Triune*, 72–4, 103–5, 114f; E. J. Fortman, *The Triune God* (Grand Rapids: Baker, 1972) 163f, 295–300. The linguistic confusion created by the parallel Greek and Latin trinitarian traditions was the occasion of Augustine's often cited epigram, according to which one speaks of three Persons, "non ut illud diceretur, sed ne taceretur omnino." *de Trinitate*, V.9. Cf. VII.4.

[44]See above, 100ff.

[45]Basil of Caesarea, *de Spiritu Sancto*, 43f. Cited Claude Welch, *The Trinity in Contemporary Theology* (London: SCM, 1953), 190.

[46]The harsh criticism which Barth has received from Pannenberg and Moltmann for this terminological decision and its underlying emphasis upon divine unity must be weighed against their equal dissatisfaction with the Western tradition in general and in Moltmann's case, a desire for rapprochement with the East. See Moltmann, 154f, 204–6 (ET, 139f, 188–90); Wolfhart Pannenberg, "Die Subjektivität Gottes und die Trinitätslehre," in *Grundfragen systematischer Theologie*, II (Göttingen: Vandenhoeck & Ruprecht, 1980), 99–101, 109–11. Cf. Pannenberg, *Theologie*, 322f.

[47]Fortman, 262.

[48]The doctrine of relations assumed its classic form in the theology of Augustine. See *de Trinitate*, V.5–14. Augustine's formulation became normative for Western theology and remained influential upon Reformed dogmatics, which forms the "confessionally determined" place of the *Kirchliche Dogmatik*. Cf. H. Heppe, *Die Dogmatik der evangelisch-reformierte Kirche: Dargestellt und aus den Quellen belegt* (Neukirchen: E. Bizer, [2]1958), VI.11. ET = *Reformed Dogmatics: Set Out and Illustrated from the Sources*, tr. G. T. Thomson (London: Allen & Unwin, 1950).

[49]See Kelly, 274f. Cf. F. C. Baur, *Die christliche Lehre von der Dreieinigkeit und Menschwerdung Gottes*, I (Tübingen: Osiander, 1841), 836–44.

[50]Barth would thus dialectically counterpoise the Anselmian (and Augustinian) *tres nescio quid* with an equally weighted assertion of the "eschatological" truth of the trinitarian dogma. Cf. Dalferth, "Theologischer Realismus," 403.

[51]On the history of the *filioque* controversy, which need not be presented here, see Jaroslav Pelikan, *The Spirit of Eastern Christendom (600–1700)* (Chicago: Univ. of Chicago, 1974), 183–98. Cf. Barth's own historical summary, KD I/1, 500–502.

[52]KD I/1, 503f. Barth places exegetical weight not only on particular instances in which the New Testament speaks expressly of the Spirit of Christ, but especially upon John 15:26 and 16:13 which describe the task of the Spirit in terms of testimony to Christ (475). Cf. Pohle-Preuss, 173f, 177f, for a defense markedly similar to Barth's. Cf. also Heppe, VI.31.

[53]The primary trinitarian appropriations for Barth are God as Creator, God as Reconciler, God as Redeemer. KD I/1, 404, 419, 470.

[54]"Heiligen Geist gibt es nämlich nur jenseits des Todes und der Auferstehung Jesu Christi bzw. in Form von Erkenntnis des Gekreuzigten und Auferstandenen, d.h. also unter Voraussetzung des Abschlusses und der Vollendung der objektiven Offenbarung." KD I/1, 474.

[55]The understanding of the inner-divine role of the Holy Spirit as the bond of communion and love between Father and Son is by no means original to Barth. Cf. Augustine, *de Trinitate*, VI.5(7), XV.17(27), XV.19(37).

[56]Cf. R. D. Williams, "Barth on the Triune God" in S. W. Sykes, ed. *Karl Barth: Studies of his Theological Method* (Oxford: Clarendon Press, 1979), 147–193, who has pointed

up the conceptual difficulties of Barth's understanding of the Holy Spirit as the eternal bond of love between the Father and the Son. "As an 'act,' the Spirit cannot be a subject of predication in any way analogous to that in which Father and Son are subjects" (170). The doctrine of *perichōrēsis* which Barth would predicate of the entire Trinity becomes problematic if now one Mode of Being "is seen primarily as a function of the other two" (170). The difficulty which Williams notes however stems not so much from Barth's notion of the Holy Spirit, but from Williams notion of the Father and Son. His complaint betrays a tendency to think the trinitarian Persons in subjective terms, i.e., as a society of three intimately interrelated subjects. Barth indeed works with the modern conception of subjectivity in relation to God, but only as a single acting subject, the one triune God. That the Holy Spirit is conceived of as an "act" within the divine life is not a deficiency within Barth's Trinity, but a clue as to the actualistic manner in which he would understand the Father and the Son as well. With regard to an overlap between the doctrine of *perichōrēsis* and the Mode of Being of the Holy Spirit it should be noted that Barth employs the doctrine as an illustration of the thesis *opera Trinitatis ad extra sunt indivisa* and not as a description of the communion of love between Father and Son.

[57]As bond of eternal love and fellowship between Father and Son, the Holy Spirit grounds the *pro nobis*. Barth can speak of a "Selbst-rechtfertigung und Selbstheiligung Gottes" which as the special function of the Spirit acts as ground and guarantee for God's salvific act in revelation. In the Spirit the whole reality of God's fatherly mercy, His self-revelation, His self-glorification in the Son, the promise, the power of the Gospel, and the whole order of the relation between the Creator and the creation find their preexistence. The creature then in a sense pre-exists in the Holy Spirit, for the Spirit makes that existence possible in and through His special trinitarian function. That function necessarily assumes the eternal common procession of the Spirit from the Son and the Father. KD III/1, 59–63.

[58]Samuel Laeuchli, "Das 'Vierte Jahrhundert' in Karl Barths Prolegomena," in *Theologie zwischen Gestern und Morgen*, ed. W. Dantine and K. Lüthi. (Munich: Kaiser, 1968), 217–34.

[59]Ibid., 225.

[60]Ibid.

[61]Ibid., 220.

[62]Ibid., 225f, 227.

[63]Here again issue must be taken with the observations of Laeuchli, who suggests that with this line of argumentation Barth has actually abandoned the criterion of Scripture for theological thought and speech which he established in the early paragraphs of *Kirchliche Dogmatik* I/1. In its place one finds the tradition of the Church, a criterion to which Barth subjects the texts of Scripture. See Laeuchli, 220. Against Laeuchli it must be observed that his own view of the history and origin of dogma which reduces a theological perspective into its historically conditioned components is one which simply does not allow for a meaningful theological hermeneutic of dogma. Moreover, his penchant for caricature noted above distorts Barth's use of the tradition as a relative secondary authority into a primary authority

and is unable to recognize the subtleties of a circular (or "spiral") hermeneutical appropriation of the tradition.

[64]"Die Trinitätslehre sagt, dass unser Gott—nämlich der in seiner Offenbarung sich zum unsrigen machende wirklich *Gott* ist. Und auf die Frage: Wer aber ist Gott? wäre dann ebenso schlicht zu antworten: eben dieser *unser* Gott." KD I/1, 401.

[65]Wilfried Joest, *Dogmatik*, I (Göttingen: Vandenhoeck & Ruprecht, [2]1987), 332f.

CHAPTER FIVE

The Trinitarian Hermeneutic as the Ground of Responsible Talk of God

In the two chapters preceding we have focused upon the method used by Barth for deriving a doctrine of the Trinity, which, as we have argued, functions hermeneutically to form a fundamental perspective for doing theology which is executed throughout the *Kirchliche Dogmatik*. We have focused particularly upon the use of philosophical and traditional elements which are employed to this end. We turn our attention now to the question of the function itself.

One of the ways in which modern hermeneutics distinguishes itself from traditional biblical hermeneutics is a concern with the way in which language functions. Generally speaking, this means a consideration of language which moves beyond a simple theory of signification to an inquiry into "linguisticality" as an essential attribute of human existence.[1] While the issues in this regard are many, they tend to revolve around the questions of the essential character of language, its relation to human existence, and how it works, that is, how it functions with regard to reference and meaning. It is the third of these which has particular relevance for Barth's doctrine of the Trinity.

In Chapter 2 it was already noted that the doctrine of the Trinity exercises a critical function within the *Kirchliche Dogmatik* in its formal role of giving account of theology's peculiar language and method. It remains however to give a material account of the hermeneutical function of the doctrine, and it is this concern which occupies the present chapter. The discussion is presented in four parts: the first offers a brief analysis of the crisis in theological language which formed the situation out of which Barth's Trinity doctrine arose; the second considers the principle of trinitarian correspondence through which Barth would enable responsible talk of God; the third contrasts

Barth's principle of correspondence with a more recent proposal from Karl Rahner; the fourth offers conclusions regarding the trinitarian ground of theological language.

Responsible Talk of God as Context of Barth's Trinity Doctrine

The Crisis Context of Barth's Early Theology

The theology of Karl Barth is a theology concerned with the fundamental problem of how one is able to speak responsibly of God. The fact that theology is the attempt to form coherent and veridical statements whose object is God and the fact that the cultural and intellectual contexts of the twentieth century represent in many respects a radical questioning of the very possibility of such statements form the backdrop against which the basic themes of Barthian theology must be interpreted. This is particularly evident within the early critical phase of Barth's theology but is no less true for the Barth of the *Kirchliche Dogmatik*. The concern of the present chapter is to delineate as precisely as possible the peculiar hermeneutical role which Barth's doctrine of the Trinity plays in coming to terms with the twentieth century crisis in theological language. This is to be achieved primarily by means of an analytical engagement with Barth's doctrine itself and its influence in the *Kirchliche Dogmatik*. Because it is the early phase of Barth's theological career, however, in which the crisis is most overtly perceived, it is worthwhile to consider the degree of continuity (and discontinuity) which obtains between the dialectical phase of Barth's work and his development of the doctrine of the Trinity which stands at the beginning of the dogmatic phase.[2]

The Influence of Ludwig Feuerbach

Among the several influences upon the shape of Barth's early thought were the writings of Ludwig Feuerbach. Barth recognized in the anti-theological polemic of Feuerbach the incisive critique of the contemporary theological situation. The work of Feuerbach set in clear relief the dire and critical situation into which the theological language of the day had fallen. The refusal of the theological establishment to take his critique seriously signaled just as poignantly for Barth the short-sightedness of so many of the recognized theologians who followed in Feuerbach's wake. In the essay entitled simply "Ludwig Feuerbach," the published fragment taken from a 1926 lecture series on the history of modern theology, Barth singled out Feuerbach from among the philosophers of the modern era for his demonstration of a theological knowledge far beyond that which was characteristic of the majority of representatives of his discipline.[3]

Barth recognized in Feuerbach's harsh critique of theological language something other than its total rejection and negation as "Unsinn, Nichts, pure Illusion."[4] Quite to the contrary, Barth affirms the genuinely positive intention in Feuerbach's thought, as the following passage would illustrate.

> Feuerbachs Absicht ist—das wird in der theologischen Berichter-stattung über ihn oft unterschlagen—so positiv wie die nur irgend-eines Theologen. Er ist kein blosser Skeptiker und Neinsager—das ist allerdings die Seite, die er den Theologen zugekehrt hat, aber nicht einmal den Theologen nur diese!—er sagt begeistert und pathetisch Ja! "Ich verneine nur, um zu bejahen."[5]

Barth emphasized what he regarded as a neglected element of Feuerbach's thought—the fact that in spite of his program of transformation of theology into anthropology, it was God about whom Feuerbach wished to speak. According to Feuerbach, the actual object of theological speech, that is, the referent which stands behind the word God, is nothing other than the essence of humanity,[6] This is not, however, intended in any derogatory sense. It is, as Barth says, the "highest honor" which Feuerbach could bestow upon God.[7] For this realization represents a purification of the concept of God which human beings rightly set up for themselves. The word God acts as focal point onto which the perfections of humanity as a whole are projected; true theology is the analytical reflection upon these perfections of the human essence. Barth designates the conclusion of this line of thought as nothing short of the apotheosis of humanity.[8]

Barth's interest in Feuerbach was determined by his conviction that what could be found explicitly in the thought of Feuerbach was equally as much the logical conclusion of the theological line of thought associated with Schleiermacher and Neo-Protestantism.[9] Feuerbach represented a line of development not alien to theology, but one which emerged out of the theological assumptions dominant in the theological culture of Feuerbach's time. The principle assumption of this theological milieu (for which Feuerbach represents the point of convergence)[10] is the assertion that *primary theological statements are statements about the human religious consciousness.* Statements about God *per se* are secondary and derivative from the primary statements. Theology was in the process of substituting its original object, the God revealed in Jesus Christ, for the transcendent ego of human being. The intentionality and blatancy with which Feuerbach pressed this thesis offered Barth a vivid illustration of the deadly threat to theological language implicit in the assumptions of the prevailing liberal theology of the early twentieth century.[11]

Dialectical Theology and the Crisis of Theological Language

In the 1922 essay, "Das Wort Gottes als Aufgabe der Theologie," which has been described as "probably the most pregnant expression of what was then called 'dialectical theology,'"[12] Barth presented a concise formulation of his earliest attempt to come to terms with the crisis in theological language which he perceived in the theological situation of the time. The thesis which he developed there represents in large degree an anticipation of the formulation of the problem as well as the attempt to overcome it which is found in the early volumes of the *Kirchliche Dogmatik*. Barth gave expression to this thesis in the now well-known formula:

Wir sollen von Gott reden. Wir sind aber Menschen und können als solche nicht von Gott reden. Wir sollen Beides, unser Sollen und unser Nicht-Können, wissen und eben damit Gott die Ehre geben.[13]

The antithetical character of the thesis is indicative of the fundamental crisis which Barth perceived within the theological status quo of the early twentieth century. That the minister should speak of God is a necessity which rises from a longing for ultimacy deep from within the human spirit.[14] Congregations call ministers just as universities commission theological faculties to deal with a basic need to resolve ultimate questions. But the simple truth is that the minister cannot speak of God. Whatever answer is given, drawn from the finitude of existence, cannot correspond to the infinitude of the question.[15] Speaking of God authentically and genuinely is an impossible task for human beings in face of the radical otherness of God. It was precisely the failure of the dominant liberal theology of the day to recognize the impossibility of its task which for Barth signaled the dire crisis into which the Church had fallen. Schleiermacher and his spiritual heirs had deceived themselves in thinking that speaking of God would become possible by "speaking of humanity in a somewhat louder voice."[16] They had failed to recognize the desperate character of the human situation and committed an absurdity in locating the place of theological language in the experience and culture of human existence.

Barth offers no easy solution to a situation which can only be described as one of "distress" (*Bedrängnis*) and "perplexity" (*Verlegenheit*). It is noteworthy, however, that the direction which Barth takes for confronting the impossibility of the task has a decidedly formal or methodological character. It is the way that one does theology and the assumptions that one makes which come to the fore of the discussion of the "impossible possibility"[17] which is authentic talk of God. Barth considers three such ways of doing theology: the dogmatic, the critical, and the dialectical. The dogmatic way, which Barth associates with orthodoxy, fails ultimately in the idolatrous manner with which its objectifications are identified with the transcendent God.[18] The critical way, associated with mysticism, fails not only in its inability to move beyond the moment of self-negation and recognition of the infinite distance between humanity and God, but equally so in the groundless way in which it arrives at this assertion.[19] The way of dialectic, while not without its own weaknesses, is the best suited for the subject-matter of theological talk. Dialectical talk of God is a language on the way. It recognizes the incompleteness of both its affirmations and its denials, and only by pressing forward does it arrive at truth. Dialectical talk cannot in and of itself guarantee authentic talk of God. When God is genuinely spoken of, it is not because of the dialectic as such, but rather it is the result of an event which happens in the midst of its affirmations and denials, an event which asserts itself. This event, which is the reality of God, creates the question which it answers and the answer which it seeks.[20] The relative advantage of dialectic over its alternatives is according to Barth to be found in its superior capacity to give full sway to an actualistic conception of authentic language of God. Humanity is unable to speak of God. Only God can speak of God.[21] The dialectical method acknowledges this unfathomable distance by recognizing the incompleteness and anticipatory character of all its statements.

In spite of the emphasis which the essay assigns to formal questions of theology, Barth stops far short of attributing an inherent capacity for conveying truth about God to any particular theological form or method. This is the meaning of the third part of his thesis: "Wir sollen Beides, unser Sollen und unser Nicht-Können, wissen und eben damit Gott die Ehre geben." For the ultimate ground of authentic talk of God resides neither in the formal rules which shape that language nor in a descriptive theory of linguistic function. Its ground resides in its object, which is of course God himself. Barth does not allow this assertion to slip into a meaningless abstraction. This object may come to expression only by means of a particular content, a content which for Barth is epitomized in the three words "God becomes human."[22] In a brief closing comment greater concretion is offered in what is an even more poignant anticipation of the direction which Barth's understanding of the ground of responsible talk of God will take in the dogmatic phase of his work:

> Ich habe das *eigentliche* Thema meiner Darlegungen einige-
> mal berührt, aber nie ausdrücklich genannt. Alle meine Gedanken
> kreisen um den einen Punkt, der im Neuen Testament Jesus
> Christus heisst. Wer "Jesus Christus" sagt, der darf nicht sagen: "es
> könnte sein", sondern: es *ist*. Aber wer von *uns* ist in der Lage
> "Jesus Christus" zu sagen? *Wir* müssen uns vielleicht begnügen mit
> der Feststellung, dass Jesus Christ *gesagt* ist von seinen ersten
> Zeugen. Auf ihr Zeugnis hin zu glauben an die Verheissung und
> also Zeugen von ihrem Zeugnis zu sein, also *Schrift*theologen, das
> wäre dann unsre Aufgabe.[23]

Here already it is God's revelation which is offered as the concrete ground upon which responsible talk of God must proceed. Here already there is an assertion of the distance which is to be found between one's words about revelation and the revelation itself. And implicit as well is the suggestion that in spite of the distance between the object and its verbalization, that which is ineffable finds its way into human words. The impossible task of the theologian is a possibility only for God.

Transition to Dogmatics

As early as 1924 Barth had hinted in a letter to Thurneysen that the doctrine of the Trinity might well hold the key for a new theological founda-tion.[24] In 1927 Barth offered a thoroughgoing elaboration of the idea with the publication of *Die christliche Dogmatik*. In this volume, which is subtitled "Prolegomena zur christlichen Dogmatik," Barth maintains the strong emphasis upon the purely formal concerns so characteristic of his dialectical phase—particularly, the unfathomable distance between God and Man and the actualistic character of the "event" of revelation which bridges that distance.[25] These formal concerns are articulated chiefly through the development of the doctrine of the Word of God, (which stands as the volume title of the work, although the series was never continued). The Word of God represents the comprehensive category within which Barth wishes to understand the divine human relationship. The relationship itself may be described as "Word": "Die Beziehung von Gott und Mensch, von der die christliche Rede in ihrer reinen Form als kirchliche Verkündigung redet, sie ist *selbst Wort*."[26] At the foundation of theology stands for Barth the self-authenticating impenetrable fact that "God has spoken." And it is this fact which must condition above all the necessity of the Church to speak about God and about the human being's relationship to God. The answer which Barth forges in *Die christliche Dogmatik* to the crisis of theological language in Protestant Christianity, is that authentic talk must allow itself to be determined at every critical juncture by the theological fact that "God has spoken." The possibility that God may be genuinely spoken of, preeminently in Christian proclamation, as well as the possibility that this speech may be humanly heard, are possibilities which reside solely in the reality of the speaking God who in the events of authentic talk of God as well as authentic hearing is the acting subject.[27]

One of the points at which *Die christliche Dogmatik* begins to diverge from the dialectical writings is the engagement with material dogmatics itself. The formal doctrine of the Word is given material content in the doctrine of the Trinity. Barth describes this methodological change of direction at the outset of the treatment of the Trinity doctrine:

> Wir haben in unserem ersten Kapitel zum allgemeinen Nach-weis der Wirklichkeit des Wortes Gottes als des Sinns und der Möglichkeit der Dogmatik den Weg von unten nach oben ein-geschlagen: vom Phänomen der christlichen Rede zum Begriff der kirchlichen Predigt, zu dessen notwendiger Voraussetzung und dann in neuem Ansatz: von der Situation des Predigers und Hörers aus zu deren Ursprung mit seiner eigentümlichen Erkenntnis-bedingung. Es wird sachgemäss sein, wenn wir nun, zur speziellen Analyse unseres Hauptbegriffs übergehend, den umgekehrten Weg einschlagen: von oben nach unten, von der diesen Begriff konstitu-ierenden Offenbarung zur Heiligen Schrift, zur kirchlichen Predigt.[28]

The contraposition of Christian talk (*christliche Rede*) and revelation (*Offenbarung*, whose analysis yields the triune God) makes clear the purpose which the doctrine of the Trinity is intended to serve in the immediate dogmatic context. The Trinity is the new foundation upon which authentic talk of God is to rest. It will root the legitimacy of human speech about God in the very being of God. That God has spoken (*Deus dixit*) shows itself to correspond to its ground in the triune being of God in that the phenomenon of the speaking God is itself triune: God is simultaneously Subject, Object and Predicate in the event in which God speaks.[29]

The doctrine of the Word as developed in *Die christliche Dogmatik* would undergo considerable transformation in Barth's new beginning with dogmatics in *Die Kirchliche Dogmatik*.[30] The basic purpose of the Trinity doctrine, and thus its context within the crisis of theological language perceived by Barth were, however, to remain intact, as we shall see in the following section.

The *Kirchliche Dogmatik* and the Problem of Responsible Talk of God

The development of a foundation for responsible talk of God is one of many prominent motifs throughout the *Kirchliche Dogmatik*. While Barth at no point offers anything akin to a philosophically articulated theory of religious language, it is evident that a particular understanding of the function and limits of authentic talk of God is operative throughout the whole.[31] This is particularly evident in the recurring theme of the *analogia fidei* or *analogia relationis* and the recurring polemic against the *analogia entis*. It is in the early volumes of the work, however, particularly *Kirchliche Dogmatik* I/1, I/2, and II/1, that the perceived crisis in theological language which was characteristic of Barth's dialectical phase finds renewed expression.[32] Consequently, it is in these volumes that the polemic against alternative understandings is particularly strong.

The opening pages of *Kirchliche Dogmatik* I/1 leave no doubt as to the author's serious concern over a proper understanding of authentic talk of God. Barth offers a definition of the task of dogmatics in terms of the discipline's responsibility for the Church's talk of God.[33] A few pages later a pair of assumptions are set out which clarify the content of the Church's characteristic speech. The dogmatic task assumes, first of all, that the content of this speech is something which "can be known."[34] Its content can be known since it corresponds to the "being of the Church," which itself is defined as "God in Jesus Christ" (KD I/1, 10f). This definition is critical for Barth's understanding of the ground and possibility of authentic Christian speech. The human event of talk of God is utterly dependent upon a prior event of divine activity in Jesus Christ. It is a divine act which is the criterion and measure of human talk of God. This thesis arises in dispute with the theological line of Schleiermacher who likewise understood the content of Christian speech as a reality corresponding to the being of the Church. He erred, however, in his failure to identify the true being of the Church with Jesus Christ and thereby with God's prior acting, and mistaking it for the phenomenon of Christian piety.[35] The second thesis like the first contains a polemical barb. Barth declares that the proper content of Christian speech not only *can* but *must* be known.[36] Knowledge of this content comes only as the product of serious investigation. The task of human appropriation of divine truth is by nature always only a fallible and relatively certain undertaking. Here Barth sets distance between himself and a traditional Roman Catholic conception of the nature of the Church's talk of God. He rejects the notion of "revealed truths" which in their very wording correspond once and for all to divine truth (14). Thus Barth identifies the demons with which he will do battle through many of the pages of the *Kirchliche Dogmatik* which follow. In Neo-Protestantism and Roman Catholicism Barth finds the Scylla and Charybdis through which he would maneuver to chart a new foundation for theological speech.

It is against the background of this crisis context which we must now attempt to consider once again Barth's doctrine of the Trinity. Barth's doctrine stands at the conclusion of years of searching for the proper foundation for responsible talk of God. How this foundation functions for Barth is the question which the remainder of the chapter must address.

Trinitarian Correspondence

The foregoing discussion has sought to sketch the theological situation out of which Barth developed the doctrine of the Trinity as presented in the *Kirchliche Dogmatik* I/1. We turn now to the doctrine itself in order to consider the doctrine's material response to the perceived crisis in theological language.

Vestigia Trinitatis and the Exclusive Ground of Theological Speech

The point in Barth's development of the doctrine at which concern for responsible theological language becomes most conspicuous is unquestionably the critique of the *vestigia trinitatis* doctrine. The *vestigia trinitatis* denote a way of explaining the doctrine of the Trinity, usually traced to Augustine,[37] in which certain phenomena of the experienced world, such as imagery of the sun, its rays and illumined objects, or a tripartite division of the human psyche (as in memory, reason, and will) are employed as analogies for the divine Trinity of Father, Son, and Holy Spirit. Barth rejects the undertaking on the grounds of its inevitable implication, namely, that a second root for the doctrine of the Trinity is being posited alongside its actual root in the event of revelation (*trinitate posita*). The *vestigia trinitatis* imply for Barth a genuine *analogia entis* according to which the creator God has left traces or vestiges of his attributes in the created order (KD I/1, 353f).

The significance of Barth's rejection extends far beyond the critique of an inappropriate model for deriving the doctrine of the Trinity. Barth himself

recognizes that he is addressing a problem which affects the very foundation
of theological speech:

> Das Problem, das uns durch die Behauptung von dem Vorhanden-
> sein und Erkennbarsein jener *vestigia trinitatis* gestellt ist, ist also
> wahrhaftig von grösstem Belang: nicht nur für die Frage nach der
> Wurzel der *Trinitätslehre*, sondern für die Frage nach der *Offen-*
> *barung überhaupt*, für die Frage nach der Begründung der Theo-
> logie allein in der Offenbarung und schliesslich geradezu für die
> Frage nach Sinn und Möglichkeit der Theologie im Unterschied zu
> einer blossen Kosmologie oder Anthropologie.[38]

In his rejection of the *vestigia trinitatis* Barth is defending a fundamental rule
for talk of God. Authentic talk of God is talk grounded in God's revelation. All
other sources are excluded. The *vestigia trinitatis* seek to talk of God with
language drawn from the human experience of the world. But this language
and imagery is inherently unsuitable for talk of God. Human language and
thought are fundamental aspects of humanity and as such share in humanity's
utter fallenness and alienation from God.[39] If one then asks how theological
speech is possible at all or even how Holy Scripture can be written since it is
the same human speech which is the medium of communication, the answer of
Barth is simply that it is indeed not possible. Human language has no inner
capacity for authentic talk of God (358f). This capacity resides not in human
speech nor in the human being *per se*, but rather resides in the event of
revelation which is the object of authentic talk of God. Language does not
seize revelation but is seized by revelation.[40]

Barth recognizes a basically correct intention behind the *vestigia trinitatis*
doctrine.[41] It represents an understandable process of casting a rational light
drawn from the world of experience upon the mystery of God. It is a process
however which is undertaken by the Church only at serious risk. At stake is the
nature of the theological task itself and the threat of a *metabasis eis allo genos*
through which that task is essentially altered (364). Barth designates this danger
as the "transition from interpretation to illustration." Recognizing fully the
subtlety and tenuousness of the distinction, Barth defines each process in the

same phraseology with which he identifies the other, with only the emphasis at variance: "Interpretieren heisst: in anderen Worten *dasselbe* sagen. Illustrieren heisst: dasselbe in *anderen Worten* sagen" (364). The precise boundary between the two is elusive. Traces of illustration are to be found within interpretation, just as interpretive language is to be found in the process of illustration. Yet, Barth recognizes a direction denoted by each which he wishes to identify and employ as a criterion for authentic talk of God. Illustrative language posits alongside revelation a second point of reference (364f). It represents a loss of confidence in the communicative power of revelation and a shift of confidence toward the inner capacity of human language and experience. Ultimately, the pursuit of illustration in theological language is nothing less than abandonment of the revelation. Interpretation is a process whereby the language of the theologian centers itself around its object, the event of revelation. Interpretation is language which allows itself to be seized and transformed by revelation. An appropriately formulated doctrine of the Trinity, as indeed all authentic talk of God, will consist of interpretive language oriented to the biblical witness to revelation.

Barth's dispute is clearly with what in other contexts is identified straightforwardly as "natural theology." A definition of natural theology representative of the years of Barth's active polemic against it may be found in *Kirchliche Dogmatik* II/1:

> Natürliche Theologie ist die Lehre von einer auch ohne Gottes Offenbarung in Jesus Christus bestehenden Gottverbundenheit des Menschen; sie entwickelt die auf Grund dieser selbständigen Gottverbundenheit mögliche und wirkliche Gotteserkenntnis und deren Konsequenzen für das ganze Verhältnis von Gott, Welt und Mensch. (189)

As the definition suggests, Barth's rejection of natural theology is rooted in his conception of revelation. Revelation comes to the human being solely on the basis of the grace of God which has become manifest in the Incarnation and the out-pouring of the Holy Spirit. There is no human capacity for revelation.

The effects of sin are such that there is no "natural" point of connection between human reality and divine reality. Natural theology is the attempt to establish this connection in the realm of human knowledge and language without the benefit of revelation. What Barth finds objectionable in natural theology corresponds to what Augustine and the Reformers found objectionable in Pelagianism.[42] Natural theology is for Barth "cognitive-linguistic Pelagianism."[43] It represents a human arrogation of a place beside God and a place equivalent with God outside of the dispensation of God's grace. Consequently, Barth was unyielding in his opposition and refused to find a place for the undertaking within the Church, which defines the boundaries of Christian theology (190f).

For Barth the rejection of the *vestigia trinitatis* signifies the rejection of natural theology. The doctrine of the Trinity as the interpretation of revelation represents the positive alternative which points to the sole possibility for authentic human talk of God, a possibility which lies actually outside the realm of the human. The doctrine of the Trinity is an attempt to ground the possibility of responsible theological language while adhering to the Reformation principle of *sola gratia*. This of course has enormous implications for the content of the doctrine, but above all, implies the demand for as intimate a connection as possible between the content of the doctrine and the assertions of the biblical witness to revelation. And, moreover, if the doctrinal assertions are to be meaningful, it must be shown to what extent the interpretation of revelation corresponds to an interpretation of the God who is its author.

Trinitarian Correspondence and Revelation as Self-interpretation

Jüngel has correctly noted the fundamental link between the interpretive hermeneutic which Barth prescribes in his rejection of the *vestigia trinitatis* doctrine and his working concept of revelation as God's own self-interpretation.[44] It is axiomatic for Barth that God's revelation is self-revelation. In the triadic pattern of revelation, God Himself is Subject, Object, and Predicate; God Himself is Revealer, Revelation, and Revealedness.[45] Barth often expresses this relation in terms of the strongest identity between the event of revelation and the eternal God, as in the following passage:

> Die Wirklichkeit Gottes in seiner Offenbarung ist nicht einzu-klammern mit einem "nur," als ob irgendwo hinter seiner Offen-barung eine andere Wirklichkeit Gottes stünde, sondern eben die uns in der Offenbarung begegnende Wirklichkeit Gottes ist seine Wirklichkeit in allen Tiefen der Ewigkeit. (503)

The event of revelation is the event of God's self-interpretation to humanity.[46] In other words, the authenticity and truth of revelation is guaranteed by the fact that who God is in His revelation, He is already in his eternal life:

> Dieser Herr kann *unser* Gott sein, er kann uns begegnen und sich uns verbinden, weil er Gott ist in diesen drei Seinsweisen als Vater, Sohn und Geist, weil die Schöpfung, die Versöhnung, die Erlösung, das ganze Sein, Reden und Handeln, in dem er unser Gott sein will, begründet und vorgebildet ist in seinem eigenen Wesen, in seinem Gottsein selber.[47]

What Barth designates here with the word "*vorgebildet*" (prefigured), Jüngel identifies as a principle of correspondence.[48] God in his revelation corresponds to Himself as He eternally is.[49] This understanding of revelation functions to warrant the legitimacy of talk of God on the basis of revelation, but only so long as that talk of God genuinely orients itself to the event of revelation and not to a secondary point of reference.

In trinitarian terms this principle may be expressed in the thesis, "the economic Trinity corresponds to the immanent Trinity."[50] For Barth this thesis functions as a hermeneutical rule, the effect of which is to ground all talk of God in the ultimate object of that talk, the eternal reality of God. The thesis does not admit of proof as such any more than the thesis that "God Himself acts in His revelation" admits of proof.[51] Nor does it represent a doctrine *per se*. It represents a summary of the way in which Barth employs the doctrine of the Trinity as a critical principle for responsible talk of God. All statements about the immanent Trinity, that is, God in Himself, must represent an interpretation of statements about the economic Trinity, that is, God in His revelation, since there is no other ground or source of knowledge of God. The language of the economic Trinity is authenticated on the basis of the immanent Trinity to which it corresponds.

The principle of trinitarian correspondence is the principle of unity by which Barth would understand the relationship between God's being and God's acting or works. Barth seeks to maintain the essential unity of God's action and God's being while simultaneously insisting on their conceptual distinction, as expressed in the following passage:

> Das Wirken Gottes ist das Wesen Gottes in seinem Verhältnis zu der von ihm unterschiedenen, zu schaffenden oder geschaffenen Wirklichkeit.... Obwohl das Wirken Gottes das Wesen Gottes ist, ist es notwendig und wichtig, sein Wesen als solches von seinem Wirken zu *unterscheiden*: zur Erinnerung daran, dass dieses Wirken Gnade, freie göttliche Entscheidung ist, zur Erinnerung auch daran, dass wir von Gott nur wissen können, weil und sofern er sich uns zu wissen gibt.[52]

This understanding of an immanent-economic identity in distinction is often brought to expression with the phrase "antecedently in himself" (*zuvor in sich selber*) when applied to each of the triune Modes of Being.[53] Jesus Christ is the Son of God for us because he is already the Son of God antecedently in Himself. Likewise the one whom Jesus reveals as Father can be Father only because he is antecedently the Father of the Son in the eternal triune relations. Yet, a distinction between God's eternal being and His salvific activity is necessary in order to remember that God's operation in His revelation is an act of free grace, a sovereign decision in which God brings his eternal love to temporal expression.

The thesis of trinitarian correspondence also finds frequent expression within the *Kirchliche Dogmatik* in the concept of the trinitarian *Urbild* or "primal pattern,"[54] according to which the events of creation and salvation history are prefigured within the immanent trinitarian life of God. Undoubtedly the pinnacle of this line of thought is to be found in the doctrine of election whereby the salvation event becomes the outworking of an eternal possibility in the very nature of God. The possibility of the human experience of grace has no ground in human psychology, experience, or culture. There is no inherent capacity for redemption, no trace of salvific truth hidden within creation waiting for human discovery. The possibility is rooted elsewhere. The reality that Jesus Christ elects humanity is grounded in a possibility that coincides with the divine nature. This possibility consists in the eternal resolve of God for election, such that the Father gives over the Son to be the executor of His grace, the Son gives Himself up in obedience to become man and thereby executor of God's grace, and the Holy Spirit resolves that the unity of Father and Son should not only preserve itself but glorify itself in the divine-human covenant (KD II/2, 109). The trinitarian *Urbild*, the correspondence of the immanent to the economic Trinity, grounds the language of God's grace in God Himself, thus constituting a profound alternative to the anthropologically centered theology to which Barth was responding.[55]

The thesis of trinitarian correspondence requires a further refinement if we are to understand aright the way in which Barth uses it as guide and ground of theological speech. The language of God in the world raises immediately the question of the objectivity of God. If there is authentic talk of God, then God has somehow become an object of human language and perception. Barth wishes to affirm the real objectivity of God in His revelation without however allowing God to be thought of as an object like other objects of perception which are at the disposal of the human being. To this end he introduces a distinction between "primary" and "secondary objectivity" (KD II/1, 14–18). The basic thesis is as follows:

> In seinem dreieinigen Leben als solchem ist Gegenständlichkeit und damit Erkenntnis göttliche Wirklichkeit, bevor es geschöpfliche Gegenständlichkeit und Erkenntnis gibt. Wir nennen dies: die *primäre* Gegenständlichkeit Gottes und unterscheiden von ihr die *sekundäre*, d.h. die Gegenständlichkeit, die er in seiner Offen-

barung auch für uns hat, in der er sich auch uns zu erkennen gibt,
wie er sich selber erkennt.[56]

In the immanent Trinity God is directly objective to Himself in the mutual
knowing of Father and Son in the unity of the Holy Spirit (52f). The reality of
the primary objectivity of God grounds the possibility of God's secondary
objectivity to the created world. The possibility of human knowledge of God
resides solely in God's own eternal self-knowing (and not in any latent capacity
of humankind). Human knowledge of God is not, however, identical to God's
knowledge of Himself. It occurs through the medium of God's secondary
objectivity, according to which God elects an objectivity within the world which
in itself is different from God. A worldly object, by virtue of God's action,
becomes a "sign" (*Zeichen*) or a "shell" (*Hülle*) which bears witness to the real
activity of God (16). Knowledge is possible only as indirect or mediate
knowledge, but it is none the less real knowledge of God. This is possible
because the secondary objectivity of God has its "correspondence and ground"
in God's primary objectivity.[57]

Secondary objectivity has a sacramental role to play in Barth's theology
as the medium of God's love and grace (56). That which is not God becomes
the medium through which God mediates His self-revelation. The human
nature of Christ, which represents the secondary objectivity of God in the event
of His self-revelation, thus represents the first sacrament, the center from
which all of God's works are to be ordered (58).

While mediated knowledge of God is true and authentic, it is not without
limitation. Human knowledge of God is always partial knowledge. This
restriction is not one however that may be interpreted in quantitative terms, for
the wholeness of God's being is indeed mediated in the event of revelation
(55). The restriction resides within the form of creaturely objectivity which God
assumes. In the secondary objectivity in which God gives Himself to be known,
He remains simultaneously hidden. The limitation is precisely the indirectness
of the knowledge.

Barth's concept of primary and secondary objectivity in God is a further indication of the relationship which he understands to obtain between the economic and immanent Trinity, a relationship we have expressed with the thesis, "the economic Trinity corresponds to the immanent Trinity." The economic Trinity is the activity of God at work in and through an objectivity which is not as such a part of God. The distinction between the objectivity of the economic Trinity and that of the immanent Trinity excludes any simple or absolute identity. The ground which the economic Trinity finds in the immanent Trinity guarantees its correspondence.[58]

Trinitarian Correspondence and the *Analogia Fidei*

A comprehensive discussion of Barth's use of analogy in the *Kirchliche Dogmatik* would carry us well beyond the scope of our present focus. Barth's concept of the *analogia fidei* or *analogia relationis* has been sufficiently considered and analyzed in a number of other places so as not to require a thorough explication here.[59] What does warrant attention is the relationship which exists between Barth's analogical understanding of theological language and the concept of trinitarian correspondence.

By *analogia fidei* we refer to Barth's insistence that the only reason that human talk of God is possible at all is that human conceptuality is made fit for talk of God's revelation by means of God's grace. There is no inherent capacity for authentic talk of God (KD II/1, 218f). God must appropriate human language to Himself in an act of grace, and thus in a sense, resurrect language from the dead to make it suitable (258f). As redeemed language, it expresses truth analogous to God's actual truth. Its designations and references are "similar" to the final truth it seeks to express (254). The truth of human talk of God is "partial" truth, which "corresponds" to God's being. Its essential character is determined by the event of grace in which the human being is received and reconciled by God. The restitution of human talk of God is but an aspect of the whole event of redemption. "Indem Gott in diesen Verhältnis, Gott seiend und bleibend, sich des Menschen annimmt, kommt es zu echter Entsprechung und Übereinstimmung" (257). It is no surprise then to find that the most thorough elaboration of the doctrine after its introduction in the doctrine of God is to be found in Barth's anthropology.[60] In the event of justification, the human being is called into correspondence to God Himself. The faith of the believer is an "echo" or "reflection" of Jesus Christ in whom it rests (KD IV/1, 710).

The relationship of correspondence at work in Christian talk of God finds its ultimate ground in a relationship of correspondence in the being of Jesus Christ. This premise of Barth is given expression by Jüngel in the formula "Das Sein des Menschen Jesus ist der Seins- und Erkenntnisgrund aller Analogie."[61] According to Jüngel, the ground of all analogies in Barth's theology is to be found in the humanity of Jesus as the being of the man Jesus for the other. As the man for others, Jesus represents a repetition and correspondence of the inner being of God. For his being for others corresponds to his being for God.

> Die Menschlichkeit Jesu, seine Mitmenschlichkeit, sein Sein für den Menschen als unmittelbares Korrelat zu seinem Sein für Gott zeigt, bezeugt, offenbart diese Entsprechung und Ähnlichkeit. Sie ist nicht nur in einem faktischen und vielleicht zufälligen Parallelismus—sie ist auch nicht nur auf Grund eines willkürlichen göttlichen Entschlusses so beschaffen und gerichtet wie sie so ist: sie folgt dem *Wesen* Gottes, seinem inneren Sein.[62]

Humanity finds correspondence to the divine being in and only in the being of Jesus Christ. In Jesus Christ humanity corresponds to God as a correspondence between a divine nature and a human nature. The humanity of Christ is not alien to fallen and sinful humanity but genuinely corresponds to it, or more precisely, the relation of human to divine in the being of Jesus Christ corresponds to the relation between the humanity of the man Jesus and all humanity. And as we have already seen, the being of Jesus Christ, as the self-revelation of God, and as a Mode of Being of the divine Subject in relationship with Himself, corresponds to the triune God in his eternal self-relation.[63] Thus by means of a series of analogical relations, human existence finds itself called into correspondence to divine being. Because God corresponds to Himself, because the immanent corresponds to the economic Trinity, it becomes possible for human existence to be called into this relation. And because human existence may be called into this relation, it is also possible for human knowledge and human language to participate in this relation of correspondence. The eternal resolve which finds expression in the doctrine of election is thus that which ultimately enables the possibility of the *analogia fidei* of Christian talk of God.

Essential to this is understanding is the character of the *analogia fidei* as an event whose possibility and realization are grounded on the side of God. The event character of Christian talk of God corresponds to the event character of Church as the "place" of God's revelation. "Das Sein der Kirche ist *actus purus, göttliche*, mit sich selbst anfangende und nur aus und durch sich selbst einsichtige, also anthropologisch nicht vorverständliche Handlung" (KD I/1, 41). It is here where theological speaking and knowing finds its starting point, in that happening in which the speaking and hearing of Jesus Christ occurs (41). The truth content of Christian talk of God is something which befalls it in an event of divine grace. "In seiner Offenbarung *verfügt* Gott über sein Eigentum, *erhebt* er unsere Worte zu dieser ihrer Eigentlichkeit, *gibt* er ihnen also Wahrheit" (KD II/1, 260). God is the acting subject in the event of truth. It is thus on the side of God that the event finds its ground. The *analogia fidei* is an *analogia relationis*.[64] The analogy between Christian talk of God and God's truth about Himself is a relation which corresponds to the relation between God in His revelation and God in Himself. The relation between God in his revelation and God in Himself is that which grounds or makes possible the analogical character of Christian speech. There is no capacity for the analogy inherent in human speech or human existence. There is no question of an *analogia entis*. "Gott wird nur durch Gott erkannt" (205). The relation is one established in divine freedom, grounded in the correspondence of the threefold self-revelation of the God who is "antecedently in Himself" triune from eternity.[65]

Correspondence vs. Identity

In recent years Barth's concept of a correspondence between the immanent and economic Trinity has often been identified as an anticipation of Karl Rahner's thesis of identity, which states, "The 'economic' Trinity is the 'immanent' Trinity and the 'immanent' Trinity is the 'economic' Trinity."[66] Kasper refers to Barth's concept of God's self-revelation as a "comparable" precursor to Rahner's thesis.[67] Pannenberg insists the whole conceptuality is already to be found implicitly in the *Kirchliche Dogmatik* I/1 in Barth's development of the Trinity doctrine from its root in revelation, since the process implies the unity of the economic and immanent Trinity.[68] A recent work on Barth's doctrine of the Trinity from the Catholic perspective makes reference to Rahner's thesis as a summary of the intention in Barth's own concept of correspondence.[69] Indeed, there is a considerable overlap and agreement in the trinitarian theologies of Rahner and Barth. Yet, such statements are all too misleading if they fail to point out the material differences in the two views of the economic-immanent relation, differences which stem from an essential divergence of intention.

Rahner's interest the economic-immanent relation arises from a concern over the isolation which has befallen the doctrine of the Trinity in recent Catholic dogmatics. Rahner observes,

> It is as though this mystery has been revealed for its own sake, and
> that even after it has been made known to us, it remains, *as a
> reality*, locked up within itself. We make statements about it, but as
> a reality it has nothing to do with us at all.[70]

Rahner contends that this need not be the case. He offers in the place of the relative isolation of the doctrine an interpretation which not only integrates the doctrine of the Trinity within the whole of systematic theology but which shifts it to the foundation of Christian thought. Rahner accomplishes this by interpreting the Trinity as a "mystery of salvation."[71] The basic thesis which establishes this relation is the thesis of identity cited above. Two significant consequences which Rahner sees for this trinitarian reconstruction are relevant for our concern here. First, Rahner wishes to assert with the thesis of identity, in a way similar to Barth, God's actual presence in the economy of salvation.[72] God's revelation is God's own "self-communication." The threefold pattern which is to be recognized in God's "self-communication" is not a "copy" or "analogy" of the inner Trinity but is itself the divine Trinity.[73] Secondly, and here the divergence from Barth becomes more apparent, the identity thesis implies methodologically for Rahner that our own experience of faith is the appropriate point of access to the doctrine of the Trinity.[74] This is possible since the immanent Trinity is already present in our experience of Jesus Christ and the Spirit. The doctrinal statements of the Trinity are warranted by the human experience of salvific reality. On this basis, then, Rahner can declare that "no adequate distinction can be made between the doctrine of the Trinity and the doctrine of the economy of salvation,"[75] and thus ultimately "that the mystery of the Trinity is the last mystery of our own [human] reality, and that it is experienced precisely in this reality."[76] Jüngel, therefore, is quite right in suggesting that in light of Rahner's proposal for the Trinity doctrine, Schleiermacher's objection that the doctrine is not a "direct statement of the Christian self-consciousness" has been overturned.[77]

Barth's intention in the thesis of correspondence arises from a different concern. Like Rahner, Barth is eager to defend the unity of God with His revelation. The human encounter with Jesus Christ through the Holy Spirit is an encounter with the eternal God. Thus, one finds throughout the *Kirchliche*

Dogmatik remarks which assert an identity of the God-revealed with God-in-Himself, such as the following:

> Gottes Offenbarung ist nach der Schrift Gottes eigenes unmittelbares Reden, nicht zu unterscheiden von dem Akt dieses Redens, also nicht zu unterscheiden von Gott selbst, von dem göttlichen Ich, das dem Menschen in diesem Akt, in dem es Du zu ihm sagt, gegenübertritt. (KD I/1, 320)[78]

This assertion of unity between God and His revelation, between immanent and economic Trinity, or between God and His works, requires qualification if Barth is not to be misunderstood. Barth insists on the unity of God and His revelation, but he also insists on a distinction. The distinction is expressed on two different planes, although we shall see that the intention is the same on each level.

Barth insists first of all on a distinction on the epistemological plane. This is especially clear if we return to the discussion already noted above which asserts the unity of being and act (*Wesen und Wirken*) in God:

> Obwohl das Wirken Gottes das Wesen Gottes ist, ist es notwendig und wichtig, sein Wesen als solches von seinem Wirken zu *unter-scheiden*: zur Erinnerung daran, dass dieses Wirken Gnade, freie göttliche Entscheidung ist, zur Erinnerung auch daran, dass wir von Gott nur wissen können, weil und sofern er sich uns zu wissen gibt. Gottes Wirken ist freilich das Wirken des ganzen Wesens Gottes. Gott gibt sich dem Menschen ganz in seiner Offenbarung. Aber nicht so, dass er sich dem Menschen gefangen gäbe. Er bleibt *frei*, indem er wirkt, indem er sich gibt.[79]

Barth speaks of this distinction as merely "heuristic" and thus not "constitutive" for the being of God (KD II/1, 389). It is a necessary distinction only for human knowledge of God. It is necessary if theology is to bring the attribute of divine freedom to expression. The unity of God's works and being implies logically that the love of God for humanity which is brought to expression in the revelation event is already an attribute of the eternal God. If act and being are not sufficiently distinguished, however, then it is quite possible to think of revelation in terms of a necessity which transcends the being of God, so that in effect God is bound to reveal Himself as He does. The distinction in works and being is what brings the freedom of God to expression. God's love for humanity is grounded in his eternal being, but the outworking of that love in God's revelation is His free and gracious decision. In other words, God could be the same loving and gracious God even without his self-revelation. God's being is not contingent upon His act.[80]

Barth also carries out a distinction between the immanent and economic Trinity on what may be called an ontological plane. The immanent is distinguished from the economic Trinity as eternity is from time. The economic Trinity represents God in His historicity, while the immanent refers to God in His eternity.[81] It is in this vein that one encounters Barth's often elusive use of the language of analogy and correspondence. The economic Trinity is analog to the immanent. But analogy entails not only similarity! At least some degree of dissimilarity is also implied. A thing does not *correspond* to itself, but simply *is* itself. In using the language of analogy, however, Barth does not thereby intend to lessen the fullness of the divine reality present in revelation. In the economic Trinity of revelation God reveals Himself and He reveals Himself as He is. The dissimilarity is to be found in the form in which God is God: the form of eternity over temporality, the form of primary objectivity over secondary, the form of essence over act. For Barth there is in each case a certain priority which belongs to the former and a certain contingency to the latter. But most importantly neither can be collapsed into the other without a reduction in responsible talk of God, that is, without what Jüngel and others have referred to as a *"Sprachverlust."*[82]

It is here that the ambiguity and danger of the thesis of identity becomes apparent. It can be understood to imply an utter collapse of the immanent Trinity into the economic, such that rather than establishing a foundation for responsible talk of God in Himself, it actually serves to abolish the very possibility. More likely is the implication of an absolute mutuality of relationship between the immanent and economic Trinity such that each becomes constitutive for the other. Not only the immanent but the economic Trinity as well would accordingly have significance for the deity of God.[83] God would not be who He is apart from His works. Barth's thesis that the economic Trinity *corresponds* to the immanent asserts not only their unity, but that antecedent to the economic Trinity is its corresponding ground. Should the immanent Trinity collapse into the immanent Trinity, or should they become mutually determinative for the deity of God, then that ground is jeopardized, to say the least. Moreover, the door is opened once again to a trinitarian or theistic speculation which takes its starting point not in the immanent but in the economic Trinity. In other words, it invites a return to the doctrine of the *vestigia Trinitatis*.

According to Kasper, "What K. Rahner sets down as a basic principle, reflects a broad consensus among the theologians of the various churches."[84] Recent literature would tend to bear this statement out.[85] On the other hand, the discussion generated by the proposal has been largely occupied not with pursuing responsible trinitarian talk of God on the basis of Rahner's proposal, but rather with clarifying its precise meaning.[86] As an unqualified statement of identity the statement leaves itself open to considerable misunderstanding. The consensus which has developed around the thesis stems from the language rule for responsible talk of God which it implies: there may be no statement about God in Himself which is not simultaneously a statement about God in His revelation. This language rule is of course already established in Barth's principle of correspondence, thus explaining the frequent references to Barth by Rahner commentators.

In terms of precision and clarity Barth's correspondence principle is clearly to be preferred to Rahner's identity thesis. In terms of their relative hermeneutical significance for responsible talk of God, Barth's correspondence principle stands as a cautionary reminder against the implications of misinterpretations to which Rahner's identity thesis lends itself, particularly the implications of a failure of theology to distinguish sufficiently God's immanent being from His salvific acts. As Barth demonstrates, such a failure means, that the free and sovereign decision in which God wills to be God for us will find difficulty in coming to view. And it means secondly, should the economic Trinity take on constitutive significance for the being of God, the subtle beginnings of a return to the doctrine of the *vestigia Trinitatis*. Rahner's own conclusions in this regard, according to which the experience of faith becomes the starting point for trinitarian inquiry, open the door to this direction.[87]

Hermeneutical Significance of the Trinitarian Ground

Barth's perception of a crisis in theological language, as we have seen, formed the theological context out of which he developed the doctrine of the Trinity and for which the doctrine was intended to represent an answer. The doctrine of the Trinity clarifies for Barth the function of theological language, and it does so in at least two respects: first, by clarifying the referential function of theological language, and secondly, by exercising a critical-polemical function over and against illegitimate modes of theological speech.

The doctrine of the Trinity clarifies the referential function of theological language by providing the ontological foundation which grounds the possibility of objective reference for theological statements. This is aided conceptually by the distinction between God's primary and secondary objectivity as well as the analogy of faith, (both considered above). How these concepts relate to one another is indicated in a summary statement of Barth on the nature of analogy.

> [Die Analogie] ist nicht anders möglich als da, wo die Analogie als Werk und Setzung der Offenbarung selber verstanden wird.... Sie ist Auslegung der Offenbarung Gottes, wenn sie sich hält an die menschlichen Worte, die uns in unserer Konfrontierung mit Gottes Offenbarung zur Verfügung gestellt und damit als zu diesem Gebrauch dienlich bezeichnet werden, wenn sie der Freiheit folgt, in welcher Gott seine Gnade, wie dem Menschen überhaupt, so auch seinem menschlichen Anschauen, Begreifen und Reden

gegenüber walten lässt. Dann wird sie etwas Bestimmtes zu sagen
haben und dieses mit gutem Gewissen, mit der Verheissung,
sachlich zu sein, d.h. in realer Beziehung zu der von ihr
Verkündigung Realität zu stehen, und mit dem berechtigten
Anspruch, mit der begründeten Aussicht Gehör zu finden. (KD
II/1, 262f)

Theological statements are constructed from human concepts and words. In the
service of theology these words are applied to God. The application, however,
is not direct. Theology speaks of God only insofar as it speaks of God in His
revelation. Human words may be applied to revelation, because revelation
assumes an objectivity within the human world of objects, namely, the
secondary objectivity of God. What gives these words truth value with regard
to God is the faith view that what is perceived in the event of revelation
corresponds to God as He is in Himself. The secondary objectivity of revelation
corresponds to the primary objectivity of God in His eternal life. In corresponding fashion, the truth of language applied to God's revelation is
analogous to its truth when applied to God in Himself. This truth is an event
which occurs insofar as language allows itself to be determined by revelation
and not by any external criteria. The analysis of revelation is of course for
Barth the root of the doctrine of the Trinity which functions for theology as
the fundamental relation of correspondence upon which other analogies stand.

Consequently, theological statements have objective reference, however
indirectly it is derived. This understanding of objective reference marks Barth's
position off from two significant alternatives, that of metaphorical reference
and that of literalism. Metaphorical theology, emphasizing the contextual
character of human language, looks for the meaning of theological language in
the secular and everyday language from which it borrows. The cultural setting
of a particular time and place becomes a determinative criterion for the
selection of the appropriate language for talk of God.[88] The focus of a
metaphorical understanding is upon its dissimilarity and incongruity with its
object. "Most simply, a metaphor is seeing one thing *as* something else,

pretending 'this,' is 'that' because we do not know how to think or talk about 'this,' so we use 'that' as a way of saying something about it."[89] Barth's doctrine of analogy rejects the metaphorical route. Theological statements do not attempt to describe God with the proviso of an "as if" (259). The emphasis is not upon dissimilarity, but similarity, a similarity rooted in the similarity between the triune God and His revelation. The criterion of language is revelation and not the *Sitz im Leben* of language itself. When "Father" and "Son" are applied to God, their "truth" is not actually found in their everyday use in familial relationships, but rather, their truth resides in their theological truth, so that their everyday use is derivative from and judged by their theological use (259f). This claim, which superficially appears as a logical absurdity, represents an axiomatic principle for Barth which asserts that *"real" truth, just as "real" reality, resides solely with God*.[90] Thus the real truth and ultimate criterion of theological language is its object and not the human world which gives language its form and initial meaning.[91]

The trinitarian ground of theological language also marks it off from a literalist understanding of theological language. Literalism for theological language denotes a positivistic understanding which inadequately distinguishes theological reference from worldly reference. Like the metaphorical understanding, literalism allows the worldly use of language to determine its meaning in application to God. Consequently, its propositions about God are understood in terms of final truths, themselves equivalent to revelation. But the doctrine of the Trinity asserts that God as He gives Himself to humanity *corresponds* to God as He is in eternity. This correspondence does not negate the moment of dissimilarity or the partiality in our talk of God. It affirms that what truth our language does bear occurs as an event, an event which defies containment within a particular set of verbal propositions.

When theological language seeks to ground itself through its own dogmatic assertions, that is, through a statement of faith as opposed to an an empirical or rational ground, then it makes itself vulnerable to the charge of fideism.[92] And indeed, there is a certain justification for ascribing a fideistic character to Barth's understanding of theological language. Barth's view does not allow for a verification of theological statements outside of the experience of faith. The venturing of a theological proposition is always *Glaubensakt* or else it is something different than Christian theology. The secondary objectivity in which God reveals Himself is one that can always be interpreted differently when observed outside of faith. But fideism is hardly the final word on Barth's view of theological language. Its fideistic character by no means divorces it from accountability, rationality, or plausibility. Rather its fideistic character means that its accountability, rationality, and plausibility are tests which likewise can only be exercised within the same perspective of faith, which is the perspective of the Lordship of Jesus Christ.[93] Here again one finds an illustration of the paradigmatic function which the doctrine of the Trinity serves within the *Kirchliche Dogmatik*. Its paradigmatic character obviates the possibility of an external accounting of its truth or falsehood. Indeed, truth or falsehood are not even the most appropriate categories for such an accounting. Accountability will be won on the basis of the rationality and plausibility which the trinitarian ground offers for those who earnestly seek to understand talk of God according to its perspective. Accordingly the trinitarian ground will not simply present itself to faith as a way of thought and speech demanding obedience, but rather will justify itself to faith on the basis of the insights which it offers to faith.

The hermeneutical significance of the principle of trinitarian correspondence extends beyond the ontological ground for theological language which it establishes outside of the experienced world. The back side of the principle of correspondence is a critical-polemical function exercised against inappropriate forms of theological language, specifically the language forms of myth and metaphysical and anthropological speculation.[94] Barth understands myth as a temporal, historical narrative which intends to convey timeless truth which is generally knowable or known to humanity.[95] Mythical talk of God is talk which is drawn from the horizons of human experience. It is talk which operates on the assumption that the highest truths with which humanity has to do are truths hidden within the human heart or reason. Myth for Barth, therefore, is but a particular form of metaphysical or anthropological speculation, none of which are capable, because humanity as such is incapable, of speaking meaningfully of God's revelation. The correspondence of the economic to the immanent Trinity is an exclusive relation. There is no legitimate *vestigia trinitatis*. The possibility of revelation is not something that can be derived from human reason or experience. Meaningful talk of God is possible because God interprets Himself in his acting as Creator, Reconciler, and Redeemer.

On the other side, the correspondence between God in His revelation and God in Himself means that the triune God comes to speech as subject, as a thou, and not as an it or a he.[96] This is the meaning of the doctrine of the Trinity for Barth over and against subordinationism on the one hand and modalism on the other. While subordinationism would transform the subject of revelation into something less than God, which must ultimately be an object in the world of other objects, modalism posits the real God somewhere on the other side of revelation, so that in revelation one encounters not God as thou, but a mere objectification of the divine. Against these traditional heresies Barth wishes to assert that the God encountered in revelation is genuinely God Himself, even if encountered indirectly.

One misunderstands the import of Barth's polemic at this point if what is heard is no more than a pious appeal for a biblically oriented theology and personalistic imagery in talk of God. Clearly Barth's primary target is a dominant line of liberal theological thinking referred to in the opening section of this chapter. In the polemic against myth, Barth implicitly accused theologians of practicing mythology who sought to ground, confirm, or support their talk of God with observations drawn from the phenomena of religious experience. Philosophical theism, whether of a Hegelian or some other variety, could come off no better. Even more or less confessional theologies which develop themselves in terms of ontology or ontic reality, such that God is conceived of as "being itself"[97] or as the "dimension of ultimacy in the secular experience,"[98] are in light of Barth's critique not merely poor theologies, but rather are not even theology at all. For each of these alternatives has chosen an object other than God in His revelation about which it wishes to speak.[99]

ENDNOTES

[1]Thus declares Palmer (influenced by Gadamer) in one of his "Thirty Theses on Interpretation,": "*The hermeneutical experience is intrinsically linguistic*. It is not possible to understand the full importance of this until language is conceived within the horizon of 'linguisticality,' that is, not as the tool of a manipulating consciousness but as the medium through which a world comes to stand before us and in us." Richard Palmer, *Hermeneutics: Interpretation Theory in Schleiermacher, Dilthey, Heidegger, and Gadamer* (Evanston: Northwestern Univ. Press, 1969), 242.

[2]The distinction between the Barth's critical (or dialectical) phase and the dogmatic (or analogical) phase is of course a widely recognized division in the development of Barth's thought. Cf. Hans Urs von Balthasar, *Karl Barth* (Einsiedeln: Johannes Verlag, [4]1976), 71, 93. ET = *The Theology of Karl Barth*, tr. J. Drury (New York: Holt, Rinehart and Winston, 1971), 48, 73; Eberhard Jüngel, "Einführung in Leben und Werk Karl Barths," in *Barth-Studien* (Zurich: Benzinger Verlag, 1982), 36–58. ET = "Barth's Life and Work," in *Karl Barth: A Theological Legacy*, tr. P. Garrett (Philadelphia: Westminster, 1986), 33–51; and T. F. Torrance, *Karl Barth: An Introduction to His Early Theology, 1910–1931* (London: SCM,1962), 48–132. The distinction represents a helpful designation of the very real and significant theological turn which occurred between 1928 and 1932 in Barth's thought. It must not be allowed, however, to overshadow the lines of continuity which unite dialectical theology with the *Kirchliche Dogmatik*. The dual principle of Barth interpretation laid down by v. Balthasar continues to prove itself reliable: Any attempt to interpret the dogmatic phase solely in terms of the dialectical period is nothing short of an absurdity and an affront to the author who himself set distance between the two approaches to theology. On the other side, however, "jene andere Deutung, die die Schriften der Frühzeit schlechthin im Schatten liesse, als abgetan betrachten und sich einzig der Frucht der reifen Jahre zuwenden wollte, würde diese zumindest nur sehr unvollkommen verstehen" (v. Balthasar, 69; ET, 46). The discussion which follows demonstrates in a modest degree at least one of the lines of influence and continuity which obtain between the early and later periods of Barth's work.

[3]"[Feuerbach] hat sich in seinen Schriften, jedenfalls was Bibel-, Kirchenväter- und besonders auch Lutherlektüre betrifft, über eine theologische Sachkenntnis ausgewiesen, die ihn wiederum vor der Mehrzahl der neueren Philosophen auszeichnet." "Feuerbach," 212.

[4]Barth citing Feuerbach, *Das Wesen des Christentums*, critical ed., ed. R. Quenzel in Reklams Universalbibliothek (1841), 42, in "Feuerbach," 215.

[5]"Feuerbach," 219. Citation from L. Feuerbach, *Das Wesen der Religion* (Leipzig: Alfred Kröner, 1851), 14.

[6]"Feuerbach," 220f.

[7]Ibid., 220.

[8]Ibid., 226.

[9]Ibid., 226–9. Cf. ProtTh, 486f. Barth wants to show that the crisis precipitated by the Protestant theology of nineteenth century which found its logical conclusion in Feuerbach

is not simply a sudden diversion from or abandonment of a time-honored orthodoxy, but a trend rooted within emphases of Luther himself. "Feuerbach," 229–31. Cf. ProtTh, 487f.

[10]"Feuerbach," 228.

[11]The iconoclastic critique of the confused and fragmented undertaking of modern Christian theology and its absolute discontinuity with Christian origins which characterized the writings of Franz Overbeck exerted a similar influence upon Barth's conviction of the crisis situation into which theological language had fallen and the necessity of a reconstruction of theological foundations. Overbeck's line of influence upon Barth has been delineated in a careful and insightful essay by Eberhard Jüngel: "Theologie als 'unmögliche Möglichkeit'. Zwischen Overbeck und den beiden Blumhardts," in *Barth Studien*, 62–83. ET = "Theology as an 'Impossible Possibility': Between Overbeck and the Two Blumhardts," in *Karl Barth: A Theological Legacy*, 54–70.

[12]Eberhard Busch, *Karl Barths Lebenslauf* (Munich: Kaiser, [2]1976), 153. ET = *Karl Barth*, tr. J. Bowden (London: SCM, 1976), 140.

[13]Barth, "Wort Gottes," 159.

[14]Ibid., 159f.

[15]Ibid., 161–65.

[16]Ibid., 165. My translation.

[17]Jüngel appropriately draws this expression from other of Barth's texts to characterize the essence of Barth's argumentation in "Wort Gottes." Jüngel, "Unmögliche Möglichkeit," 71f. ET, 61f.

[18]Barth, "Wort Gottes," 169f. It is interesting to note that Barth mentions here the doctrine of the Trinity in a negative light as an example of an orthodox response which in effect denies or negates the human question it is supposed to answer. Why, asks Barth rhetorically, is it insufficient to simply and reverently accept the traditional answers of theology? "Weil da die Frage des Menschen nach Gott durch die Antwort einfach niedergeschlagen wird. Nun soll er nicht mehr fragen, sondern an Stelle der Frage die Antwort haben" (169). The recognition that dogma threatens toward idolatry when allowed an objective identity with the reality of revelation persists throughout the *Kirchliche Dogmatik*. What shifts is the recognition of its decisive hermeneutical possibility for bringing the reality of God to speech.

[19]Ibid., 171f.

[20]Ibid., 175.

[21]Ibid., 177.

[22]Ibid., 167.

[23]Ibid., 179.

[24]The following passage is taken from a letter of April 20, 1924: "Das Problem der 'natürlichen' Offenbarung und Religion macht mir immer wieder viel Kummer. Die alten Reformierten haben sehr lebhaft damit gerechnet. Ich weiss noch nicht definitiv, wo und wie ich es unterbringen kann. Hier greift die 'Väterlichkeit' Gottes ein und zwar gleich von mehreren Seiten: Logos, Schöpfung, Vorsehung. Mit der Menschwerdung gilt es jedenfalls vorsichtig umzugehen, damit man sich nicht in das exklusive 'Jesus Christus'-Loch der Lutheraner verrent. Alles steht natürlich auf diesem Nenner, aber dieser Nenner dann 'irgendwie' unter Allem. *Wesen*trinität, nicht nur ökonomische! Überhaupt die Trinitäts-lehre! Wenn ich da den rechten Schlüssel in die Hand bekäme, wäre einfach alles gut, aber immer wieder gerät man auf Kurzschlüssigkeiten, die sich dann irgendwo rächen." A few weeks later on the eighteenth of May, Barth declares, "Ich verstehe die Trinität als das Problem *der unaufhebbaren Subjektivität Gottes in seiner Offenbarung* und kann dem Athanasius, der überhaupt ein ganzer Kerl gewesen muss, meinen Beifall nicht versagen. Die Modernen sind natürlich auch da traurige Brüder: Sabellianer und andere ungute-ianer!" *Briefwechsel: Barth—Thurneysen*, II (Zürich: TVZ, 1974), 245, 253f. Cited, Wolfhart Pannenberg, "Die Subjektivität Gottes und die Trinitätslehre," *Grundfragen systematischer Theologie*, II (Göttingen: Vandenhoeck & Ruprecht, 1980), 97.

[25]Cf. v. Balthasar, 79–93. ET, 58–73.

[26]CD, 25.

[27]Ibid., 62–5, 73–9.

[28]Ibid., 126. The references here to phenomenological and existential methodology are indicative of the elements from which Barth wished to distance himself in the *Kirchliche Dogmatik*. Cf. KD I/1, 128–30.

[29]CD, 127, 131–40.

[30]Cf. T. F. Torrance on Barth's transition from *Die christliche Dogmatik* to *Die Kirchliche Dogmatik* in Torrance, *Karl Barth*, 133–47.

[31]Numerous studies have appeared which seek to take account of a position on the problem of religious language in the later Barth. Those which assume a sympathetic position toward the contribution of linguistic analysis to religious language tend to be critical of the viability or even coherency of Barth's understanding. See, for example, John Macquarrie, *God-Talk* (London: SCM, 1967), 41–50; Ian Ramsey, "Paradox in Religion," in J. Gill, ed., *Christian Empiricism* (Grand Rapids: Eerdmans, 1974), 113f; and D. D. Evans, "Barth on Talk about God," Canadian Journal of Theology 16 (1970) 175–92. (For a brief statement of the function of linguistic analysis in relation to confessional theology, see Ingolf Dalferth, *Religiöse Rede von Gott* [Munich: Kaiser, 1981], 22.) More constructive are those studies which work from a positive estimation of the place of analogy in theological speech: cf. Horst Georg Pöhlmann, *Analogia entis oder Analogia fidei?* (Göttingen: Vandenhoeck & Ruprecht, 1965), a detailed study of Barth's analogy concept; v. Balthasar, 116–23, 175–81 (ET, 93–100, 147–50); Walter Kreck, "Analogia Fidei oder Analogia Entis?" *Antwort* (Zurich: Evangelischer Verlag, 1956), 272–286; and Karl Hammer, "Analogia Relationis

gegen Analogia Entis," *Parrhesia* (Zurich: Evangelischer Verlag, 1966), 288-304. Perhaps the best indication of the far-reaching significance of analogy for the *Kirchliche Dogmatik* is to be found in Eberhard Jüngel, "Die Möglichkeit theologischer Anthropologie auf dem Grunde der Analogie. Eine Untersuchung zum Analogieverständnis Karl Barths," *Barth-Studien*, 210-232.

[32]Cf. Pöhlmann's observation that with the temporal development of the *Kirchliche Dogmatik*, Barth's positive formulation of the analogy concept (*analogia fidei* or *analogia relationis*) is referred to with increasing frequency, while reference to its unacceptable formulation (*analogia entis*) declines in frequency. Pöhlmann, 114.

[33]"Dogmatik ist als theologische Disziplin die wissenschaftliche Selbstprüfung der christlichen Kirche hinsichtlich des Inhalts der ihr eigentümlichen Rede von Gott." KD I/1, 1.

[34]"Dogmatik als Forschung setzt voraus, dass der rechte Inhalt christlicher Rede von Gott vom Menschen erkannt werden *kann*." KD I/1, 10.

[35]"Die Bedeutung *Schleiermachers* besteht vor allem darin, dass er in seiner Lehre von der christlichen Frömmigkeit als dem Sein der Kirche dieser Häresie [i.e., 'Lehre von der "Religion"'] eine die Zeit vor ihm ebenso erfüllende wie die Zeit nach ihm weissagende formale Begründung gegeben hat." KD I/1, 35.

[36]"Dogmatik als Forschung setzt voraus, dass der rechte Inhalt christlicher Rede von Gott vom Menschen erkannt werden *muss*." KD I/1, 12.

[37]Cf. Augustine, *De Trinitate*, VIII-XV.

[38]KD I/1, 354. Cf. 360: the problem of the *vestigia trinitatis* is "das Problem der theologischen Sprache."

[39]Cf. KD IV/3, 544f, where Barth portrays human language as the most prominent manifestation of the human situation of guilt, misery and separation from God.

[40]KD I/1, 359. Barth's conception of authentic talk of God as talk which is habilitated in an act of divine appropriation (*analogia gratiae*) finds its fullest expression in KD II/1, §27.

[41]Barth can describe this original sense of the doctrine as a "interessanten, erbaulichen, lehr- und hilfreichen Hinweis zum Verständnis der christlichen Lehre," not as a proof or alternative source of the doctrine, but rater a "nachträgliche unverbindliche, aber doch dankbar entgegenzunehmende Illustration des christlichen Credo." KD I/1, 357f.

[42]Barth suggests this parallel in "Nein! Antwort an Emil Brunner" (Munich: Kaiser, 1934), 38f.

[43]Natural theology is then a theology which may dispense with grace: "Gerade der für die Bereitschaft Gottes verschlossene Mensch kann und wird es sich ja nicht nehmen lassen, dass ihm selbst eine Bereitschaft für Gott auch ohne Gottes Gnade zur Verfügung stehe. Sein Versuch, sich selbst zu bewahren und zu behaupten—wir sahen, dass eben dieser

Versuch nicht nur die Möglichkeit, sondern die tiefste Wirklichkeit seiner Existenz und zwar gerade seiner in das Licht der göttlichen Offenbarung gerückten, gerade auch seiner gläubigen Existenz ist—dieser sein Versuch kann gar nicht anders endigen als in der Behauptung, dass er auch *ohne* Gottes Gnade, der Gnade Gottes immer schon *zuvor*kommend, sie immer schon *vorweg*nehmend, für Gott bereit, dass ihm also Gott auch anders als aus und durch sich selbst erkennbar sei." KD II/1, 150.

[44]Eberhard Jüngel, *Gottes Sein ist im Werden* (Tübingen: Mohr, 1965), 26. ET= *The Doctrine of the Trinity* (Grand Rapids: Eerdmans, 1976), 14f.

[45]"Die Offenbarung ist wohl Prädikat Gottes, aber so, dass dieses Prädikat restlos mit Gott selber identisch ist." KD I/1, 315.
"Es ist Gott selber, es ist in unzerstörter *Einheit* der gleiche Gott, der nach dem biblischen Verständnis der Offenbarung der offenbarende Gott ist *und* das Ereignis der Offenbarung *und* dessen Wirkung am Menschen." KD I/1, 315.

[46]Cf. Jüngel, *Gottes Sein*, 32f. ET, 21.

[47]KD I/1, 403f. Cf KD II/1, 51f.

[48]"Gott entspricht sich. In der Tat ist die Barthsche Dogmatik im Grunde eine ausführliche Exegese dieses Satzes." Jüngel, *Gottes Sein*, 35. ET, 23.

[49]"Der Einigkeit des Vaters, des Sohnes und des Geistes unter sich *entspricht* ihre Einigkeit nach aussen." KD I/1, 391. "Aber daraus, dass er in Jesus und nur in Jesus als Schöpfer und also als unser Vater offenbar wird, geht hervor, dass er das *Entsprechende* schon zuvor und an sich ist,..." (412). (Emphasis mine)

[50]This is the meaning which Jüngel wishes to expresses with his summary thesis of Barth's theology: "Gott entspricht sich." Jüngel, *Gottes Sein*, 35. ET, 23. The statement, "The economic Trinity corresponds to the immanent Trinity," as such, is not to be found in the *Kirchliche Dogmatik*, perhaps in part because of Barth's reluctance to use the "immanent—economic" phraseology itself which tends to imply an essential distinction within God, one which Barth would prefer to avoid. (The "immanent—economic" designation occurs only three times in the whole of KD I/1: 179, 352, and 503.)

[51]KD I/1, 320f.

[52]KD I/1, 391; cf. 179, KD II/1, 291.

[53]See KD I/1, 412, 437, 490, 502–4.

[54]That a trinitarian *Urbild* prefigures and grounds the *opera ad extra* is a running theme of the *Kirchliche Dogmatik*: the possibility of ethics, (which for Barth is the realization of human love), finds its ontological basis in the inner love of the trinitarian fellowship (KD I/2, 415); knowledge of God is possible because of the mutual knowledge of Father and Son in the fellowship of the Holy Spirit (KD II/1, 52, 175–7); each of the divine attributes are grounded in the triune life of God: omnipresence (KD II/1, 527), omnipotence (595), and eternity (693f); election is prefigured in a trinitarian *Urentscheidung* (KD II/2, 82); the

possibility of creation finds its prior ground in the eternal love of Father for Son (KD III/1, 53); the humility of the Son is a possibility prefigured in the Trinity (KD IV/1, 220–2); the humanity of Christ is grounded in an *Urentscheidung* of the eternal triune God (KD IV/2, 34f), just as his humility finds its *Urbild* in the relationship of Son to Father (46f). The trinitarian *Urbild* applies not only to the *opera ad extra* but equally as well to the divine Modes of Being (*Seinsweisen*): God comes to us as Father, Son, and Holy Spirit because he is already (*zuvor in sich selber*) Father, Son, and Holy Spirit in his eternal being (KD I/1, 404, 419, 470).

[55]It is from this perspective that the correspondence thesis must be understood lest it be interpreted as a lapse into speculation. Cf. Ted Peters, "Trinity Talk: Part I," Dia 26 (1987) 45f, who describes the undertaking as a "pseudo-problem," unnecessary for a theologian who takes the biblical claim for revelation seriously. By presenting Barth's development of the concept against the background of the theological crisis which he observed within Neo-Protestantism, we have sought to give clarity to the theological hermeneutical function of the doctrine (and particularly the principle of correspondence) which allows revelation to be interpreted solely as God's *self*-revelation, excluding alternative foundations.

[56]KD II/1, 15f. The distinction between God's primary and secondary objectivity corresponds to Barth's conception of the "form" of revelation. In assuming "form" God remains veiled in His revealing. God in His revelation is His own "Doppelgänger." KD I/1, 333f; cf. 339.

[57]"Gott ist sich selber *unmittelbar*, er ist aber uns *mittelbar* gegenständlich: nicht direkt, sondern indirekt, nicht unbekleidet, sondern bekleidet, unter dem Zeichen und unter der Hülle *anderer* von ihm verschiedener Gegenstände. Er ist es auch so in voller Wahrheit, weil diese seine sekundäre Gegenständlichkeit in seiner primären ihre Entsprechung und ihren Grund hat,...." KD II/1, 16.

[58]In spite of the parallels, Barth's thought in this regard may not be reduced to a Platonic style dualism, (the most recent attempt of which is to be found in Jean-Louis Leuba, "Platonisme et Barthisme: Quelques Perspectives Théologiques," *Archivio di Filosofia* 53 (1985) 153–72, who finds in Barth's use of analogy a Platonic dualism which falls ultimately into an *Identitätsphilosophie* and consequently into a monistic vision of reality). Trinitarian correspondence functions for Barth to emphasize both the unity of God with Himself and the way of His being with the world which is characterized by the act of taking the objectivity of the world on Himself. In the suffering and death of the Son on the cross Barth sees far more than a worldly manifestation of an eternal reality. God takes upon in himself in the course of created time the fallenness of the creation which He has called into being. The conception defies any monistic reduction. Cf. Jüngel, *Gottes Sein*, 44ff. ET, 33ff.

[59]Cf. note 31, above.

[60]See especially KD III/2, 244ff, 262f; IV/1, 709–11.

[61]Jüngel, "theologische Anthropologie," 212.

[62]KD III/2, 262. Cf. I/1, 341.

[63]See Jüngel, "theologische Anthropologie," 213-16.

[64]Cf. Jüngel, "Einführung," 49. ET, 43.

[65]Against the suggestion that the *analogia fidei* is simply a variant of the *analogia entis* (as per, eg., v. Balthasar, 175-81; ET, 147-50) Jüngel demonstrates the radical otherness of the two conceptions. Jüngel, "theologische Anthropologie," esp. 216-22, 224-27.

[66]Karl Rahner, "Der dreifaltige Gott als transzendenter Urgrund der Heilsgeschichte," *Mysterium Salutis*, II (Einsiedeln: Benziger, 1967), 328. ET = *The Trinity*, tr. J. Donceel (New York: Herder and Herder, 1970), 22. In an earlier text Rahner articulates the identity thesis although without a systematic development of its methodological implications. See *Schriften zur Theologie*, IV (Einsiedeln: Benzinger, 1960), 103-133; ET = *Theological Investigations*, IV, tr. K. Smith (London: Dartman, Longman & Todd, rpt. 1974 [=1966]), 77-102.

[67]Walter Kasper, *Der Gott Jesu Christi* (Mainz: Matthias Grünewald Verlag, 1982), 333. ET = *The God of Jesus Christ*, tr. M. J. O'Connell (London: SCM, 1984), 273f.

[68]Wolfhart Pannenberg, *Systematische Theologie*, I (Göttingen: Vandenhoeck & Ruprecht, 1988), 356f.

[69]Isidro García-Tato, *Die Trinitätslehre Karl Barths als dogmatisches Strukturprinzip* (Bad Honnef: Bock u. Herchen, 1983), 572. Similarly in Robert Theis, "Die Lehre von der Dreieinigkeit Gottes bei Karl Barth," *Freiburger Zeitschrift für Philosophie und Theologie* 24 (1977) 269.

[70]Rahner, "Der dreifaltige Gott," 323. ET, 14.

[71]Ibid., 327. ET, 21.

[72]Ibid., 338-40. ET, 36-8.

[73]Ibid., 337. ET, 35

[74]Ibid., 340. ET, 39f.

[75]Ibid., 329. ET, 24.

[76]Ibid., 346. ET, 47.

[77]Eberhard Jüngel, "Das Verhältnis von 'ökonomischer' und 'immanenter' Trinität," ZThK 72 (1975) 355; citing F. Schleiermacher, *Der christliche Glaube*, ed. M. Redeker, II (1960), 458 (§170).

[78]Cf. note 45 above. See also KD I/1, 402f, 435. Cf. Barth also on the unity of God's works and God's essence: KD I/1, 391f, 450.

[79]KD I/1, 391. Cf. I/1, 442; II/1, 291, 389.

[80]Cf. Robert Jenson, *God After God* (Indianapolis: Bobb Merrills, 1969), 112, who makes a similar point. Cf. also the sympathetic analyses of Barth on this point in Claude Welch, *The Trinity in Contemporary Theology* (London: SCM, 1953 [=1952]), 185–7; and John Dillenberger, *God Hidden and Revealed* (Philadelphia: Huhlenberg Press, 1953), 132–39.

[81]Cf. KD IV/1, 223, in which the humiliation of the Son in history is depicted in analogy to the eternal inner life of God. "Er ist nur auch in der *Zeit*, was er in Ewigkeit ist (und gerade vermöge seines ewigen Seins auch in der Zeit sein kann)." This he does "nicht ohne Grund in seinem Wesen, in seinem eigenen inneren Leben, nicht ohne Entsprechung zu der Geschichte—vielmehr in wunderbar konsequenter letzter Fortsetzung eben der Geschichte, in der er Gott ist." See also KD II/1, 64: "...Geschichte ist ein Prädikat der Offenbarung."

[82]Jüngel, *Gottes Sein*, 22–25. ET, 11–13. Cf. Hans Geisser, "Der Beitrag der Trinitätslehre zur Problematik des Redens von Gott." ZThK 65 (1968) 237.

[83]This is the direction which has been taken by Pannenberg and Moltmann. Pannenberg, *Theologie*, 356–8. Jürgen Moltmann, *Trinität und Reich Gottes* (Munich: Kaiser, 1980) 176f. ET = *The Trinity and the Kingdom of God*, tr. M. Kohl (London: SCM, 1981), 160f.

[84]Kasper, 333. ET, 274.

[85]Cf. T. F. Torrance, "Toward an Ecumenical Consensus on the Trinity," TZ (1975) 337–50, for an elaboration of the widespread acceptance of Rahner's thesis.

[86]See Kasper, 335f, ET, 275f; Josef Wohlmuth, "Zum Verhältnis von ökonomischer und immanenter Trinität—eine These," ZKTh (1988) 139–162; Wolfhart Pannenberg, "Problems of a Trinitarian Doctrine of God," Dia 26 (1987) 250–57. Orig. = "Probleme einer trinitarischer Gotteslehre," in *Weisheit Gottes—Weisheit der Welt*, I, FS J. Ratzinger, ed. W. Baier (St. Ottilien: 1987); and Moltmann, *Trinität*, 176f. ET, 160f.

[87]It is the service of Jüngel that he has demonstrated the possibility of thinking of God's historical being, that is, of God as becoming, such that it represents a real becoming in the being of God which corresponds to a divine inner, eternal becoming of God, and this he does within Barth's own theological framework. God's becoming in the death of Jesus Christ signifies a genuine threat for the eternal being of God (Jüngel, *Gottes Sein*, 91; ET, 78); but in so far as the being of God has its ontological locus in an eternal becoming, the being of God can confront non-being, expose itself to it, and prevail in such exposure as suffering being. In this sense then, Jüngel would want to assert a mutual relatedness between the economic and immanent Trinity, but without thereby sacrificing the ground which the immanent provides the economic. Thus, can Jüngel affirm Rahner's identity thesis and still add the following proviso: "Die Einheit von 'immanenter' und 'ökonomischer' Trinität zu behaupten ist theologisch nur dann legitim, wenn diese Einheit nicht in dem Sinne *tauto-logisch* verkannt wird, dass die *Freiheit* und ungeschuldete *Gnade* der Selbstmitteilung Gottes und also deren *Ereignishaftigkeit* undenkbar wird. Es sollte deshalb, gerade um die *reale* Identität von 'immanenter' und 'ökonomischer' Trinität als *Geheimnis aussagen* zu können,

die *distinctio rationis* von 'ökonomischer' und 'immanenter' Trinität theologisch beibehalten werden." E. Jüngel, "Verhältnis," 364.

[88]Cf. chapter one of Sallie McFague, *Metaphorical Theology* (London: SCM, 1983), 1–29.

[89]Ibid., 15.

[90]Methodologically this means that the *principium essendi* takes priority to the *principium cognoscendi*, since the ontic reality of God precedes the noetic rationality of human knowledge. Cf. Ch. 2, note 73.

[91]Cf. Pannenberg's critique of recent theology's rejection of the notion of God as Father. In a few lines which could easily have come from the pen of Barth himself, Pannenberg sees the rejection as a throwback to Feuerbach's view of theological language according to which anthropology is determinative. Pannenberg, *Theologie*, (Göttingen: Vandenhoeck & Ruprecht, 1988), 285f.

[92]This is precisely Pannenberg's critique of Barth's method for constructing the doctrine of the Trinity, which according to Pannenberg amounts to an extreme form of the very subjectivism and anthropocentrism which Barth sought to reject. Pannenberg, "Subjektivität Gottes," 103f.

[93]There are remarkable similarities between Barth's view of theological language and the philosophical concept of "language game" as developed in the later writings of Wittgenstein. "Language games" refer to a particular form of life or, as it were, a world of meaning, within which a language system functions. Verification outside of the "language game" is neither necessary nor possible. Two analyses of the relationship between Barth and Wittgenstein in this regard are available in D. M. Lochhead, "The Autonomy of Theology: A Critical Study with Special Reference to Karl Barth and Contemporary Analytical Philosophy" (Ph.D. diss., McGill Univ., 1967), and A. A. Glenn, "The Relationship Between Theology as a Special Science and Analytic Philosophy with Special Reference to the Theology of Karl Barth" (Ph.D. diss., Northwestern Univ., 1967).

[94]This aspect of the doctrine of the Trinity, which is explicit in Barth's discussion (KD I/1, 354), has been given careful analysis by Jüngel. Jüngel suggests that the polemical-critical character of Barth's Trinity doctrine parallels the concern for a responsible theological language in Bultmann's program of demythologization. Jüngel's intention thereby is to offer a bridge between the two divergent theological programs which would alleviate the "either-or" alternative usually associated with them. See Jüngel, *Gottes Sein*, 22f, 33f, 71f. ET, 11f, 21f, 58–60.

[95]"Mythus heisst ja in Form von Erzählung gebrachte, aber an sich raum- und zeitlos wahr sein wollende Darstellung gewisser immer und überall bestehender Grundverhältnisse der menschlichen Existenz in ihren Beziehungen zu ihren eigenen Ursprüngen und Bedingungen im natürlichen und geschichtlichen Kosmos bzw. in der Gottheit, in Form von Erzählung gebracht unter der Voraussetzung, dass der Mensch um alle diese Dinge weiss und sie so oder so darstellen kann, dass er ihre mächtig ist, dass sie letzten Grundes seine eigenen Dinge sind." KD I/1, 346.

[96]KD I/1, 401–3. Cf., Jüngel, *Gottes Sein*, 34. ET, 22f.

[97]Paul Tillich, *Systematic Theology*, I (Chicago: Univ. of Chicago, 1951), 235.

[98]Langdon Gilkey, *Reaping the Whirlwind* (Indianapolis: Bobbs Merrill, 1969), 305.

[99]It is one of the remarkable insights of Barth's theology that it is only in granting the objectivity of God that objectification is to be avoided. By removing God *in toto* from the realm of objective reality, as Tillich does, for instance, with the concept of God as "being itself," God becomes ultimately an ineffable "it" standing beyond His revelation(s). In granting a qualified (sacramental) objectivity to God Barth secures the "real presence" of God in His revelation and the possibility of personal (subjective) encounter.

CHAPTER SIX
The Trinitarian Hermeneutic and
the Interpretation of
Human Existence

The historical development of the general field of hermeneutics may be characterized in terms of a dual emphasis.[1] On the one hand is the hermeneutical problem in its narrow focus, that is, the problem of the historical distance between text and interpreter. On the other is hermeneutics in its broader sense, that is, the problem of human understanding itself and the conditions under which understanding becomes possible. Hermeneutics in its narrow focus may be thought of as a special instance of hermeneutics in its broader focus, since both tasks share the common objective of bringing to light the process of human understanding with the final aim of helping that process to reach its goal. It is thus a particular phenomenon of human existence, the phenomenon of understanding, which is the object of hermeneutical inquiry. Theological reflection upon hermeneutics in each of its stages of historical development has shared this common goal of aiding the process of understanding, whether it be in the form of rudimentary rules of biblical exegesis or in the form of an anthropological ontology which offers a theoretical description of the structures of existence which enables and effects genuine understanding.

As seen in chapter one, it is this anthropological focus of hermeneutical inquiry, and thus the implication of an anthropological starting point for theological reflection that stands primarily behind Barth's suspicion of hermeneutically oriented theology. The function which philosophically articulated hermeneutics fulfills is not, however, abandoned by Barth, but rather, as we have endeavored to point up throughout this work, is a function executed from within material dogmatics, specifically by means of a particular understanding of the doctrine of the Trinity. It is the burden of the present chapter to demonstrate how the doctrine of the Trinity executes this peculiar anthropological function for Barth. Clarity may be gained in this regard if Barth's understanding is contrasted with the methodological assumptions of an explicit hermeneutical theology. Ideal for this purpose is the hermeneutical thought associated with Bultmann, Ebeling, and Fuchs, not only because of the anthropological emphasis which is to be found there, but also, and just as importantly, because of certain shared theological aims which characterize both lines of thought. The chapter proceeds in three parts: 1) an overview of the role of the analysis of human existence in hermeneutical theology; 2) a discussion of the place which Barth finds for human existence in the doctrine of the Trinity; and 3) conclusions regarding Barth's doctrine of the Trinity as a hermeneutic of human existence and its relation to hermeneutical theology as such.

Hermeneutical Theology and Human Existence

The line of recent hermeneutical thought associated with Bultmann, Fuchs, and Ebeling is far-reaching in its scope and complex in its subject-matter. Our concern here is to offer neither a comprehensive summary nor a thoroughgoing critique (both of which have been sufficiently undertaken in other places),[2] but rather to touch upon a few salient features which will offer a point of comparison with the hermeneutical dimension of Barth's Trinity doctrine.

It is Rudolf Bultmann who more than any other has elevated the hermeneutical problem to a place of such prominence for twentieth century Christianity. As Barth declares at the beginning of his now (in)famous essay, "Rudolf Bultmann—Ein Versuch, ihn zu verstehen," "The name of Rudolf Bultmann is inseparably linked with the idea of 'understanding.'"[3] Bultmann's program of existential interpretation of the New Testament seeks to relate the theological task of careful scrutiny of the biblical word of revelation specifically to the possibility of human understanding of that word.

Bultmann's work operates upon the assumption that the biblical witness to revelation wants to relate to us in the depth of our existence as a word for us, and as a word which transforms us. The heartbeat of the New Testament for Bultmann is the kerygma, the proclamation or message, which can only be understood as a personal message. The New Testament is not understood properly if one thinks to draw from it general or theoretical knowledge of God, or neutral, historical data. If such things are to be found in the New Testament, they are of secondary interest only. The New Testament kerygma is an event in which the hearer participates with the wholeness of his being, or else it is a message which has either not been heard or has been rejected.[4]

To this extent, Bultmann's assumptions are at one with contemporary theology and indeed with the Christian tradition as a whole. What distinguishes Bultmann is the vigor with which he seeks to focus upon the moment of reception of the kerygmatic word and the conditions which are necessary to make that possibility a reality. This emphasis is justified for Bultmann preeminently by the fact that the kerygma encounters us not directly but through the mediation of Scripture, an historical document which can rightly be understood only when its historicity, that is, the fact that its expression is rooted within the particularities of human cultures, philosophies, world-views, etc., which are very much different from our own, is properly taken into account. Thus the problem of hermeneutics presses itself upon the interpreter of Scripture if the kerygma is to be rightly heard.

Bultmann's conception of this hermeneutical task for theology is given particular clarity in his 1950 essay, "Das Problem der Hermeneutik."[5] Following Dilthey, Bultmann suggests that the problem of hermeneutics is "the question of the possibility of attaining to *objectivity in understanding individual human being,* namely, of the past."[6] Bultmann continues, "This question is basically an enquiry into the possibility of understanding historical phenomena at all, in so far as they are testimonies to individual human being: thus hermeneutics would be the science of understanding history in general."[7] For Bultmann the problem of hermeneutics is the problem of conveying existentially relevant truth from the past into the present of its contemporary hearers. It is insufficient, however, if one attempts to overcome this problem simply by means of philological, structural, and historical analysis. Such analysis is indispensable if the process of interpretation is to be advanced, but it is by no means sufficient—it does not guarantee the possibility of genuine understanding of the content of a particular text.

Once the necessary historical and philological questions are resolved, genuine understanding is to be achieved only after the reader is brought into a right relation with the subject-matter of the text. The possibility of this right relation is one governed by Bultmann's concept of *pre-understanding* (*Vor-verständnis*). The basic idea of pre-understanding is described by Bultmann as follows:

> A comprehension—an interpretation—is, it follows, *constantly orientated to a particular formulation of a question, a particular "objective"*. But included in this, therefore, is the fact that it is never without its own presuppositions: or, to put it more precisely, that it is *governed always by a prior understanding of the subject*, in accordance with which it investigates the text. The formulation of a question, and an interpretation, is possible at all only on the basis of such a prior understanding (*Vorverständnis*).[8]

The basic idea of pre-understanding is thus not prescriptive but simply descriptive. One's understanding of a text is always determined at least in some degree by the pre-understanding which he brings to its subject-matter. The prescriptive portion of Bultmann's program is to be found in the fundamental role he assigns the concept for theological hermeneutics. Pre-understanding is hardly something which must be eliminated before genuine understanding is possible.[9] It represents rather that which must be cultivated. It is by virtue of a pre-understanding that a reader or hearer of a text is brought into a "life-relation" with the text's subject-matter.[10] The pre-understanding constitutes a living relation between text and interpreter.

For the New Testament this means that a pre-understanding regarding God is at work if the subject-matter of the text is to be comprehended. By this Bultmann does not mean to suggest that a theistic belief necessarily precedes authentic encounter with the text, since,

> in human existence an *existentiell* knowledge about God is alive in the form of the inquiry about "happiness", "salvation", the meaning of the world and of history; and in the inquiry into the real nature of each person's particular "being".[11]

The pre-understanding which one brings to the text will indeed encounter correction as it allows itself to become subject to the message of the text. It can, however, "only receive such a correction if the basic intention of the inquiry, as comprised in the concept of 'salvation', coincides with the intention of the answer given in the New Testament."[12]

It is then for Bultmann of decisive and determinative significance how one fashions the inquiry into the text. If the questions are not properly posed, then the answers will surely be distorted. It is therefore incumbent upon scientific exegesis that it devote itself to reflection upon the proper interpretation of its inquiry, which means, of course, a proper interpretation of human existence.[13] Exegetical science must conduct itself on the basis of a careful, conceptually delineated philosophical or existential analysis of human being, if the kerygma is to be brought into a "life-relation" with modern hearers. It is this basic understanding of the hermeneutical task which lies at the foundation of Bultmann's existential exegesis as well as the program of demythologization, which rather than removing myth from the pages of Scripture, seeks to interpret or translate mythical language into the existentially relevant kerygma which lies beneath it.

We must carry this foundational element of Bultmann's hermeneutic one step further. The careful conceptual analysis of the pre-understanding which corresponds most closely to the kerygma proclaimed in the New Testament is a fundamental inquiry about one's self. This is the essential motivation, the fundamental "life-relation" between interpreter and the biblical text.

> Man's life is moved by the search for God because it is always moved, consciously or unconsciously, by the question about his own personal existence. The question of God and the question of myself are identical.[14]

The exposition of the biblical witness to revelation must be understood accordingly as the inquiry into a particular understanding existence. The kerygma is significant for me as the transformation of my own self-understanding. It proclaims the new self-understanding of authentic existence, or in more theological terms, eschatological existence. This new self-understanding is not a latent possibility simply awakened by a new insight, but arises out of the encounter with Scripture as the Word of God and out of a hearing of the kerygma which addresses and calls me from without.[15]

In an observation registered by Barth (and later confirmed by Bultmann himself) Bultmann's understanding of the kerygma may be thought of as the unifying principle between soteriology and christology, even though within this unity a certain ordering takes place.[16] Soteriology precedes christology and becomes its interpretive frame of reference. To press the point as far as Barth does, however, that christology is for Bultmann derived from soteriology is an ambiguous overstatement which refuses to take seriously the fact that it is after all the New Testament witness which is the object of Bultmann's hermeneutic and exegesis.[17] What may be said in a fair estimation of Bultmann's intention is that the analysis of human existence is the essence of the hermeneutical task in its broader dimension and thus forms the basis for the interpretation of the Christ event (which for Bultmann means the *existentiell* event of encounter with Jesus Christ).

Fuchs and Ebeling represent a further development of the hermeneutical focus given prominence in the writings of Bultmann. Like Bultmann, the later hermeneutical theologians are concerned with the question of understanding and the conditions which allow understanding to happen. Implicit within their work is likewise an engagement of the notion of pre-understanding with similar implications for the theological task.[18] It is not the existential analysis of the early Heidegger which characterizes their work, however, but the linguistic analysis of the later Heidegger. Language becomes the primal category which tends to replace the concept of "being" as employed by Bultmann. This primacy of language is expressed by Fuchs in a reflection upon Heidegger's lament upon the inauthenticity into which language has fallen:

> For the lament as *language* no longer belongs to lostness, but rather supplies man with the plus that as the *essence* of language reminds him that he belongs to a communication, a...*nearness* to the power at work in language prior to all human participation. For it is not true that man has given birth to language. Rather man is born out of language. That man then has made language a means of usurped existence merely proves that man is accustomed to exist in daily life having missed the mark.[19]

Hermeneutics, then, is a science not concerned strictly with the interpretation of language, but with language itself. This concern is expressed *in nuce* by Ebeling:

> If hermeneutics, in order to be an aid to understanding, has to reflect on the conditions under which understanding is possible, then it has to reflect on the nature of words. *Hermeneutics as the theory of understanding must therefore be the theory of words.*[20]

For both Ebeling and Fuchs understanding is an event which is executed in what is referred to as the word-event (*Wortgeschehen*) or language-event (*Sprachereignis*) respectively. The understanding of language and word operative here is not that of a tool or mechanism which merely facilitates communication. The notion of word is taken to a deeper level to designate the event of understanding itself and thereby underscore the linguistic character of the event of human illumination. "Where word happens rightly, existence is illumined."[21]

Theological hermeneutics is concerned with how the word-event happens, particularly when the word-event in question is the Word of God.

This word-event takes place, Christians confess, in the Gospel. It
is savingly related to the word-event which always proceeds from
God and strikes the foolish man as the law which kills. But for that
reason, too, it is only in the light of the Gospel that we can grasp
what God's Word really means and how far the law is God's Word.
For God's Word must not on any account be reduced to a formal
concept which would be indifferent towards any intrinsic definition
of the Word of God. For God's Word is not various things, but
one single thing—the Word that makes man human by making him
a believer, i.e. a man who confesses to God as his future and
therefore does not fail his fellowmen in the one absolutely
necessary and salutary thing, viz. true word.[22]

Theological hermeneutics then is the "theory or doctrine of the Word of
God."[23] Its task consists in removing the obstacles which hinder the word-event
from taking place.[24] It executes this task by "a deeper penetration into the
linguistic realm" to enhance the understanding of language.[25] And because word
and language are not merely the designations of verbal mechanisms, but
designate the very essence of human being, then hermeneutics will undertake
the elucidation of not only the human relation to verbal statements, but of
human relationships as such—in the person's relation to his fellow, as well as his
relationship to God.[26]

Hermeneutical theology does not want to think of itself as a mere
precursor to theology but as a necessary part of doing theology itself.[27] As such
it would appear at times to understand itself as fundamental theology, that is,
prolegomena,[28] and at other times as anthropology or soteriology.[29] Both foci
are integral to the task which hermeneutical theology has set for itself. The
primary problem which it seeks to overcome is a problem rooted in the
historicity of human being. Understanding is approached as a human
phenomenon which is to be enhanced by an explication of the linguistic
character of human being. This explication entails further the elucidation of the
human being in his relationships with other human beings, with himself, and
ultimately with God. By means of this explication, hermeneutics represents a
"clearing the way" which desires to offer a fresh hearing to the Word of God,

and which seeks to that end to mold the totality of theological and ecclesial language in such a way that the word-event which was characteristic of the ministry of Jesus is repeated again and again in our own linguistically diseased era of history.

The Trinity and Human Existence in the *Kirchliche Dogmatik*
The Trinitarian Critique of Anthropocentric Theology

A superficial familiarity with Karl Barth's doctrine of the Trinity suggests little if anything that it might hold in common with the concerns of hermeneutical theologians. Indeed, the same observation can be extended to Barth's theology as a whole, at least from the time of the *Römerbrief*. A number of Barthian slogans which bring to expression the critique of anthropocentric theology tend but to reinforce this impression:

> Es gibt einen Weg von der Christologie zur Anthropologie. Es gibt aber keinen Weg von einer Anthropologie zur Christologie. (KD I/1, 135)

> [Der Mensch ist] nicht nur ein kranker, sondern ein Toter. (KD I/2, 280)

> Es gibt anthropologische und ekklesiologische Sätze nur in Form von Lehnsätzen aus der Christologie. (KD II/1, 166)[30]

We have already seen in the previous chapter that the doctrine of the Trinity stands for Barth as an extended polemic against the attempt to employ a general concept of human being or experience as the foundation for theological statements. The rejection of the doctrine of the *vestigia trinitatis* leaves no room for talk of God upon any basis other than that laid down by God Himself in the event of His self-revelation. Other aspects of Barth's Trinity doctrine also contribute to the polemic. In an explicit dialogue with Friedrich Gogarten's critique of *Die christliche Dogmatik* (a discussion which is apparent at many points throughout the writing of KD I/1), Barth makes the point that the danger of anthropocentric theology forms an external justification for the distinction between the immanent and economic Trinity. Barth rejects a theology of correlation which would posit a mutual contingency between God and humanity. If this rejection is in order, argues Barth,

> dann bleibt es nicht nur sinnvoll, sondern notwendig, mit der ganzen älteren Theologie zwischen der Trinität Gottes, wie sie uns im offenbarten, geschriebenen und verkündigten Wort Gottes erkennbar ist und seiner immanenten Trinität, also zwischen "Gott an sich" und "Gott für uns", zwischen der "ewigen Geschichte Gottes" und seinem zeitlichen Handeln bewusst und scharf unterscheiden, immer wieder daran zu erinnern, wie das "Gott für uns" sich gar nicht selbstverständlich von dem Hintergrund des "Gott an sich" abhebt, wie es wahr ist nicht als ein Zustand Gottes, den wir vom Begriff des seiner Offenbarung teilhaftigen Menschen aus fixieren und behaupten könnten, sondern als eine Tat, als ein Schritt Gottes, den er dem Menschen entgegentut, und durch den dieser erst ein seiner Offenbarung teilhaftiger Mensch *wird*. (KD I/1, 179)

Trinitarian theology represents for Barth the assertion not only of the objectivity of God but of an objectivity which transcends human subjectivity. The necessary distinction between the economic Trinity and the immanent Trinity, that is, God as He enters into human history and God in His eternal self-sufficiency, is a distinction which is necessary if this objectivity is to be preserved. If God is to be spoken of, even the experience of God, it will not be possible on the basis of any aspect of human existence.[31]

The most prominent feature of this disparity, however, arises not from the content of the doctrine *per se*, but from its "place" in Barth's dogmatic scheme.[32] The doctrine of the Trinity, which is itself the fullest statement of the doctrine of God, is offered as prolegomena, as the initial, if not preparatory word of a systematic and comprehensive presentation of Christian theology, and thus precisely at that point at which one would most likely expect to encounter hermeneutical reflections. As we have seen in Chapter 2, Barth is quite intentional in offering talk of God in the place where one would expect talk of either the role and limits of human reason and understanding or else a doctrine of Scripture as a guaranty for the veracity of the statements which follow.

The clearest expression of the implicit polemic in Barth's trinitarian prolegomena occurs in a discussion of the relationship of the Word of God, that is, God's triune self-revelation, to human existence and experience. Barth acknowledges that indeed the event of the Word of God is an event which cannot be thought apart from the humanity to which it is addressed (198f). There is then a sense in which "*logisch und sachlich*" a possibility and capacity within human existence corresponds to this event (201). But this capacity must not be thought of as something innate to human experience, just as the event is not one alongside the many other events and realities which the human being may encounter. The *Erkenntnismöglichkeit* (possiblity for knowing) which is presupposed in the event of the Word is rather one that is imported or created by the object of its knowing. This *Erkenntnismöglichkeit*, which is indeed a possibility for the human being, is

> im Unterschied zu allen anderen nur vom Erkenntnisgegenstand bzw. von der Erkenntniswirklichkeit her und durchaus nicht vom Erkenntnissubjekt, also durchaus nicht vom Menschen her als solche verständlich zu machen.... (201)

Assertions to the contrary represent nothing less than a denial of grace.

> Gottes Wort ist nicht mehr Gnade oder Gnade selbst ist nicht mehr Gnade, wenn man dem Menschen eine Hinordnung zu diesem Wort, eine ihm selbständing und an sich eigene Erkenntnis- möglichkeit diesem Wort gegenüber zuschreibt. (202)

The realization of this possibility for encounter with the Word of God and a consequent knowledge of God occurs indeed in concrete human experience. But the human experience is not as such the experience of the Word of God. This puzzle is resolved for Barth by the positing of dual planes upon which human existence may be determined. The experience of the Word of God involves an act of human self-determination (207f). Within this act of self-determination occurs the act of divine-determination which alone constitutes the experience of the Word. The two dimensions intersect in the experience of the Word, but there can be for Barth no question of mutual dependency. There is no "simultaneity," no "interwovenness," no "unity in tension" (*Spannungseinheit*) (207). Such theories err in mistaking the two types of determination at work here as events of the same kind, as competing or rival events, and such is simply not the case. Self-determination is utterly subordinate to divine-determination. Self-determination is dependent upon divine-determination if it is to be experience of the Word of God (208). This does not, however, constitute for Barth an impingement upon the reality of the self-determination. Rather, it is in self-determination that obedience or disobedience to the Word takes place (209).

> Ist das Wort Gottes nicht zu Tieren, Pflanzen oder Steinen gesprochen, sondern zu Menschen und ist also Bestimmtheit durch das Wort Gottes wirklich eine Bestimmtheit menschlicher Existenz, in was sonst soll sie dann bestehen, als darin, dass eben die Selbstbestimmung, in der der Mensch Mensch ist, in der Bestimmung durch Gott ein ihr schlechthin überlegenes Oberhalb bekommt, dass sie als Selbstbestimmung und ohne als solche im geringsten angetastet oder gar zerstört zu werden, eine Weisung empfängt, unter ein Urteil gestellt wird, einen Charakter aufgeprägt erhält, kurz, ebenso bestimmt wird, wie ein sich selbst bestimmendes Wesen durch ein Wort und wie nun eben der Mensch durch das Wort Gottes bestimmt wird. (210)

The consequences which Barth draws from this understanding are significant. First, it is neither possible, nor necessary to determine the precise faculty (*anthropologischer Ort*) through which the experience of the Word of God occurs (210f). Barth has in mind the ancient debate over the question of whether will, conscience or emotion constitute the point of contact to the divine. Secondly, it is unnecessary to disparage any particular anthropological faculty with regard to its role in religious experience, as has been particularly the case with the intellect in recent history (211f). Thirdly, it is unnecessary to isolate any unusual or hidden human capacity for divine encounter (212f). In sum, it is human existence in its wholeness which is determined for its encounter with the Word of God, and it is human existence in its wholeness which is totally dependent upon the determination of God for its experience of His Word.

For Barth, the "anthropological question" posed by the Word of God is not one that may be resolved on the anthropological level. The disparity between Barth's concern and that of the hermeneutical theologians comes to the fore in that the problem of understanding posed by hermeneutical theology assumes an interplay of divine and human determination which Barth will not allow. The problem of understanding the Word of God can according to Barth not be illuminated on the plane of philosophical anthropology, since it represents an event in the life of the human being which is effected solely by its object. It would appear therefore that the superficial conclusion for a total disparity between the aims of hermeneutical theology and those behind Barth's doctrine of the Trinity has found a substantial confirmation. But the rejection of the "anthropological" approach does not constitute a rejection of the problem of human understanding which it seeks to address. As we shall see in the discussion which follows, the problem of understanding constitutes a significant impetus within Barth's trinitarian development.

Revelation as Objective-Subjective Reality

For Karl Barth human participation in the event of God's self-revelation is trinitarian. The doctrine of the Trinity represents the sufficient ground for the possibility and reality of human participation in and knowledge of God in His revelation.[33] Barth unfolds the concept of this trinitarian ground in terms of the objective-subjective reality of revelation, such that human participation in revelation becomes a bipolar event held together in the unity of the one God.

In Jesus Christ, the self-revelation of the Father *pro nobis* becomes objective reality (KD I/2, 1). This becoming is the becoming of the incarnation.

The incarnation is the "simple reality" of God's revelation (13). It is simple in the sense of a "bestimmten, zeitlichen umgrenzten, nicht wiederholten und gar nicht wiederholbaren Geschehens" (13). As such, it is also a unique reality, unique not only in its historical non-repeatable character, but unique in the sense of God's own uniqueness. The witness to this reality in the New Testament articulates itself in the double assertion, "The Son of God is Jesus of Nazareth. Jesus of Nazareth is the Son of God."[34] The dialectic in these assertions finds its (penultimate) place in human understanding in the confession to the *vere Deus, vere homo* of Jesus Christ (28f). It is because Jesus Christ is both, true God and true humanity, that the reality of God "for us" is grounded eternally in the second person of the Trinity.[35]

As the objective reality of revelation, the incarnation represents theologically an expression of the extent to which God is free "for us," which is another way of saying the extent to which he is free to reveal Himself to humanity (2). Its recognition signals the awareness that prior to all human knowledge and acknowledgement of what is appropriate to God and what is salvific for humanity, God has already determined and revealed what is appropriate to Himself and what is salvific for humanity (5). The objective reality of this event itself raises the question of its possibility, a possibility which is in turn grounded in the reality itself (30f). The question of the possibility is not one that may be engaged prior to an acknowledgement of the reality. The objective reality is not available to human inquiry outside of the objectivity of the event itself. The very awareness that human existence stands apart from God, "dass Gott verborgen und der Mensch blind ist," is rooted in the objectivity of the revelation.[36]

The objective reality of revelation then confirms the human face of God, that is, the readiness of God to make Himself known to humanity and thereby reconcile humanity to Himself. But this is an incomplete picture of revelation. It is a polarity which requires the complement of a subjective reality if the biblical witness to revelation is to be expressed in its fullness. If the objective reality of revelation confirms the extent to which God is free to be "for us" and to reveal Himself to us, it is the subjective reality of revelation which confirms the extent to which God is also free to be within us, "mit uns umzugehen als mit den Seinigen, den zu ihm Gehörigen und ihm Gehörenden, obwohl wir doch Menschen, und zwar sündige Menschen sind" (2f). As the subjective reality, however, it confirms simultaneously the extent to which human existence is ready for a reception of the Word of God. The freedom of the human being to encounter revelation is a freedom created in the event of revelation itself and given to the human being (223f). The process, therefore, whereby human understanding of God's Word of address arises, that is, the process whereby human faith becomes a reality, itself belongs to the event of revelation, and more specifically to revelation as a subjective reality. At this polar end of the single event belongs the work of the Holy Spirit. "Gottes Offenbarung in ihrer subjektiven Wirklichkeit ist die Person und das Werk des Heiligen Geistes, das heisst aber die Person und das Werk Gottes selbst" (254). This assertion of Barth is misunderstood if interpreted merely as a pious homage to ecclesial language or as a refusal to speak further of the transition to faith. It is rather a declaration, much in keeping with the general character of Barth's theological method, that with the subjective reality of revelation, just as with the objective reality in Jesus Christ, we come upon a basic theological fact which may only function as an assumption. In other words, the fact that there are men and women who relate to the revelation of God in faith and obedience is a fundamental aspect of the biblical witness to revelation itself, behind which there is no higher authority or deeper ground to which inquiry may be directed (cf. 226).

The subjective pole is developed further by Barth into its own objective and subjective dimension. God's revelation in its subjective reality consists of particular signs given by God of its objective reality. By signs are meant biblically recognized events, relationships, and orders inside the world (such as circumcision, prophecy and the sacraments of the Church) which are instruments of revelation (245-7). These signs have no inherent capacity for revelation in themselves. "Die Instrumente des Wortes Gottes werden allein durch das Wort Gottes selbst das, was sie in seinem Dienst sein sollen" (243). God himself is the one who grants the signs. They serve as the worldly instruments through which the subjective reality of revelation is communicated to human beings.

> Sie verhüllen die objektive Wirklichkeit der Offenbarung in eine geschöpfliche Wirklichkeit; aber eben damit enthüllen sie sie auch: eben in Form solcher geschöpfliche Wirklichkeit bringen sie sie den Menschen, die ja selber auch geschöpfliche Wirklichkeit sind, nahe. (244)

It is on the basis of the signs that human existence finds itself led to and instructed in the objective reality of revelation. (If a bridge is to be built between Barth and hermeneutical theology it is here where it must begin, i.e., with Barth's hermeneutic of the objective signs of the subjective reality of revelation, as we shall see below.)

The subjective dimension of the subjective reality of revelation consists for Barth in the existence of persons who know and acknowledge that God is "for them" precisely in the objective revelation in Jesus Christ. The question of how the mediation occurs and of how God reveals Himself through the medium of external signs may be referred only to the work of the Holy Spirit, with a further or deeper inquiry excluded since it is an *opus Dei ad extra* which is in question. Or, to say the same thing differently, one is referred to the fact of conversion, to the event in which human beings have and do encounter God in His revelation.

> Was dazwischen liegt, kann darum nicht ausgesprochen und angegeben werden, weil es uns nicht offenbar ist. Und es ist uns darum nicht offenbar, weil es die Offenbarung selber ist. (255)

Only through the outpouring of the Holy Spirit does it become possible for the human being in his freedom to encounter revelation, because the Word is only brought to hearing for humanity in revelation (269f). The work of the Holy Spirit is the sufficient foundation for a hearing of the Word, because it is nothing other than a communication of the Word of God itself.

The subjective and objective realities of revelation represent for Barth polarities of a single indivisible event. The abstraction of a single pole and its development as though it were a reality that could be considered in itself *in toto* is a delusion which leads to nothing short of theological aberrations. If the objective reality is taken in itself apart from the subjective, the consequence is a christology which functions as an arbitrarily constructed ontology or even as a myth constructed upon the basis of Scripture and tradition (cf. KD IV/1, 136f). Particularly damaging in the history of dogma has been the alternative danger of isolating the subjective element as though the event of human reception could itself become an object of reflection in abstraction. It is however always the objective reality, the Word, Jesus Christ, who is heard in the subjective event. There can be no separation (KD I/2, 272). A neglect of the objective ground in Jesus Christ in favor an emphasis on the subjective work of the Spirit is precisely the error which according to Barth led to the excesses of the spiritualist movement among the followers and disciples of Francis of Assisi (273f). This aberration which has found counterparts in libertarian movements throughout the history of the Church, has found its modern representative in Neo-Protestantism. "Auch [der Neu-Protestantismus] wollte und will ja zunächst nur das Anliegen des Subjektivwerdens der objektiven Offenbarung gegenüber einem wirklich oder angeblich toten Objektivmus vertreten" (275).[37]

It is in this context that one of Barth's fundamental aims in addressing the *filioque* controversy becomes apparent. In asserting that the Holy Spirit proceeds from the Father *and the Son*, Barth wishes to bind in the strongest terms the witness of the Holy Spirit to the saving work of Jesus Christ (272f). Because the Holy Spirit is from eternity the Spirit of Christ, because the Spirit is the fellowship of Father and Son in the eternal triune life of God, it is possible for God to address humanity through the Spirit and through the Spirit to beckon humanity to His Son. The trinitarian doctrine of *perichōrēsis* which Barth applies to the *opera trinitatis ad extra* complements this conception in its declaration of a mutual indwelling of the trinitarian Persons in the outward works of God.[38] The subjective working of the Holy Spirit remains always and simultaneously the working of the Son and the Father.

The relation of objective and subjective polarities in the single event of revelation may be thought of as bringing to expression the unity and ordering of soteriology and christology. Countering Bultmann, Barth asserts that this relationship requires a particular structuring.

> Ich verstehe es aber nicht, wie man es unterlassen kann, diese Einheit, das Christusgeschehen, als eine in sich *unterschiedene* Einheit zu verstehen, in der die *Christologie*, ohne sich deshalb von der Soteriologie trennen zu lassen, *vorangeht*, die *Soteriologie* aber—in jener enthalten, von jener umfasst—ihr *folgen* muss.[39]

Once this objective-subjective unity is given the proper weight and balance, only then is it possible for theology to recognize the very real place which human existence occupies in God's revelation (and thus in God's eternal election). From this perspective it is possible to see human existence in the fullness of its dignity, as an "I" or a "we" loved and eternally elected by God for reconciliation to Himself. From this perspective it is actually possible for Barth to recognize a positive function for the "I" language not only of pietism but of existential theology as well. For only from this perspective is it possible to speak of the event of faith without slipping into the abstraction whereby the whole faith event becomes a latent possibility of existence. By speaking of the objective-subjective reality of revelation, Barth finds a way to affirm the "I" character, the experiential character, of the event, even if the "I" must constantly be "demythologized" as does Paul in Galatians 2:20: "It is no longer I who live, but Christ who lives in me" (KD IV/1, 845).

The Trinitarian History of God

In order to progress further into the understanding of human existence which is at work in Barth's trinitarian hermeneutic it is necessary to give attention to the relationship between God and history implicit within the doctrine of the Trinity. At the core of the problem of hermeneutics is the fact of human historicity.[40] The discipline of hermeneutics problematizes the phenomenon of human historicity with regard not only to texts but also with regard to the possibility of understanding history at all. The hermeneutical implication of this constitutive feature of human existence is a gap (expressed by Gadamer as the "two horizons")[41] which must be bridged either by a bringing together of two different historical worlds (i.e., that of the past and that of the present) or by means of the discovery of a unifying theme which is common to both horizons, such as a fundamental "self–understanding."

Barth's understanding in this regard runs in quite a different direction. He too is aware of the constitutive significance of historicity for human existence.[42] It does not for Barth, however, constitute a problem whose solution is to be found either in a particular understanding of history or in a particular "self-understanding." Rather, whatever theological and hermeneutical problems are given occasion by the historicity of human existence must be understood against the background of the historicity of God to which human historicity corresponds. The motif of the historicity of God is a major theme of the *Kirchliche Dogmatik* and one to which we can hardly do justice here. We restrict ourselves therefore to an overview of Barth's understanding of the historicity of God as it comes to expression in its trinitarian formulation.

The previous chapter identified Barth's concept of the trinitarian *Urbild* as a feature of the trinitarian ground of theological language.[43] This same concept also functions to illustrate the relationship of the eternal triune God to human history. The most profound expression of this concept is to be found in Barth's doctrine of election where it is given the following succinct expression.

> Dass der Vater den Sohn liebt und der Sohn dem Vater gehorsam wird, dass Gott sich in dieser Liebe und diesem Gehorsam an den Menschen dahingibt, des Menschen Niedrigkeit auf sich nimmt, um ihn auf seine Höhe zu erheben, dass der Mensch in diesem Geschehen frei wird, indem er seinerseits den Gott wählt, der ihm erwählt hat, das ist eben schlechterdings eine Geschichte, die als solche nicht in eine ruhende Ursache irgendwelcher Folgen umgedeutet werden kann. Ist sie der Inhalt der Ewigkeit vor der Zeit, dann kann diese Ewigkeit nicht vor der Zeit zurückbleiben, dann ist sie *per se* in der Zeit wie vor der Zeit, dann kann sie auch in der Zeit nur Geschichte sein. (KD II/2, 206)[44]

God's history with humanity is developed by Barth in unity with an eternal history of God with Himself.[45] It is preeminently the event of Jesus Christ which gives expression in human history to what is from eternity the very nature and being of God. As Jenson says, "What God does in the history of Jesus Christ on earth is the *implementation* and *revelation* of the eternal act of choice."[46] Temporal history corresponds to eternal history, (a Barthian thesis which must be pursued further in the following section).

This historical correspondence may be extended to the subjective dimension of the event of revelation, as well. Revelation in the Scripture always occurs as "historical event" (*geschichtliches Ereignis*) (KD I/1, 343). By "historical" in this context Barth does not have in mind that which may be fixed with certainty by historical science (in which case on would expect the German word "*historisch*"). Nor does that mean that it is an event which is fully explainable in historical categories, that is, as a particular instance of that class of events designated as "historical."[47] It is historical in the sense of its relatedness to human existence in its historicity, or in Barth's words, in the sense of a "*konkrete Beziehung zu konkreten Menschen*" (343). In other words, it is in the particularity of concrete human life that God encounters humanity with His revelation. And it is in this event that particular men and women in particular and various historical situations find themselves determined by the Word of God and enabled to respond to its address in an authentic act of obedience (cf. 349). This aspect of revelation is one which Barth identifies *per appropriationem* with the Holy Spirit. As Barth declares, "Das *pneuma* ist das Wunder des Dabeiseins wirklicher Menschen bei der Offenbarung"; (350) and elsewhere,

> Um [den Menschen] selber, um sein Dabeisein bei Gottes Offen-barung, geht es ja in dem Problem des Geistes innerhalb des Offenbarung, geht es ja in dem Problem des Geistes innerhalb des Offenbarungsbegriffes (490).

The work of the Spirit in the world corresponds to the inner work of the Spirit in the eternal life of the triune God. Thus, what occurs as the subjective pole of the one event of revelation, namely, that which happens in the event in which the Word of God occurs and human understanding is the result, must be understood for Barth as the temporal implementation and expression of that which happens eternally in God's inner life.

In a reflection upon the identity of the Holy Spirit late in the *Kirchliche Dogmatik*, Barth offers a brief observation on the trinitarian character of the peculiar Christian history. Three decisive features are named of the "little history" (KD IV/2, 373), which for Barth is the "central history" in relation to all others: (1) the existence of the man Jesus as the foundation and beginning of this history, (2) the Church, that is, the Christian community, as the goal of this work of God begun in Christ, and (3) God's self disclosure as transition between the two. In each of the three decisive factors of history, one encounters God himself, three times God (375f). Here Barth would find a correspondence to the doctrine of the Trinity, a purely formal correspondence which is admittedly a *vestigium trinitatis*, and one upon which Barth wishes to lay no dogmatic weight.[48] Yet, within the third point of reference Barth notes not only a formal correspondence, but a material correspondence as well, namely, in the principle of transition which corresponds formally to the principle of historicity in the analysis of revelation and which corresponds materially as the principle of mediation not only between God and humanity, but more fundamentally between God and God. This formal and material correspondence acts for Barth as confirmation of the thesis that God's salvific history must be understood within the light of the trinitarian understanding of God (377).

The mystery of the Holy Spirit's being and work in our earthly history is a repetition, representation, and out-working of what the triune God is in Himself (381). As the mediator between humanity and Jesus Christ, the Holy Spirit is God himself creating fellowship between Himself and humanity.

> Eben mit Gottes Einigkeit und so mit ihm selbst haben wir es zu tun, wenn wir es im Geschehen des Übergangs, der Kommunikation, der Vermittlung zwischen Jesus und uns mit dem *Heiligen Geist* zu tun haben (381).

As the mediator in the eternal life of the triune God it is the Spirit who founds the fellowship, the unity, and the love in which Father and Son relate mutually to one another. The problem, then, of human understanding and of the hermeneutical gap, or "das Problem der Geschichte zwischen dem Menschen Jesus und uns anderen Menschen" (382) is not for Barth a problem primarily of human, earthly, and historical proportions. It is rather primarily a divine problem,

> das Problem von Gottes *eigenem* Sein, *seine* Beantwortung und Lösung, in und mit der er—eben indem er selbst im Heiligen Geist bei uns auf den Plan und dazwischen tritt—auch *unser* Problem beantwortet und löst. (383)

We have, however, touched upon here an issue in Barth's understanding which requires further discussion if the full scope of the trinitarian hermeneutic's relevance for the anthropological question is to come to light. And that is the doctrine of correspondence which unites the relationships in the historical event of revelation with relationships in the eternal life of the triune God.

The Trinitarian *Analogia Relationis* and the Ontology of Human Existence

The trinitarian hermeneutic of human existence employed by Barth finds a further justification and confirmation in the ontology of human existence which Barth grounds christologically in the eternal life of the triune God. Eberhard Jüngel, who has carefully scrutinized and defended Barth's understanding of the ontological function of christology for anthropology on the basis of an *analogia relationis*, identifies the three critical analogical relations which lie at the foundation of this conception:[49] (1) the humanity of the man Jesus corresponds to humanity itself; (2) this relation of correspondence corresponds to the relationship between the human and divine natures of Jesus Christ; (3) the relationship between the human and divine natures of Jesus Christ corresponds to the relation of correspondence between the being of Jesus and the inner life of God (which is to say, the correspondence between the economic and the immanent Trinity). The focal point for Barth in this series of analogically related analogies, as evident here in the summary from Jüngel, is Jesus Christ. From Jesus Christ the relations of correspondence move both in the direction of humanity and in the direction of God. It is on this basis that Jüngel suggests the following principle at the root of Barth's doctrine of theological analogy: "Das Sein des Menschen Jesus ist der Seins- und Erkenntnisgrund aller Analogie."[50] It is the *humanity* of the *man* Jesus which is of critical significance here for the question of anthropological ontology. For it is the humanity of Jesus which grounds the possibility of a relationship between divine reality and human existence, and which thereby functions as an implicit anthropological ontology.

The humanity of Jesus consists in the being of Jesus as the man for others. In this sense his humanity is nothing less than "die Wiederholung und

Nachbildung Gottes selber,"[51] and in this sense is quite simply the *imago Dei*. The humanity of the man Jesus is the form which the inner being of God assumes in the outward work of the incarnation, so that one is justified in speaking of an analogous relation between God's inner being and the humanity of Christ. But because the humanity of the man Jesus also corresponds to humanity itself, a double analogy is at work, or rather, a double set of relations. The togetherness and relatedness of divine and human natures in Christ corresponds to the relation between the human being and his fellow human beings, just as surely as it corresponds to the being of God as the one who is for Himself, that is, in the relatedness of the triune being of God. This double relation of correspondence functions to ground the essence of human existence in a possibility of the divine life.

> Es ist ja auch in [Gott] ein Zusammensein, ein Miteinandersein, ein Füreinandersein. Gott selber in sich ist ja nicht nur einfach, sondern in der Einfachheit seines Wesens auch dreifach: der Vater, der Sohn und der Heilige Geist...Gott selber in sich ist ja der ewige Liebende, der ewig Geliebte, die ewige Liebe und in dieser seiner Dreieinigkeit das Urbild und die Quelle alles Ich und Du. (KD III/2, 260f)

In this way Barth proceeds to develop a thoroughgoing christological (trinitarian-christological!) ground for anthropological ontology.

The various sets of relationships which obtain in this series of analogies are described by Barth as constituting an *analogia relationis*, which appears as the structural or ontological variant of what in other contexts Barth describes as an *analogia fidei*.[52] We have already given attention in the previous chapter to the *analogia fidei* as Barth's conceptual basis for responsible theological language which is itself rooted in the correspondence of the immanent and the economic Trinity.[53] We need here only to reiterate that the analogy which obtains is according to Barth one which resides in the freedom of God to create in correspondence with Himself.

> Die Entsprechung und Ähnlichkeit der beiden Beziehungen [die Beziehung im Sein Gottes und die Beziehung zwischen dem Sein

> Gottes und dem des Menschen] besteht darin, dass die Freiheit, in der Gott sich selber setzt als der Vater und durch sich selber gesetzt ist als der Sohn und sich selber bestätigt als der Heilige Geist, dieselbe Freiheit ist, in der er des Menschen Schöpfer ist, in der der Mensch sein Geschöpf sein darf, in der dies Verhältnis Schöpfer-Geschöpf vom Schöpfer her begründet ist.[54]

Disallowed is any notion of being which functions as the comprehensive category for which the being of God and the being of humanity are particular instances. There can be no question of an *analogia entis*. The possibility of comparison and correspondence is one that is enabled in the eternal life of the triune God.[55]

On the basis of the correspondence which obtains between the being of Jesus Christ as *verus Deus, verus homo* and the being of the eternal God, it is possible for Barth to speak even further of the mystery of the triune God which enables the correspondence which ultimately grounds human existence. For the exaltation of humanity, or more specifically of the human nature of Jesus Christ, which was an event in history, has its "first and final foundation in God's eternal election of grace."[56] The humanity which is exalted in Jesus Christ in his life, death, and resurrection, is an historical realization of an eternal reality in the triune life.

> Eben die wahre Menschheit Jesu Christi als die Menschheit des Sohnes war, ist und bleibt nämlich primärer Inhalt von Gottes ewiger *Gnadenwahl*, d.h. eben: derjenigen göttlichen Entscheidung und Aktion, der ausser dem trinitarischen Geschehen des inneren Lebens Gottes keine höhere vorangeht, der vielmehr alle anderen göttlichen Entscheidungen und Aktionen folgen und zugeordnet sind. (KD IV/2, 33)

What happens in history is the *Ausführung* and *Offenbarung* of the eternal will of God (33). Accordingly, the humanity which is revealed there can in nowise be a secondary thing, a kind of afterthought in the eternity of divine contemplation. Rather, on the basis of the *verus homo* of Jesus Christ, it is necessary to see humanity as a reality already present with God from eternity.[57]

> Gott war auch in jenem Anfang aller seiner Wege und Werke nicht allein und auch nicht allein wirksam: *nicht ohne den Menschen.* Und es brauchte der Mensch nicht erst geschaffen, geschweige denn zum Sünder zu werden, dem Tode zu verfallen, gewchweige denn, in dieser Situation allerhand Gegenbewegungen zu versuchen, um für Gott und vor ihm da zu sein, von ihm geliebt zu werden und ihn wieder zu lieben. (34)

This does not mean of course that the human being is God.[58] He is a creature, not eternal as God is, bound to time. By asserting the co-eternity of humanity and God, Barth grounds the theological necessity of the humanity of Christ, but not only that. The very reality of humanity is assured and grounded. Humanity as such is real, and that so because that which is the "really real," the eternal reality of God, has prefigured the reality of humanity from eternity.

> [Der Mensch] ist aber als dieses Geschöpf, weil von Gott ersehen und gewollt, *vor* aller, auch *vor* dem Anbruch seiner eigenen Zeit, als primärer Gegenstand und Inhalt seines Schöpferwillens bei, mit und vor Gott in seiner Weise so real wie Gott es in der seinigen ist: in Gottes alle Realität begründendem Ratschluss auch er *grundreal.*" (34)[59]

To summarize, Barth wants to understand human existence as a reality grounded in an eternal possibility within the triune life of God. The possibility of an encounter between God and human beings is a possibility contingent ultimately only upon the ground of the communion of the two natures of Christ in the eternal Logos. The historical realization is linked to its eternal *Urbild* by the *analogia relationis*, a similarity with no legitimacy outside of the good pleasure of the Creator. Theological inquiry into the conditions of the divine-human encounter finds itself misdirected if it occupies itself with an analysis of the phenomenon of human existence *per se*, since the conditions of the encounter are conditions met already in the divine essence and borne witness to in the pages of Scripture.

Hermeneutical Implications

What has hopefully become clear in the preceding pages is the characteristic way in which Barth wishes to address the theme of human understanding in encounter with the Word of God. While Barth is operating on a materially different plane than that of explicit hermeneutical inquiry, the function of the trinitarian interpretation of human existence parallels with remarkable similarity the hermeneutical task of aiding genuine understanding by means of an exposition of the effective conditions and factors which contribute to that process.

The pattern of correspondence employed by Barth to interpret human existence, however, particularly the trinitarian rooted *analogia relationis*, raises the question of what was noted in a previous context as Barth's "evangelical Platonism."[60] What happens in history is the implementation and revelation of what happens eternally. God's salvific acts are interpreted as a repetition, a representation, and out-working of God's own eternal, triune history. The incarnation and the out-pouring of the Spirit are historical manifestations not only corresponding to but enabled by eternal, divine dispositions. Human existence is capable of knowledge of the divine because human nature is already prefigured in the eternal Logos. Each of these assertions bears a remarkably striking resemblance to the Platonic theory of the Forms. The problematic which this similarity implies is the same twofold problematic in any Platonic scheme of thought: (1) the implication of an impervious dualism, in this case, between the eternal, divine world and the human world of history, and (2) the dissolution of that dualism into a monistic principle which relativizes and compromises the integrity of the manifest world, in this case, both human history and God's working within that history.[61]

This relationship between divine and human reality is a significant one for the trinitarian hermeneutic. In a recent article, Ingolf Dalferth has helped to put Barth's understanding of this relationship into the proper perspective.[62]

Dalferth depicts the theology of Barth in terms of "theological realism." Theology has to do with the reality of the resurrected, living Jesus, a reality which oversteps our experience of the givens of reality.[63] This reality which escapes our conception is for Barth "eschatological reality" which is in fact the "real reality" (*wirkliche Wirklichkeit*). Worldly realities are not the fundamental reality. By means of a process of eschatological *assumptio* they are able to become real (or not real). The world of our experienced reality has *enhypostatic reality*—its existence is contingent upon its anchoring in the concrete reality of the history of God.[64] This conception of eschatological reality is a critique, if not an attack, upon our contemporary reality consciousness. What conventional understanding calls abstract, Barth calls concrete, and vice versa.[65] From this perspective, then, it becomes apparent that the trinitarian analysis of human existence is an effort to interpret humanity in its most real form, that is to understand it as it "really" is, a reality which is to be found only as God's self-revelation bears witness to it. It is in the human participation in the event of revelation and ultimately in the presence of humanity in the eternal life of the triune God where the "real reality" of humanity has its "place."[66]

For Barth then, there is no question of a simple dualism, at least not in the strict sense of a "radical and irreducible difference in the world," or of "an insuperable gulf between two realms of being."[67] What is finally and ultimately real is the immanent Trinity of God. The world of human history, is neither a competing second principle of ultimacy, nor is it a mere reflection of a higher ontological plane which in its transiency will pass away without significance. The monism which Barth represents is a thoroughgoing eschatological monism. The point of connection between the historical and eternal worlds is the event of revelation in the world, in which God reveals Himself to the world by taking worldly objectivity upon Himself with all the humiliation which that entails even to death on the cross. The goal of revelation is redemption. Revelation reveals not only what is truly real, the triune God, but it reveals the divine plan for worldly reality, a reality in the eschatological presence of God. The analogy of relation in human history and existence bears witness to this final destiny of human existence, a destiny which bears witness to its integrity as an object of divine love. That this destiny is rooted in the eternal, triune history of God by no means, then, implies a denigrating relativizing of the reality of worldly history. That relativizing occurs is obvious. But it is relativizing in the sense of setting the world into relation with its eschatological destiny.

The hermeneutical implication of this trinitarian interpretation of human existence is a negative critique of a theological hermeneutic which seeks to enlighten itself with regard to the event of human encounter with the Word of God by an analysis (whether philosophical, linguistic, sociological, or cultural) of human existence or some aspect of human existence outside of revelation. The point of the critique is twofold. First, it casts suspicion upon the conventional hermeneutical enterprise as an attempt to establish a point of contact or a potentiality within human existence as such for an encounter with God. The critique reveals the fine line that exists between the necessary work (which Barth heartily affirms) which makes an ancient text understandable to modern readers and the (perhaps tacit) assertion of an innate human capacity to hear the "real" content of the biblical witness, which would necessarily assume that the "real" content was a content already present within the world of human experience and not an in-breaking of the Word of God. Secondly, the trinitarian critique trivializes conventional hermeneutics, regardless of whether it falls victim to the first critique. To use a distinction which Barth makes in his anthropology, hermeneutics applies itself to the *phenomenon* of humanity, but fails to treat the *reality* of humanity which can only be read from revelation (KD III/2, 27). In this sense, the work of hermeneutics is seen as neutral with regard to the work of theology. It poses no threat. Yet, the significance of its work for theology becomes questionable. Hermeneutics becomes an auxiliary science useful for exegesis and homiletics, but with only the most relative critical significance for the content of theology proper.

Here it becomes particularly evident that any attempt to bring Barth's trinitarian prolegomena under the same roof with theological hermeneutics can only happen under substantial qualification. When Jüngel declares that Barth's doctrine of the Trinity and Bultmann's program of demythologization carry out essentially the same fundamental aim,[68] one must be quite clear as to the level of generalization that one has reached in order for the statement to be true. Both Barth's doctrine of the Trinity and Bultmann's demythologization program (as a function of his existential exegesis) aim at a critical polemic which identifies and excludes inauthentic theological language thereby aiding the event of human understanding in relation to the biblical witness to revelation. The assertion must not be allowed, however, to disguise the critical significance of Barth's undertaking for conventional hermeneutical work such as that of Bultmann's (or vice versa!). The fundamental aim is the same; the assumptions which underlie the material course of each are quite different.

It may be argued that what Barth has achieved in his trinitarian interpretation of human existence is nothing less than an obliteration of the responsible human self. By turning to God to resolve the problem of human understanding, Barth has actually turned his back on concrete human reality. The humanity revealed in the human nature of Jesus Christ is not an equivalent to concrete and historical human existence.[69] The "really real" humanity which Barth uses to ground the structures of human existence and thus the possibility of an encounter with the Word of God is an alienating concept which does little to prepare the way for a genuine engagement between the modern reader and the historical text of Scripture. Furthermore, the humanity which preexists in the Son is a thoroughly passive construction which must mute if not ultimately silence altogether the call for radical decision which is so characteristic throughout the Bible. Divine determination deprives concrete, historical humanity of its dignity and autonomy.[70]

Such criticism can carry no more than superficial weight, however.[71] By focusing the hermeneutical question upon "eschatological reality," Barth is simply carrying through the theological task with the utmost consistency. Barth recognizes that theological truth does not belong to a restricted province, as though theological truth could be set down beside other areas of truth such as sociological truth, or anthropological truth, and then compared and contrasted. Theology is rather the task of thinking the world, that is, experienced reality in its most comprehensive form, together with God in His revelation. It entails the formation of a perspective of universal inclusiveness, a paradigm, which relates the revealed truth of God to the world in its complexity and pluriformity.[72] It does not thereby do violence to the self-understandings of the world, but rather insists on setting these within the light of its own unique perspective. The acting human self is not obliterated by the trinitarian hermeneutic, but is, as Barth says, demythologized. The trinitarian interpretation stands as a critique and challenge to existing "self-understandings" which claim some basis other than Jesus Christ. The interpretation offered by Barth is not of course one that may be proved for its veracity. But neither does it represent a fideistic leap away from responsible talk of humanity. As Dalferth reminds us, interpretations live from the plausibility of their perspective. "They enlighten, therefore, not because someone decides in their favor, but rather one decides in their favor because they enlighten."[73]

With this assessment in view, and only with this assessment in view, we venture a reservation with regard to the trinitarian interpretation of human existence which is intended to function as a correction to a perceived overstatement in the position. Barth allows the shadow of suspicion which the doctrine of the Trinity casts upon the hermeneutical undertaking to function as a rejection of its theological integrity—as anthropological analysis of the subjective pole of revelation, a *vestigium trinitatis* is implied, which for Barth is a direct road back to natural theology. This need not, however, be the case. The critique of hermeneutical theology need not imply its rejection. And it is even possible to find potential points of contact within Barth's own trinitarian interpretation of existence which would justify not only a peaceful coexistence, but indeed, a meaningful dialogue between the two approaches.

In Barth's initial discussion of the event of human experience of the Word of God in *Kirchliche Dogmatik* I/1, he differentiates, as we have shown above, between two levels or planes of human determination.[74] Experience of the Word of God always happens within an act of human self-determination (KD I/1, 207f). But the human act is not constitutive for the experience of the Word. It is neither identical with the divine determination, nor does it belong together with the divine determination in a cooperative relationship. For the coming together of God's Word and human experience is not something which happens on the same plane. It is solely the determination of the Word of God which makes the experience an experience of the Word. Nevertheless, the self-determination, that is, human experience as normally understood, is always there in an experience of the Word (209). In spite of its subordination to the divine determination of the Word, it is necessarily present (as the *Unter-liegende*); otherwise talk of a *human* experience or of *human* existence would be utterly meaningless (210). Here, however, is where the problem arises. That the Word of God is and remains the ultimately constitutive and determinative reality in the experience of the Word of God need not imply that theology is restricted to the divine determination of the Word in its explication of the event of human encounter with the Word. It remains unclear why the form and content schema, applied vigorously by Barth in so many other contexts, may not have an application here. It remains unclear why the human act of self-determination, which is the act of faith, might not be thought of as the shell through which the transcendent Word becomes real event. And if this is the case, it remains unclear from Barth's exposition why theology should not also occupy itself with the outward aspects of this event. Barth would seem already to have conceded this point in his own explicit reflections on hermeneutics in which the thoroughgoing historical character of Scripture is acknowledged.[75] If the Word of God addresses humanity through the vehicle of the human and historical account of Scripture, then it must remain incumbent upon theology, if it is to maintain responsibility in its own language, to gain clarity with regard to the very human and historical process of understanding which will always underlie the event of the Word in its ultimate dimension. To use Barth's own logic, if theology has nothing meaningful to say about the self-determination which underlies the event of the Word, is it meaningful to speak of it as a human experience for human existence at all?

A second point of contact suggests itself from within Barth's discussion of the subjective pole of the revelation event. As we have seen, Barth distinguishes an objective and subjective dimension within the subjective pole. While the subjective dimension is represented simply by women and men convicted by God that the reality of revelation is there for them in such a way that they must understand their own existence as transformed (KD I/2, 253), the objective dimension is represented by the signs (*Zeichen*) given by God (243–53). Barth speaks of signs in a broad sense to embrace the whole creaturely form which God's revelation has taken within the history of salvation. In the Old Testament, the election of Israel, the rite of circumcision, the institution of the prophets, kings, priests, tabernacles, and temples may all be spoken of as signs. Likewise, The New Testament offers a world of signs—in the appearance of Christ, in his words and deeds. Preeminently for the Church are the signs of baptism and the Lord's Supper (247).

In taking on a reflection upon the signs of revelation Barth has entered in an overt way the realm of hermeneutics.[76] Barth, of course, endeavors to bind the signs as closely as possible to the objective pole of revelation. They are not creaturely inventions. Their communicative power resides neither within themselves nor within their interpreters.

> Die Instrumente des Wortes Gottes werden allein durch das Wort Gottes selbst das, was sie in seinem Dienst sein sollen. Und so ist es auch allein das Wort Gottes selbst, das es Menschen ermöglicht, sie über die immanente Sicht hinaus auch in transzendeter Sicht zu sehen, das heisst aber Zeichen entgegenzunehmen und sie zu verstehen. Dass sie Zeichen sind, beruht also nicht auf einer diesen bestimmten geschöpflichen Wirklichkeiten als solchen innewohnenden Fähigkeit, Zeugnisse der Offenbarung zu sein oder doch zu werden, nicht auf einer *analogia entis*, sondern auf göttlicher Stiftung und Einsetzung,.... (244)

As the objective dimension of the subjective pole of revelation, the giving of signs belong to the work (*per appropriationem*) of the Holy Spirit. Theology is concerned with the "thatness" of the signs and not with the "how" of their communicative power. Yet, a few paragraphs later, Barth makes the remarkable observation.

> Und sicher muss diese Zeichengebung (so gewiss sie ja eben Zeichengebung ist, die auf sehende Augen, auf hörende Ohren immer neuer Menschen wartet) in der Kirche von Geschlecht zu Geschlecht immer wieder neu erkannt und verstanden werden, und zwar so, dass die Kirche nie auch nur teilweise meinen kann, schon mit ihr fertig zu sein, schon zu wissen, was Christus durch die Botschaft der Apostel nun eigentlich von uns will, was also Predigt und Sakrament unter uns eigentlich sollen, vielmehr so, dass jederzeit in der Kirche...aufgefordert ist, sich selber *ab ovo* darüber Rechenschaft zu geben und von Grund aus darüber Verantwortung abzulegen: ob es sich mit dieser Zeichengebung so verhält, wie sie es zunächst gemeint hatte. (248f)

Here in rhetorical fashion is the hermeneutical task *in nuce*, a task which hermeneutical theology in its variety of forms has undertaken—*Rechenschaft* and *Verantwortung* with regard to the Christian signs, which far from seeking to master them or "*mit [ihnen] fertig zu sein*," seeks to rediscover their newness and their vitality for every succeeding generation of believers. Indeed, as Barth seems close to recognizing here, the demand is unavoidable for theology to consider the creaturely side of the signs and the understanding of signs, of the words and understanding of words, which parallel the event of divine determination when God speaks through the signs. And there remains no convincing reason why a trinitarian hermeneutic which interprets the subjective dimension of revelation from the fundamental perspective of divine freedom and sovereignty, should not affirm the complementary reflection upon the event which occurs in the realm of creaturely autonomy whose claim to reality has no less authority than the *analogia relationis* in which created reality has its being.

ENDNOTES

[1] Richard Palmer, *Hermeneutics* (Evanston: Northwestern Univ. Press, 1969), 67f.

[2] While the secondary literature is vast, it is worthwhile to mention the thorough introduction of James M. Robinson: "Hermeneutic Since Barth," *The New Hermeneutic*, ed. J. M. Robinson & J. B. Cobb, New Frontiers in Theology, II (New York: Harper & Row, 1964), 1–77. A thorough analysis and critique of the hermeneutics of Bultmann is to be found in Anthony Thiselton, *The Two Horizons* (Exeter: Paternoster, 1980), especially Chs. 8–10, and with regard to Fuchs and Ebeling in Ch. 12. Cf. also the very fair introduction to and critique of Fuchs and Ebeling in Anthony Thiselton, "The New Hermeneutic," *A Guide to Contemporary Hermeneutics*, ed. D. K. McKim, (Grand Rapids: Eerdmans, 1986), 78–107 [orig. publ. in I. H. Marshall, ed., *New Testament Interpretation: Essays on Principles and Methods* (Grand Rapids: Eerdmans, 1977), 308–33]; and the more critical appraisal of John B. Cobb, "How New is the New Hermeneutic?" ThT 22 (1965) 218–35. A worthwhile comparison of the hermeneutical understanding of Barth and Ebeling is to be found in William V. Puffenberger, "The Word of God and Hermeneutics in the Theologies of Karl Barth and Gerhard Ebeling," Ph.D. diss., Boston Univ. Graduate School, 1968 (Ann Arbor: UMI, 1967). Puffenberger argues that the respective understandings of the Word of God in the theologies of Barth and Ebeling determine the form and content of their respective hermeneutics. The work is limited by a working concept of hermeneutics which restricts itself to principles of biblical interpretation.

[3] "Rudolf Bultmann—Ein Versuch ihn zu verstehen," in ThStn 34, 3. Citation from ET, "Rudolf Bultmann—An Attempt to Understand Him," in *Kerygma and Myth*, 2, ed. H.-W. Bartsch, tr. R. H. Fuller (London: SPCK, 1962), 83.

[4] Cf. Barth's summary of the *Absicht* behind Bultmann's efforts in "Versuch," 4f; and Butlmann's basic agreement with the assessment in *Briefwechsel: Barth—Bultmann*, 173.

[5] *Glauben und Verstehen*, II (Tübingen: Mohr, 1952), 211–35. ET = "The Problem of Hermeneutics," *Essays: Philosophical and Theological* (London: SCM, nd), 234–61.

[6] Ibid., 211f. ET, 234f.

[7] Ibid., 212. ET, 235.

[8] Ibid., 216. ET, 239.

[9] Ibid., 228. ET, 255f.

[10] Ibid., 217. ET, 240.

[11] Ibid., 232. ET, 257.

[12] Ibid., 232. ET, 258.

[13] Ibid., 232f. ET, 258f.

[14] Rudolf Bultmann, *Jesus Christ and Mythology* (New York: Scribners, 1958), 53.

[15]Bultmann, *Mythology*, 70f. Here Bultmann would clearly wish to emphasize the *extra nos* character of that which effects human faith. Direct reference to God or the Holy Spirit as agent of this transformation risks the introduction of mythical categories as well as a shift away from the human self addressed in the call to decision. Cf. Bultmann's more candid remark in a 1952 personal letter to Barth: "Das Ja, kraft dessen das Verstehen Glaube und die Auslegung selbst schon Predigt würde, kann doch nur als das Geschenk des Hl. Geistes verstanden werden. Auf dieses habe ich aber in der methodologischen Besinnung nicht zu reflektieren. Ich kann doch in meinen exegetischen Vorlesungen nicht mit dem Bewusstsein oder mit dem Gefühl der Verpflichtung auftreten, dass ich mich als Glaubenden zu produzieren hätte. Ich kann auch nicht meine Auslegung als *direkte* Predigt darbieten. Sondern ich kann mich nur bemühen, die im Text gestellte Entscheidungsfrage als eine mir und meinen Hören gestellte deutlich zu machen, und so wird meine Auslegung (falls sie einigermassen gelingt) *indirekt* Predigt sein." *Briefwechsel: Barth—Bultmann*, 173.

[16]Barth, "Versuch," 17f. For Bultmann's response, see *Briefwechsel: Barth—Bultmann*, 178.

[17]Barth, "Versuch," 18. Cf. also the more restrained critique of Bultmann's existential exegesis in KD III/2, 531-7.

[18]For Fuchs and Ebeling, however, the analysis of self-understanding and the consequent appropriate pre-understanding which forms the framework for a new hearing of the text is qualified by a high regard for the interpretive power of the text and a concerted effort to overcome the deadening effects of the Cartesian subject-object schema. The subjectivity or experience of the interpreter is necessarily engaged if understanding is to arise. "Words produce understanding only by appealing to experience and leading to experience. Only where word has already taken place can word take place. Only where there is already previous understanding can understanding take place. Only a man who is already concerned with the matter in question can be claimed for it." Gerhard Ebeling, "Wort Gottes und Hermeneutik," (1959) *Wort und Glaube*, I (Tübingen: Mohr, 1967), 336. ET = "Word of God and Hermeneutics," *Word and Faith*, tr. J. W. Leitch (Philadelphia: Fortress, 1963), 320. The role of the subjectivity of the interpreter, however, must be understood in context with the priority of the text. This entails an eschewal of the subject-object schema according to which the text becomes an object which is mastered by the interpreting subject. In its place is a regard for the subjectivity of the text which is allowed to address the listening interpreter. Thus says Fuchs, "The truth has us ourselves as its object." Ernst Fuchs, "Das neue Testament und das hermeneutische Problem," ZThK 58 (1961) 225. ET = "The New Testament and the Hermeneutical Problem," *New Frontiers in Theology, II: The New Hermeneutic*, ed. J. M. Robinson and J. B. Cobb, Jr. (New York: Harper & Row, 1964), 143. Cited Thiselton, "New Hermeneutic," 86; and, "The texts must translate us before we can translate them." Ernst Fuchs, "Das Hermeneutische Problem," *Zeit und Geschichte*, ed. E. Dinkler (Tübingen: Mohr, 1964). ET = "The Hermeneutical Problem," *The Future of Our Religious Past*, ed. J. M. Robinson, (London: SCM, 1971), 277. Cited, Thiselton, "New Hermeneutic," 86.

[19]Ernst Fuchs, *Hermeneutik* (Bad Cannstatt: Müllerschön, 1954), 63. Cited and tr., Robinson, "Hermeneutic Since Barth," 49f.

[20]Gerhard Ebeling, "Wort Gottes," 335. ET, 319.

[21]Ibid., 342. ET, 327.

[22]Ibid., 343. ET, 327f.

[23]Ibid., 338. ET, 323.

[24]Ibid., 334. ET, 318f.

[25]Ibid., 334. ET, 319.

[26]Cf. Ibid., 336. ET, 320.

[27]Cf. Robinson, "Hermeneutic Since Barth," 67.

[28]Gerhard Ebeling, "Hermeneutische Theologie?" *Wort und Glaube*, II (Tübingen: Mohr, 1969), 104-9.

[29]See Fuchs, "Das Hermeneutische Problem," 365. ET, 276f. Cf. Fuchs' dialogue with Karl Barth in the opening pages of his *Hermeneutik*, where he argues that the "text" of revelation must not be restricted, as does Barth, to the "document" of the biblical witness, but must rather be read, if revelation is to be a living reality, from the liberation of our own existence as realized in the encounter with the "source" of revelation, namely, the Scripture (*Hermeneutik*, 9f).

[30]It is noteworthy that even in Barth's landmark essay, "Die Menschlichkeit Gottes," hailed by many as the "second turn" in Barth's theology which signaled a warming to the necessity of a "positive" theological attitude toward human existence, Barth does not hesitate to distance himself once again from existential theology. To those who would suggest a growing similarity between the two approaches, Barth offers a harsh critique of the "Bultmannian" approach charging that far from articulating a human fellowship with God through Jesus Christ it degenerates into a lonely anthropocentrism. Barth notes that it is indeed no accident that neither the children of Israel nor the Christian congregation have any constitutive significance for existential theology. While existentialism has the merit of reminding us of the ancient truth that one does not speak of God without speaking of humanity, it runs the serious risk of leading us back into the error of believing that we can speak meaningfully of the humanity without first speaking of the living God. ("Menschlichkeit Gottes," 19f)
    While Barth remained adamantly opposed throughout his career to the possibility of an "anthropologically" centered theological method or of a theological anthropology derived from a source other than reflection on Jesus Christ, an undeniable shift did in fact occur with regard to the theological estimation of human nature, such that by 1957 Barth could speak of "theanthropology" as a more appropriate designation of the theological task. Barth signaled thereby a willingness to allow a place of greater methodological significance to the fundamental theological observation that Christian theology has to do with the God who has freely made the human being the object of His love. See "Evangelische Theologie im 19. Jahrhundert," ThStn 49 (1957) 3; Einführung, 18. Cited Eberhard Jüngel, "Einführung in Leben und Werk Karl Barths," *Barth-Studien* (Zurich: Benzinger, 1982), 53. ET = "Barth's Life and Work," *Karl Barth: A Theological Legacy*, tr. P. Garrett (Philadelphia: Westminster, 1986), 46. A profound and interesting illustration of the shift emerges from the *Kirchliche*

Dogmatik in Barth's attitude toward the hymnbook. Cf. the rejection of "anthropocentric" hymns in KD I/2, 275–80 (trinitarian criterion, p. 276!) and the modification if not renunciation of that critique in Kd IV/1, 844–6. The case is also plausible that while Barth may never have become a Bultmannian, there was certainly a growing similarity between his anthropological theses and those of Emil Brunner in the years following the publication of "Nein!". See Emil Brunner, "Der neue Barth," ZThK 48 (1951) 89–100. On the significance of existentialist motifs in the later Barth, albeit in a christologically bound form, Paul Jacobs, "Barth in den Sielen der existentialen Interpretation," EvTh 16 (1956) 310–19.

[31]Cf. Barth's reflection on the nature of faith: faith is not the primary datum of the event of reconciliation—the primary datum is the object of faith, Jesus Christ. KD IV/1, 826–46.

[32]See above, Chapter 2, for a fuller exposition of the hermeneutical significance of the place of the doctrine of the Trinity in the prolegomena of the *Kirchliche Dogmatik*.

[33]"Die Trinitätslehre selbst, sofern sie die Gottheit auch des Sohnes, auch des heiligen Geistes in ihren besonderen Seins- und Handlungsweisen neben der Gottes des Vaters lehrt, bedeutet die Aufforderung, das eigentliche Werk der Offenbarung nach seiner objektiven und subjektiven Seite, das heisst aber das Werk des Sohnes und des Heiligen Geistes nun auch noch besonders zu würdigen und so den Begriff der göttlichen Offenbarung in seiner Ganzheit zu erfassen." KD I/2, 2.

[34]Brought to expression by the Gospel of John and the synoptic Gospels respectively. KD I/2, 18.

[35]"Ist [*Der Sohn*] *für uns*, dann heisst das ja eben—und eben das heisst dann letztlich ganz allein: dass wir—und nun wirklich in ewiger, in der dem Sohne Gottes eigenen Gewissheit—auch dabei, dessen, was er ist und getan hat, wirklich *teilhaftig* sind." KD II/1, 175.

[36]The objectivity of revelation in Jesus Christ is thus a fundamental principle for Christian theology. The "*trinitarisch-christologische Erkenntnis*" must be on the "*Spitze*" of theology and thereby form the foundation upon which all its statements rest (KD I/2, 136). It is the "*Ausgangspunkt*" of theology behind which there is no further inquiry (137).

[37]Cf. the virtually identical criticism directed by Barth to Bultmann in "Versuch," 12f. Cf. also *Briefwechsel: Barth—Bultmann*, 198f. One must thus assume that it is here that Barth perceived the offense of hermeneutical theology most acutely.

[38]On Barth's affirmation of the doctrine of *perichōrēsis*, see KD I/1, 390f, 417, and 509.

[39]"Versuch," 18.

[40]Gerhard Ebeling, "Hermeneutik," [3]RGG, III, 244.

[41]See Hans Georg Gadamer, *Wahrheit und Methode* (Tübingen: Mohr, [2]1965), 286–90.

[42]Cf. §47, "Der Mensch in seiner Zeit," KD III/2, 524–780, esp. 616–71.

[43]See above, 192ff.

[44]Cf. also KD IV/2, 32–38.

[45]The relation of eternal history and human history in the theology of Barth has been given thorough and thoughtful treatment in Robert Jenson's, *Alpha and Omega: A Study in the Theology of Karl Barth* (New York: Thomas Nelson, 1963). See esp. Ch. 3, "Eternal History and Jesus of Nazareth," 84–93.

[46]Jenson, *Alpha and Omega,* 85.

[47]This is given terse expression by Barth in the now famous dictum, "Offenbarung ist nicht ein Prädikat der Geschichte, sondern Geschichte ist ein Prädikat der Offenbarung." KD I/2, 64.

[48]The function of Jesus Christ as the origin of Christian history corresponds formally to the trinitarian function of the Father as *fons et origo totius Deitatis.* The function of the Church as the goal of the Christian history, which corresponds to its origin and which refers back to its origin, corresponds formally to the function of the Son as the one loved by the Father who eternally responds in love and obedience. The function of the principle of transition between origin and goal corresponds formally (and materially) to the Holy Spirit who in eternity mediates the love and fellowship uniting Father and Son. KD IV/2, 378f.

[49]Eberhard Jüngel, "Die Möglichkeit theologischer Anthropologie auf dem Grunde der Analogie," (1962) *Barth-Studien* (Zürich: Benzinger Verlag, 1982), 210–32.

[50]Jüngel, "theologische Anthropologie," 212.

[51]KD III/2, 261. Cited Jüngel, "theologische Anthropologie," 214.

[52]So Eberhard Jüngel, "Einführung in Leben und Werk Karl Barths," in *Barth-Studien*, 49. ET = "Barth's Life and Work," in *Karl Barth: A Theological Legacy* (Philadelphia: Westminster, 1986), 43.

[53]See above, 195ff.

[54]KD III/2, 262. Cited Jüngel, "theologische Anthropologie," 220.

[55]"Die analogia relationis Barths unterscheidet sich also darin von der analogia entis, dass sie nicht Seiendes in seinem Sein mit anderem Seienden in seinem Sein vergleicht, sondern das dem geschöpflichen Seienden vorausgehende, ja das geschöpfliche Seiende in sein Sein rufende Ja Gottes in Entsprechung zu dem Ja Gottes sieht, mit dem dieser sich selbst sein Sein zuspricht." Jüngel, "theologische Anthropologie," 220f.

[56]KD IV/2, 32. My translation.

[57]In the context of the doctrine of creation, Barth portrays the Holy Spirit as the inner possibility in the eternal triune life for the reconciliation and redemption of humanity. As the Spirit who binds Father and Son in their eternal and mutual resolve for the election of

grace, it is He who prefigures the entire order of relationship between Creator and creature. In this sense, the creature as such may be said to preexist. "Es ist Gott der Heilige Geist, in welchem die Kreatur als solche präexistiert. Will sagen: Es ist Gott der Heilige Geist, der die *Existenz* der Kreatur als solcher—indem er ihre Versöhnung mit Gott und ihre Erlösung durch ihn in der Vereinigung des Vaters und des Sohnes in jenem Ratschluss vorwegnimmt und garantiert—*möglich* macht, der ihr das Existieren erlaubt, der sie in ihrem Existieren trägt, auf den sie in ihrem Existieren angewiesen ist." KD III/1, 60. This is yet another dimension of the trinitarian foundation which grounds and interprets human existence and need not be understood in tension with the christological rooted preexistence of the *humanum*. The Son grounds the essence of humanity. Only the Son was incarnated, and only the Son entered into a hypostatic union, and thus only in the Son does the possibility of human nature preexist. The act of creation and the plan of reconciliation and redemption are expressions of the divine love which is the reality of the Holy Spirit. That the delineation is imprecise is testimony to the limits of the trinitarian "appropriations" and the *perichōrēsis* or mutual indwelling of the trinitarian Persons in all of the outward works.

[58]Barth understands the eternal presence of humanity with God in terms of the traditional doctrine of the *anhypostasis* (and *enhypostasis*) of the human nature of Christ (KD IV/2, 52f; cf KD I/2, 178ff). According to the doctrine of the *anhypostasis*, the human nature of Christ has no independent existence, that is, it does not constitute a *hypostasis* alongside the three divine *hypostases*. It is thus *anhypostatos*. The doctrine of the *enhypostasis* states the same concept positively. The humanity of Christ subsists only in the hypostatic union of the two natures and thus is appropriately ascribed solely to the *hypostasis* of the Son, the eternal Logos. The doctrine not only helps guard against a deification of humanity but has critical significance for Barth as a statement of the decisive significance of the existence of Jesus Christ for all of humanity. The *enhypostasis* of human nature in the Logos means that the incarnation and the existence of Jesus Christ concerns all humanity as a ground of the promise of reconciliation and redemption. KD IV/2, 51f.

[59]This is not merely an extension of Barth's own theological logic. The exegetical foundation is taken from Col 1:15f; Joh 1:1-3, 10, 14; Heb 1:2f; I Pt 1:20; Eph 1:4, *et al*. KD IV/2, 35f.

[60]A phrase from Regin Prenter, "Karl Barths Umbildung der traditionellen Zweinaturenlehre in lutherischer Beleuchtung. Einige vorläufige Beobachtungen zu Karl Barths neuester Darstellung der Christologie," StTh 11 (1957) 78. See above, 109f.

[61]Cf. Jean-Louis Leuba, "Platonisme et Barthisme: Quelques Perspectives Théologiques," *Archivo di Filosofia* 53 (1985) 167-9, 171f.

[62]Ingolf Dalferth, "Theologischer Realismus und realistische Theologie bei Karl Barth," EvTh 46 (1986) 402-22.

[63]Ibid., 407.

[64]Ibid., 409-11.

[65]Ibid., 410.

[66]Cf. the analysis of Jüngel, which speaks of the secondary objectivity of God in His revelation as "*anthropologisches Existential.*" Eberhard Jüngel, *Gottes Sein ist im Werden* (Tübingen: Mohr, 1965), 67–72. ET = *The Doctrine of the Trinity*, (Grand Rapids: Eerdmans, 1976), 55–60.

[67]Roland Hall, "Monism and Pluralism," *The Encyclopedia of Philosophy*, V.

[68]Jüngel, *Gottes Sein*, 22f, 33f. ET, 11f, 21–3.

[69]Cf. Brunner, "Der neue Barth," 92f, 95f.

[70]Such is the position of N. H. G. Robinson, "Trinitarianism and Post-Barthian Theology," JThSt 20 (1969) 186-201, who contends that Barth's doctrine of the Holy Spirit eliminates the responsible "I" which St. Paul has no problem affirming in Gal 2:20 (198f). Richard Roberts in "Karl Barth" in *One God in Trinity: An Analysis of the Primary Dogma of Christianity*, ed. P. Toon and J. D. Spiceland (Westchester, Ill.: Cornerstone, 1980), 78-94, extends the same line of thought by suggesting that the "potential weakness" of Barth's doctrine is its tendency to "encircle and absorb...the whole scheme of creation, incarnation and reconciliation, that is, reality as a whole" (86). Roberts observes that the divine life functions for Barth as prototype of all temporal reality. This gives rise negatively to what Roberts describes as an "ontological compression." "Barth in positing the contingent historical order upon the basis of the putative contingency and historicity of God, attempts to recreate the natural order but by doing so effects a resolution and extinction of that order in the trinitarian abyss of the divine being" (88). R.D. Williams, in "Barth on the Triune God" in S.W. Sykes, ed. *Karl Barth: Studies of his Theological Method* (Oxford: Clarendon Press, 1979), 147-193, observes an epistemological function at work in Barth's Trinity doctrine which betrays a major impulse within Barth's work, namely, a quest for certainty with regard to human knowledge of divine truth. The price he pays for this certainty, however, is the dissolution of human freedom. For, "to allow any positive place of human freedom of response (in the usual sense of these words) is at once to abandon certainty, to say that the eternal unity of God's utterance is, as it were, adulterated by the plurality and confusion of human minds and hearts" (188).

[71]That Barth's pneumatology (i.e., the subjective pole of revelation) has undermined the possibility of human freedom rests upon a particularly unfortunate misreading of Barth who actually endeavors to safeguard the reality of human decision-making. It is a misunderstanding, declares Barth, "wenn man die Situation des Menschen in der Erfahrung vom Worte Gottes als Aufhebung seiner Selbstbestimmung, als einen Zustand teilweiser oder völliger Rezeptivität und Passivität verstehen wollte." KD I/1, 209. The fact that faith stands always in relation to its object, Jesus Christ, in no way takes away from its character as human action, an action of which the human being is the sole subject. Cf. KD IV/1, 828f. Cf. also Colin Gunton, "Barth, the Trinity, and Human Freedom" ThT 63 (1986) 316-30. While Gunton detects a threat to human freedom in a christological dominance which Barth allows for the doctrine of the Trinity, the trinitarian ground for human freedom is found essentially intact. Cf. esp. 322-25.

[72]Dalferth, 412.

[73]Ibid. My translation.

[74]The determination of human existence is simply Barth's working definition of experience. "Wenn Erkenntnis des Wortes Gottes Menschen möglich wird, dann muss das heissen: es wird ihnen eine Erfahrung vom Worte Gottes möglich. Wir definierten ja Erkenntnis als diejenige Bewährung menschlichen Wissens um einen Gegenstand, durch den sein Wahrsein zu einer Bestimmung der Existenz des erkennenden Menschen wird. Eben diese *Bestimmung der Existenz des erkennenden Menschen* nennen wir Erfahrung" KD I/1, 206.

[75]"Die Forderung, dass man die Bibel *historisch* lesen, verstehen und auslegen müsse, ist also selbstverständlich berechtigt und kann nicht ernst genug genommen werden. Die Bibel selbst stellt diese Forderung: sie ist auf der ganzen Linie, auch da, wo sie sich ausdrücklich auf göttliche Aufträge und Eingebungen beruft, in ihrem tatsächlichen Bestand menschliches Wort, und dieses menschliche Wort will offenbar eben als solches ernst genommen, gelesen, verstanden und ausgelegt sein." KD I/2, 513. Nevertheless, a philosophical hermeneutics which grapples precisely with this demand in a radical way leads inevitably for Barth to a deformation of the gospel and an attempt to become its master. Cf. KD IV/3, 939f.

[76]More specifically, it is the field of the hermeneutics of signification. Cf. E. Buess, "Symbol," [3]RGG, VI, 546f; G. Lanczkowski, "Symbolismus: I. Religionsgeschichtlich," [3]RGG, VI, 548–50; William P. Alston, "Sign and Symbol," *The Encyclopedia of Philosophy*, VII, 437–41. Cf. also Jüngel's observation that the linguistic implications of Barth's rejection of the *vestigium trinitatis* represent an entry into the hermeneutics of signification. Jüngel, *Gottes Sein*, 18f. ET, 7f.

CONCLUSIONS

Throughout we have sought to describe and analyze the hermeneutical function executed by the doctrine of the Trinity within the *Kirchliche Dogmatik*. In the present section we shall bring together in summary fashion the conclusions already set forth in each of the preceding chapters.

Chapter One sought to establish in a general way the relationship between Barth's theology and the hermeneutical question. Here we noted that this relationship was for Barth not historically constant and that it is necessary to distinguish two phases of this relationship which correspond to the two most generally recognized phases of Barth's thought, the dialectical and the analogical phases, or the critical and dogmatic phases respectively. While Barth's relationship to the hermeneutical question during the critical phase was largely positive, consisting a contribution to hermeneutical understanding by means of a critique of the historical-critical method which emphasized the priority of the subject-matter of the text, the relationship of the analogical phase was largely negative, consisting of a cloud of suspicion cast over "hermeneutical theology." Barth's suspicion of explicit hermeneutical work in theology was shown to consist of a perception of an implied human capacity for faith which for Barth is contrary to the biblical-evangelical witness, of a seminal "natural theology," of a usurping of the place and hermeneutical function of the subject-matter by anthropologically determined concepts (philosophy), a diversion of theology from its object, and a displacement of the role of the Holy Spirit. Barth's negative critique of "hermeneutical theology" provided the critical perspective from which an assessment of Barth's positive alternative to explicit hermeneutics followed.

The remainder of the work explored this positive alternative to an explicit hermeneutical focus for theology, the doctrine of the Trinity. That the doctrine of the Trinity functions in this way for Barth was established initially in *Chapter Two* by means of an identification of the "place" of the doctrine within the

Kirchliche Dogmatik, that is, its functional place in relation to the primary parts of Barth's systematic treatise. During periods of vigorous trinitarianism within the history of Christian dogma, it was shown that three broad functions of the doctrine are identifiable: the doxological summary of salvation-history, anti-heretical polemic, and metaphysical speculation on the being of God. The first two of these find renewed expression in Barth's theology. The third function is not only disallowed by Barth but becomes the object of his own trinitarian critique. None of these traditional functions of the doctrine, however, bring to expression the most characteristic place which the doctrine occupies within the *Kirchliche Dogmatik*. By means of a critical analysis of the function of the doctrine in relation to theological prolegomena, which included a careful delineation of the doctrine's identity in relation to Barth's revelation concept, it was argued that the doctrine constitutes for Barth a fundamental theological perspective from which not only the biblical text but all human experience may be interpreted. We designated this fundamental perspective as a theological paradigm, analogous to the paradigm concept as it has been identified and understood in the philosophy of science with the aid of insights from linguistic analysis.

Chapters *Three* and *Four* undertook an investigation of the structure of Barth's Trinity doctrine. *Chapter Three* took up an identification and description of the function which various streams of philosophical thought assume within the doctrine and sought to relate these philosophical elements to Barth's own biblical hermeneutic (including its critical-polemical aspect). An exposition of Barth's biblical hermeneutic as formulated in *Kirchliche Dogmatik* I/2, followed by an exposition of Barth's model for deriving the doctrine of the Trinity, illustrated numerous hermeneutical principles at work in Barth's trinitarianism: intrabiblical fidelity, the self-vindicating "fiduciary" character of the biblical witness, loyalty to the biblical subject-matter, the non-specialized character of biblical hermeneutics, and the special authority which belongs to the dogmatic tradition. In light of this intentional hermeneutic, we described the dominant streams of philosophical thought which are tacitly employed by Barth in the process of constructing a doctrine of the Trinity. These were identified as existentialism, Hegelianism, and Platonism. The presence and influence of philosophical elements, while appearing to stand in serious tension with Barth's hermeneutical aim in the Trinity doctrine, are actually quite reconcilable with Barth's stated theological method as well as the critique of hermeneutical theology. The refusal, however, to explicitly recognize the philosophical elements operative in the doctrine would tend toward an unwarranted identification of the doctrine with the divine self-revelation which it seeks to interpret.

Chapter Four expands the discussion of the structure of Barth's doctrine to include the role bestowed upon the dogmatic tradition. The chief distinction in Barth's appropriation of traditional materials over and against his use of philosophical materials is the explicit and intentional character of the process. Nevertheless, a similar tension is at work in both appropriation processes. The aim of the chapter was a description of the function of the tradition in light of Barth's claim to locate the root of the doctrine in revelation, and a clarification of the status which Barth's trinitarian hermeneutic would afford the tradition for theological method. We observed that the authority which Barth recognizes in the tradition stems from a particular conception of the Church which emphasizes its event-character initiated from the side of God. The actualistic conception of a trans-historical communion of the saints proffers a view of the tradition which overcomes a historical relativizing which would diminish its worth and authority for the contemporary Church. Having established its authority, Barth appropriates the tradition by means of a hermeneutical spiral which would avoid the rigid confessionalism that would characterize a linear hermeneutic. The appropriation process is one which moves strongly in the direction of the Western tradition in which Barth himself was rooted, a fact entirely consistent with Barth's confessionalism. Nevertheless, the process is characteristically creative and selective. The criteria of selection derive from the biblically won concept of revelation, although again a rigid linear hermeneutical process is avoided. Barth oversteps and thereby harms the process he has set into motion, however, by the unnecessary suggestion of a necessity for the Church doctrine of the Trinity which is inconsistent with his much emphasized recognition elsewhere of its very human and conditioned character. Barth's failure may be understood as a failure to adequately distinguish the trinitarian confession from the *doctrine* of the Trinity. This failure also stems in part from the pervasive "commentary" metaphor used by Barth to understand the function of the tradition. The metaphor fails to describe adequately the role of the tradition in Barth's trinitarian construction. "Reflection" offers the better alternative for a description of the Church's self-understanding in the formulation of the tradition, as well as the process at work in Barth's own trinitarian hermeneutic.

Chapters Five and *Six* focused upon a description the hermeneutical function *per se* of the Trinity doctrine within the *Kirchliche Dogmatik. Chapter Five* explored this function with a view to its implications for responsible talk of God. Following a presentation of the historical situation of a perceived crisis in theological language out of which Barth's trinitarianism arose, the various linguistic aspects of Barth's doctrine were identified. Most visible is the rejection of the *vestigia trinitatis* doctrine which provided Barth with a trinitarian ground for the rejection of "natural theology." The rejection of the *vestigia trinitatis* represents positively for Barth the defense of a fundamental axiom for responsible language about God: responsible talk of God is grounded solely in God's revelation. The doctrine of the Trinity as developed by Barth stands as the material out-working of this rule. That responsible talk of God is at all possible is itself grounded in the divine Trinity. Barth grounds this possibility in the assertion of a trinitarian correspondence, according to which the economic Trinity corresponds to the immanent Trinity. This assertion of an identity in distinction identifies the economic Trinity as the source of statements about the eternal God, and the immanent Trinity as their ground. This principle finds a direct extension in the *analogia fidei* doctrine, whereby the correspondence of human statements to divine reality is insured by the correspondence of God to Himself in the analogical relation between immanent and economic Trinities. In addition, the correspondence principle exercises a critical-polemical function with regard to inauthentic talk of God, which it identifies as myth, cosmology, and speculative anthropology. In *Chapter Five* it was also demonstrated that Barth's thesis of correspondence has not been advanced upon with Karl Rahner's assertion of an identity between the economic and the immanent Trinity. Indeed the latter begs for a clarity that the former can offer if it is taken as a point of reference for interpreting the thesis of identity. Barth's principle of correspondence points to the theological weaknesses of any attempt to assert a reciprocal determination between the economic and immanent Trinity.

Chapter Six takes as its focus the view of human existence which comes to expression in the trinitarian hermeneutic, particularly with a view to the problem of human understanding. It is the sustained anthropological focus of hermeneutically oriented theology which stands largely behind Barth's suspicion of its integrity. The doctrine of the Trinity is employed by Barth as a critique of the human starting point for theology. An exposition of the subjective aspect of Barth's revelation concept, however, demonstrates that Barth's aversion to the anthropological starting point does not thereby include a rejection of the demand for the anthropological relevance. The objective reality of revelation in the incarnation of the Son is an incomplete concept without the subjective reality which is the out-pouring of the Holy Spirit into the lives of concrete human beings. This anthropological dimension is further developed through the identification of a trinitarian ground for an ontology of existence. Barth would understand human existence as a reality grounded in an eternal possibility within the triune life of God. The hypostatic union of the incarnation and its ground in the pre-existence of human nature in the eternal Logos insures the possibility of an encounter between God and human beings. Barth links the historical manifestation of this encounter to its eternal *Urbild* by means of the *analogia relationis*. The correspondence resides solely in the grace of God and may not be derived as a general characteristic of existence. This conception entails an *enhypostatic* vision of reality, whereby the world of human experience is viewed as a reality contingent upon its anchoring in the trinitarian history of God. Final reality is "eschatological reality," so that human existence in its present condition, in spite of its eternal ground, remains incomplete. This conception entails nothing short of a radical critique of hermeneutical theology's preoccupation with the analysis of human existence in this fallen and incomplete state. Objections that Barth has no place for the responsible human self in his theological perspective completely miss the point. The trinitarian interpretation of human existence represents the consistent extension of the hermeneutical-heuristic aspects of the trinitarian paradigm to embrace not only talk of God and human existence, but the whole world of human history and experience, as well. It does not intend thereby to deny the possibility of alternative self-understandings but insists on setting these within the light of its own comprehensive perspective. This position, however, also entails an ambiguous overstatement which begs correction. Barth's critique of hermeneutical theology need not imply its rejection. Barth's own distinction between divine and human determination in the encounter with the Word as two real and concomitant dimensions of a single event would appear to justify theological inquiry into both levels. Barth's concern with the visible signs which mediate the encounter with revelation further confirm a necessity for a theological view drawn from a direct reflection upon the hermeneutical media upon which human understanding is dependent. There is room, even within

Barth's fundamental perspective which interprets human existence from the side of the free and sovereign triune God, for a dialogue between the trinitarian hermeneutic and the philosophically articulated hermeneutics which Barth finds so objectionable.

BIBLIOGRAPHY

WORKS BY KARL BARTH

Barth, Karl. "Das Bekenntnis der Reformation und unser Bekennen." (1935) TFA, 257-81.

____. *Die christliche Dogmatik im Entwurf*, I. Die Lehre vom Worte Gottes: Prolegomena zur christlichen Dogmatik. (1927) Zurich: TVZ, 1982.

____. *Credo*: Die Hauptprobleme der Dogmatik, dargestellt im Anschluss an das Apostolische Glaubensbekenntnis. Munich: Kaiser, 1935.

____. *Dogmatik im Grundriss*. (1947) Zurich: TVZ, 1987.

____. *Einführung in die evangelische Theologie*. (1962) Zurich: TVZ, 1985.

____. "Evangelishce Theologie im 19. Jahrhundert." ThStn 49. Zollikon-Zurich: Evangelischer Verlag, 1957

____. *Fides Quaerens Intellectum*. Ed. E. Jüngel & I. Dalferth. Karl Barth Gesamtausgabe, Abt. 2: Akademische Werke. (1931) Zurich: TVZ, ²1986.

____. *Karl Barth's Table Talk*. Ed. J. Godsey. London: Oliver & Boyd, 1962.

____. "Die Kirche—die lebendige Gemeinde des lebendigen Herrn Jesus Christus." *Die Schrift und die Kirche*, ThStn 22. Zollikon-Zurich: Evangelischer Verlag, 1947.

____. *Die Kirchliche Dogmatik* I/1. Die Lehre vom Wort Gottes: Prolegomena zur Kirchlichen Dogmatik. (1932) Zurich: TVZ, ¹¹1985.

____. *Die Kirchliche Dogmatik* I/2. Die Lehre vom Wort Gottes: Prolegomena zur Kirchlichen Dogmaitk. (1938) Zurich: TVZ, ⁷1983.

____. *Die Kirchliche Dogmatik* II/1. Die Lehre von Gott. (1940) Zurich: TVZ, ⁶1982.

____. *Die Kirchliche Dogmatik* II/2. Die Lehre von Gott. (1942) Zurich: TVZ, ⁶1981.

____. *Die Kirchliche Dogmatik* III/1. Die Lehre von der Schöpfung. (1945) Zurich: TVZ, ⁴1970.

____. *Die Kirchliche Dogmatik* III/2. Die Lehre von der Schöpfung. (1948) Zurich: TVZ, ⁴1979.

____. *Die Kirchliche Dogmatik* III/3. Die Lehre von der Schöpfung. (1950) Zurich: TVZ, ³1979.

____. *Die Kirchliche Dogmatik* III/4. Die Lehre von der Schöpfung. (1951) Zurich: TVZ, ³1969.

____. *Die Kirchliche Dogmatik* IV/1. Die Lehre von der Versöhnung. (1953) Zurich: TVZ, [4]1982.

____. *Die Kirchliche Dogmatik* IV/2. Die Lehre von der Versöhnung. (1955) Zurich: TVZ, [3]1978.

____. *Die Kirchliche Dogmatik* IV/3. 1-2. Die Lehre von der Versöhnung. (1959) Zurich: TVZ, [3]1979.

____. *Die Kirchliche Dogmatik* IV/4. Die Lehre von der Versöhnung (Fragment). Zurich: EVZ, 1967.

____. "Ludwig Feuerbach," *Die Theologie und die Kirche*. Karl Barth: Gesammelte Vorträge, II. Munich: Kaiser, 1928. 212-39.

____. "Die Menschlichkeit Gottes." Zollikon-Zurich: Evangelischer Verlag, 1956.

____. "Nein! Antwort an Emil Brunner." Theologische Existenz Heute 14. Munich: Kaiser, 1934.

____. "Offenbarung, Kirche, Theologie." (1934) TFA, 158-184.

____. *Die protestantische Theologie im 19. Jahrhundert*. (1947) Zurich: TVZ, 1985.

____. *Der Römerbrief*. (1919) Zurich: TVZ, 1985.

____. *Der Römerbrief*. ([2]1922) Zurich: TVZ, [15]1989.

____. "Rudolf Bultmann—Ein Versuch ihn zu verstehen." ThStn 34. Zollikon-Zurich: EVZ, 1952. ET = "Rudolf Bultmann—An Attempt to Understand Him." *Kerygma and Myth*, II. Ed. H.-W. Barthsch, tr. R. H. Fuller. London: SPCK, 1962. 83-132.

____. *Theologische Fragen und Antworten*. Gesammelte Vorträge, III. (1957) Zurich: TVZ, [2]1986.

____. "Das Wort Gottes als Aufgabe der Theologie." *Das Wort Gottes und die Theologie*. (1922) Munich: Kaiser, 1924.

PUBLISHED LETTERS

Barth, Karl, & Adolf von Harnack. "Ein Briefwechsel mit Adolf von Harnack," TFA, 7-31.

Barth, Karl. *Briefe*, 1961-1968. Ed. J. Fangmeier & H. Stoevesandt. Karl Barth Gesamtausgabe, Bd. 6. Zurich: TVZ, [2]1979.

Karl Barth—Eduard Thurneysen, Briefwechsel, II, 1921-1930. Ed. E. Thurneysen. Karl Barth Gesamtausgabe, Bd. 3. Zurich: TVZ, 1973.

Karl Barth—Rudolf Bultmann, Briefwechsel, 1922-1966. Karl Barth Gesamtausgabe, Bd. 1. Zurich: TVZ, 1971. ET = Karl Barth—Rudolf Bultmann: Letters, 1922-1966. Ed. B. Jaspert. Tr. & ed. G. Bromiley. Grand Rapids: Eerdmans, 1981.

CLASSICAL WORKS CITED

Anselm of Canterbury. *Epistola de Incarnatione Verbi. Opera Omnia,* I. Ed. F. S. Schmitt. Edinburgh: Nelson, 1938. 277-90. ET = "On the Incarnation of the Word." Tr. L. Gibbs, *et al. Anselm of Canterbury: Theological Treatises,* II. Ed. J. Hopkins & H. Richardson. Cambridge, MA: Harvard Divinity School Library, 1966.

Augustine. *De Trinitate. Patrologiae Latinae Cursus Completus.* Ed. J. P. Migne. 3rd rpt. of Benedictine ed. Paris, 1845. 42.819-1098. ET = *St. Augustine: The Trinity.* Tr. S. McKenna. The Fathers of the Church, XLV. Washington D. C.: Catholic Univ. of America, 1963.

Basil of Caesarea. *De Spiritu Sancto.* Sources chrétiennes, Nr. 17. Ed. B. Pruche. Paris, 1945. ET = *St. Basil of Caeserea: On the Holy Spirit.* Tr. B. Jackson. Nicene & Post-Nicene Fathers, 2nd Series, VIII. Grand Rapids: Eerdmans, 1983.

Gregory, Bishop of Nyssa. *Contra Eunomium Libri. Opera,* I-II. Ed. W. Jaeger. Leiden: Brill, 1960. ET = "Against Eunomius." Tr. W. Moore & H. A. Wilson. Nicene & Post-Nicene Fathers, 2nd Series, V. Grand Rapids: Eerdmans, 1983.

Luther, Martin. "The Three Symbols or Creeds of the Christian Faith." (1538) *Luther's Works,* American Edition, XXXIV, 197-229. Tr. R. R. Heitner from Weimar Ausgabe 50, (255) 262-283.

Melanchthon, Phillip. *Introductio,* in *Loci Communes,* 1521. Melanchthons Werke, II/1. Gütersloh: Bertelsmann, 1952. 5-8. ET = "Basic Topics of Theology, or Christian Theology in Outline." *Loci Communes Theologici.* Tr. L. J. Satre. The Library of Christian Classics, XIX. London: SCM, 1969. 20-22.

Thomas Aquinas. *De Veritate. Quaestiones Disputate,* I. Ed. R. Spiazzi, O. P. Rome: Marietti, 1964. German trans. = *Untersuchungen über die Wahrheit.* 2 Vols. Tr. E. Stein. Louvain: E. Nauwelaerts, 1952 & 55.

THEOLOGY (AND HERMENEUTICS) OF KARL BARTH

Bakker, Nico T. *In der Krisis der Offenbarung: Karl Barths Hermeneutik, dargestellt an seiner Römerbrief Auslegung.* Neukirchen: Neukirchen, 1974.

Balthasar, Hans Urs von. *Karl Barth: Darstellung und Deutung seiner Theologie.* (1962) Einsiedeln: Johannes, [4]1976. ET = *The Theology of Karl Barth.* Tr. J. Drury New York: Holt, 1971.

Berkouwer, G. Cornelius. *The Triumph of Grace.* Tr. H. R. Boer. (German trans., 1952) Grand Rapids: Eerdmans, 1956.

Bouillard, Henri. *Karl Barth: Genèse et évolution de la théologie dialectique*. Paris: Aubier, 1957.

Bradshaw, Timothy. "Karl Barth on the Trinity: A Family Resemblance." SJTh 39 (1986) 159-61.

Bromiley, G. W., and T. F. Torrance. "Editor's Preface." *Church Dogmatics* I/1. Edinburgh: T. & T. Clark, ²1975., vii-ix.

Brunner, Emil, "Der Neue Barth." ZThK 48 (1951) 89-100.

Busch, Eberhard. *Karl Barths Lebenslauf*. Munich: Kaiser, ²1976. 206-11. ET = *Karl Barth*. Tr. J. Bowden. London: SCM, 1976. 193-98.

Eichholz, Georg. "Der Ansatz Karl Barths in der Hermeneutik." *Antwort*. Zollikon-Zürich: EVZ, 1956. 52-68.

Evans, D. D. "Barth on Talk about God." *Canadian Journal of Theology* 16 (1970) 175-92.

Ford, D. F. "Barth's Interpretation of the Bible." *Karl Barth: Studies of his Theological Method*. Ed. S. W. Sykes. Oxford: Clarendon Press, 1979. 55-87.

Frey, Christofer. *Die Theologie Karl Barths: Eine Einführung*. Frankfurt: Athenäum, 1988.

García-Tato, Isidro. *Die Trinitätslehre Karl Barths als dogmatisches Strukturprinzip*. Bad Honnef: Bock & Herchen, 1983.

Gogarten, Friedrich. "Karl Barth's Dogmatik." TR 1 NF (1929) 60-80.

Gunton, Colin. "Barth, the Trinity, and Human Freedom." ThT 63 (1986) 316-30.

Hammer, Karl. "Analogia Relationis gegen Analogia Entis." *Parrhesia*. Zurich: EVZ, 1966. 288-304.

Jacobs, Paul. "Barth in den Sielen der existentialen Interpretation." EVTh 16 (1956) 310-19.

Jenson, Robert. *Alpha and Omega: A Study in the Theology of Karl Barth*. New York: Thomas Nelson, 1963.

____. *God After God*. Indianapolis: Bobbs Merrill, 1969.

Joest, Wilfried. "Barth, Bultmann und die 'existenziale Interpretation.'" *Theologie zwischen Gestern und Morgen*. Ed. W. Dantine & K. Lüthi. Munich: Kaiser, 1968.

Jüngel, Eberhard. *Barth-Studien*. Zürich: Benzinger, 1982. ET (partial) = *Karl Barth: A Theological Legacy*. Tr. G. Paul. Philadelphia: Westminster, 1986.

____. *Gottes Sein ist im Werden*. Tübingen: Mohr, 1965. ET = *The Doctrine of the Trinity*. Grand Rapids: Eerdmans, 1976.

Kreck, Walter. "Analogia Fidei oder Analogia Entis?" *Antwort*. Zurich: EVZ, 1956. 272-286.

Laeuchli, Samuel. "Das 'Vierte Jahrhundert' in Karl Barths Prolegomena." *Theologie zwischen Gestern und Morgen*. Ed. W. Dantine & K. Lüthi. Munich: Kaiser, 1968. 217-34.

Leuba, Jean-Louis. "Platonisme et Barthisme: Quelques Perspectives Théologiques." *Archivio di Filosofia* 53 (1985) 153-72.

Lindbeck, George A. "Barth and Textuality." ThT 43 (1986) 361-376.

Lochhead, D. M. "The Autonomy of Theology: A Critical Study with Special Reference to Karl Barth and Contemporary Analytical Philosophy." Ph.D. Diss., McGill Univ., 1967.

Lüthi, Kurt. "Theologie als Gespräch." *Theologie zwischen Gestern und Morgen*. Ed. W. Dantine & K. Lüthi. Munich: Kaiser, 1968. 302-32.

Maurer, Ernstpeter. *Sprachphilosophische Aspekte in Karl Barths "Prolegomena zur Kirchlichen Dogmatik"*. Frankfurt: Lang, 1989.

Meckenstock, Günter. "Karl Barth's Prolegomena zur Dogmatik: Entwicklungslinien vom 'Unterricht in der christlicher Religion' bis zur 'Kirchlichen Dogmatik.'" NZThR 28 (1986) 296-310.

Moltmann, Jürgen, ed. *Anfänge der dialektischen Theologie*, Teil I. Munich: Kaiser, 1962. ET = *The Beginnings of Dialectical Theology*, I. Ed. J. Robinson. Tr. K. Crim, *et al.* Richmond: John Knox, 1968.

Nielson, Bent Flemming. *Die Rationalität der Offenbarungstheologie: Die Struktur des Theologieverständnisses von Karl Barth*. Aarhus: Aarhus University Press, 1988.

Pöhlmann, Horst Georg. *Analogia entis oder Analogia fidei?* Göttingen: Vandenhoeck & Ruprecht, 1965.

Prenter, Regin. "Dietrich Bonhoeffer und Karl Barths Offenbarungspositivismus." *Die mündige Welt*, III. Munich: Kaiser, 1960. 11-41.

_____. "Karl Barths Umbildung der traditionellen Zweinaturenlehre in lutherischer Beleuchtung. Einige vorläufige Beobachtungen zu Karl Barths neuester Darstellung der Christologie." StTh 11 (1957) 1-88.

Provence, Thomas E. "The Sovereign Subject-Matter: Hermeneutics in the Church Dogmatics." *A Guide to Contemporary Hermeneutics*. Ed. D. McKim. Grand Rapids: Eerdmans, 1986. 241-62.

Puffenberger, William V. "The Word of God and Hermeneutics in the Theologies of Karl Barth and Gerhard Ebeling." Ph.D. diss., Boston Univ. Graduate School, 1968. Ann Arbor: UMI, 1967. 68-18,098.

Roberts, Richard H. "Karl Barth's Doctrine of Time: Its Nature and Implications." *Karl Barth: Studies of his Theological Method*. Ed. S. W. Sykes. Oxford: Clarendon Press, 1979. 88-146.

Roberts Richard H. "Karl Barth." *One God in Trinity: An Analysis of the Primary Dogma of Christianity*. Ed. P. Toon and J. D. Spiceland. Westchester, Ill.: Cornerstone, 1980. 78-94.

Robinson, James M. "Hermeneutic Since Barth." *The New Hermeneutic*. Ed. J. M. Robinson & J. B. Cobb. New Frontiers in Theology, II. New York: Harper & Row, 1964. 1-77.

Robinson, N. H. G. "Trinitarianism and Post-Barthian Theology." JThSt 20 (1969) 186-201.

Schmid, Friedrich. *Verkündigung und Dogmatik in der Theologie Karl Barths*. Munich: Kaiser, 1964.

Smend, Rudolf. "Nachkritische Schriftauslegung." *Parrhesia*. Zurich: EVZ, 1966. 215-37.

Theis, Robert. "Die Lehre von der Dreieinigkeit Gottes bei Karl Barth." *Freiburger Zeitschrift für Philosophie und Theologie* 24 (1977) 251-90.

Thompson, John. "On the Trinity." *Theology Beyond Christendom*. Ed. J. Thompson. Princeton Theological Monograph, Series 6. Allison Park, PA: Pickwick Pubiications, 1986. 13-32.

Thomson, G. T. "Note by the Translator." *Church Dogmatics* I/1. Edinburgh: T. & T. Clark, 1936. v-vi.

Torrance, T. F. "The Legacy of Karl Barth." SJTh 39 (1986) 289-308.

____. *Karl Barth: An Introduction to His Early Theology, 1910-1931*. London: SCM, 1962.

Wallace, Mark. "The World of the Text: Theological Hermeneutics in the Thought of Karl Barth and Paul Ricouer." USQR 41 (1986) 1-15.

Welch, Claude. *The Trinity in Contemporary Theology*. London: SCM, 1953.

Williams, R. D. "Barth on the Triune God." *Karl Barth: Studies of his Theological Method*. Ed. S. W. Sykes. Oxford: Clarendon Press, 1979.

HERMENEUTICS AND LANGUAGE

Alston, William P. "Sign and Symbol," *The Encyclopedia of Philosophy*, VII. Rpt., 1972.

Buess, E. "Symbol." ^{3}RGG, VI.

Bultmann, Rudolf. *Jesus Christ and Mythology*. New York: Scribner's, 1958.

____. "Neues Testament und Mythologie." (1941) *Kerygma und Mythos*. Ed. H.-W. Bartsch. Hamburg: Reich u. Heidrich, 1948. 15-53. ET = "New Testament and Mythology." *Kerygma and Myth*, I. London: SPCK, 1953. 1-44.

____. "Zum Problem der Entmythologisierung." *Kerygma und Mythos*, II. Ed. H.-W. Bartsch. Hamburg: Reich u. Heidrich, 1952. 177-208. ET = "On the Problem of Demythologizing." *New Testament & Mythology and Other Basic Writings*. Ed. & tr. S. Ogden. London: SCM, 1984. 95-130.

____. "Das Problem der Hermeneutik." (1950) *Glauben und Verstehen*, II. Tübingen: Mohr, 1952. 211-35. ET = "The Problem of Hermeneutics." *Essays Philosophical and Theological*. London: SCM, 1955. 234-61.

Bush, Randall. "The Hermeneutical Spiral and the Revelation of God as Trinity." PRSt 14 (1987) 11-27.

Cobb, John B. "How New is the New Hermeneutic?" ThT 22 (1965) 218-35.

Crockett, William R. "The Hermeneutics of Doctrine." *The Future of Anglican Theology*. Ed. M. D. Bryant. Toronto Studies in Theology, 17. New York: Edwin Mellen Press, 1984. 59-71.

Dalferth, Ingolf. *Religiöse Rede von Gott*. Munich: Kaiser, 1981.

____. "Theologischer Realismus und realistische Theologie bei Karl Barth." EvTh 46 (1986) 402-22.

Dulles, Avery. "The Hermeneutics of Dogmatic Statements." *The Survival of Dogma*. Garden City: Image Books, rpt. 1973.

Ebeling, Gerhard. "Hermeneutik." ^{3}RGG, III.

____. "Hermeneutische Theologie." (1965) *Wort und Glaube*, II. Tübingen: Mohr, 1969. 99-120.

____. "Wort Gottes und Hermeneutik." (1959) *Wort und Glaube*, I. Tübingen: Mohr, ^{3}1967. 319-348. ET = "Word of God and Hermeneutics." *Word and Faith*. Tr. J. W. Leitch. Philadelphia: Fortress, 1963. 305-32.

Fuchs, Ernst. *Hermeneutik*. (1954) Tübingen: Mohr, ^{4}1970.

____. "Das Hermeneutische Problem." *Zeit und Geschichte* Ed. E. Dinkler. Tübingen: Mohr, 1964. 357-66. ET = "The Hermeneutical Problem." *The Future of Our Religious Past*. Ed. J. M. Robinson. London: SCM, 1971. 267-78.

____. "Das neue Testament und das hermeneutische Problem." ZThK 58 (1961) 198-226. ET = "The New Testament and the Hermeneutical Problem." *New Frontiers in Theology, II: The New Hermeneutic*. Ed. J. M. Robinson and J. B. Cobb, Jr. New York: Harper & Row, 1964. 111-145.

278   **Bibliography**

Gadamer, Hans Georg. *Wahrheit und Methode*. Tübingen: Mohr, ²1965.

Glenn, A. A. "The Relationship Between Theology as a Special Science and Analytic Philosophy with Special Reference to the Theology of Karl Barth." Ph.D. Diss., Northwestern University, 1967.

Kuhn, Thomas. *The Structure of Scientific Revolutions*. International Encyclopedia of Unified Science, II, 2. Chicago: Univ. of Chicago Press, ²1970.

Macquarrie, John. *God-Talk*. London: SCM, 1967.

Marlé, René. *Das theologische Problem der Hermeneutik*. Tr. N. Rocholl. Mainz: Grünwald, 1965.

McFague, Sally. *Metaphorical Theology*. London: SCM, 1982.

Mudge, Lewis S. "Hermeneutical Circle." *A New Dictionary of Christian Theology*. Ed. A. Richardson and J. Bowden. London: SCM, 1983.

Palmer, Richard. *Hermeneutics: Interpretation Theory in Schleiermacher, Dilthey, Heidegger, and Gadamer*. Northwestern University Studies in Phenomenology & Existential Philosophy. Ed. J. Wild. Evanston: Northwestern Univ. Press, 1969.

Ramsey, Ian. "Paradox in Religion." *Christian Empiricism*. Ed. J. Gill. Grand Rapids: Eerdmans, 1974. 98-119.

Robinson, James M. "Hermeneutic Since Barth." *The New Hermeneutic*. Ed. J. M. Robinson & J. B. Cobb. New Frontiers in Theology, II. New York: Harper & Row, 1964. 1-77.

Schäfer, Rolf. "Die hermeneutische Frage in der gegenwärtigen evangelischen Theologie." *Die hermeneutische Frage in der Theologie*. Ed. O. Loretz & W. Strolz. Freiburg: Herder, 1968. 426-66.

Thiselton, Anthony. "The New Hermeneutic." *A Guide to Contemporary Hermeneutics*. Ed. D. K. McKim. Grand Rapids: Eerdmans, 1986. 78-107. [Orig. publ. in *New Testament Interpretation: Essays on Principles and Methods*. Ed. I. H. Marshall. Grand Rapids: Eerdmans, 1977. 308-33.]

_____. *The Two Horizons: New Testament Hermeneutics and Philosophical Description with Special Reference to Heidegger, Bultmann, Gadamer, and Wittgenstein*. Exeter: Paternoster, 1980.

THE TRINITY

Baur, Ferdinand Christian. *Die christliche Lehre von der Dreieinigkeit und Menschwerdung Gottes in ihrer geschichtlichen Entwicklung*, I-III. Tübingen: Osiander, 1843.

Bracken, Joseph. *The Triune Symbol*. Lanham: Univ. Press of America, 1985.

Brown, David. *The Divine Trinity*. London: Duckworth, 1985.

Bush, Randall. "The Hermeneutical Spiral and the Revelation of God as Trinity." PRSt 14 (1987) 11-27.

Fortman, Edmund J. *The Triune God*. Grand Rapids: Baker, 1972.

Franks, Robert S. *The Doctrine of the Trinity*. London: Gerald Duckworth, 1953. 178-80.

Geisser, Hans. "Der Beitrag der Trinitätslehre zur Problematik des Redens von Gott." ZThK NF 65 (1968) 231-55.

Geisser, Hans. "Die Trinitätslehre unter den Problemen und in den Prolegomena christlicher Theologie." Unpubl. Diss., Tübingen, 1962.

Hill, William. *The Three-personed God*. Washington D.C.: Catholic University of America, 1982.

Jenson, Robert. "The Triune God." *Christian Dogmatics*, I. Ed. C. Braaten & R. Jenson. Philadelphia: Fortress, 1984. 83-191.

____. *The Triune Identity*. Philadelphia: Fortress, 1982.

Jüngel, Eberhard. "Das Verhältnis von 'ökonomischer' und 'immanenter' Trinität." ZThK 72 (1975) 353-64.

Kasper, Walter. *Der Gott Jesu Christi*. Mainz: Matthias Grünewald, 1982. ET = *The God of Jesus Christ*. Tr. M. J. O'Connell. London: SCM, 1983.

Kelly, J. N. D. *Early Christian Doctrines*. New York: Harper, [3]1965.

Kretschmar, Georg. *Studien zur frühchristlichen Trinitätstheologie*. Beiträge zur historischen Theologie, 21. Ed. G. Ebeling. Tübingen: Mohr, 1956.

LaCugna, C. M., and K. McDonnell. "Returning from 'The Far Country': Theses for a Contemporary Trinitarian Theology." SJTh 41 (1988) 191-215.

Mackey, James P. *The Christian Experience of God as Trinity*. London: SCM, 1983.

Moltmann, Jürgen. *Trinität und Reich Gottes*. Munich: Kaiser, 1980. ET = *The Trinity and the Kingdom of God*. Tr. M. Kohl. London: SCM, 1981.

Pannenberg, Wolfhart. "Person und Subjekt." *Grundfragen systematischer Theologie*, II. Göttingen: Vandenhoeck & Ruprecht, 1980. 80-95.

____. "Probleme einer trinitarischer Gotteslehre." *Weisheit Gottes—Weisheit der Welt*, I. FS J. Ratzinger. Ed. W. Baier. St. Ottilien: 1987. ET = "Problems of a Trinitarian Doctrine of God." Dia 26 (1987) 250-57.

_____. "Die Subjektivität Gottes." *Grundfragen systematischer Theologie*, II. Göttingen: Vandenhoeck & Ruprecht, 1980. 96-111.

_____. *Systematische Theologie*, I. Göttingen: Vandenhoeck & Ruprecht, 1988.

Peters, Ted. "Trinity Talk." Parts 1 & 2. Dia 26 (1987) 44-8, 133-8.

Pohle, Joseph. *The Divine Trinity*. Adapted & ed. A. Preuss. St. Louis: Herder, 1950.

Porter, Lawrence B. "On Keeping 'Persons' in the Trinity: A Linguistic Approach to Trinitarian Thought." ThS 41 (1980) 530-48.

Rahner, Karl. "Der dreifaltige Gott als transzendenter Urgrund der Heilsgeschichte." *Mysterium Salutis*: Grundriss heilsgeschichtlicher Dogmatik, II. Einsiedeln: Benziger, 1967. 317-401. ET = *The Trinity*. Tr. J. Donceel. New York: Herder & Herder, 1970.

_____. *Schriften zur Theologie*, IV. Einsiedeln: Benzinger, 1960. ET = *Theological Investigations*, IV. London: Dartman, Longman & Todd, 1966.

Ritter, A. M. "Dogma und Lehre in der alten Kirche." *Die Lehrentwicklung im Rahmen der Katholizität*. Handbuch der Dogmen- und Theologiegeschichte, I. Ed. C. Andresen. Göttingen: Vandenhoeck & Ruprecht, 1983. 99-283.

Schlink, Edmund. "Trinität, III." ³RGG, VI.

Schwarz, Hans. "Die Aktualität des Trinitarischen im christlichen Gottesglauben." TZ 44 (1988) 211-21.

Torrance, T. F. "Toward an Ecumenical Consensus on the Trinity." TZ (1975) 337-50.

Welch, Claude. *The Trinity in Contemporary Theology*. London: SCM, 1953.

Wohlmuth, Josef. "Zum Verhältnis von ökonomischer und immanenter Trinität—eine These." ZKTh (1988) 139-162.

Wolfson, Harry Austryn. *Faith, Trinity, Incarnation*. The Philosophy of the Church Fathers, I. Cambridge, Mass.: Harvard, 1956.

OTHER WORKS CITED

Bauckham, Richard J. "Tradition in Relation to Scripture and Reason." *Scripture, Tradition and Reason: Essays in Honour of Richard P. C. Hanson*. Edinburgh: T & T Clark, 1988.

Brunner, Emil. *Dogmatik*, I. Zürich: Zwingli-Verlag, 1946. ET = *Dogmatics*, I. Tr. O. Wyon. Philadelphia: Westminster, 1949.

Congar, Yves, O. P. *Tradition and Traditions*. (1960) Tr. M. Naseby & T. Rainborough. London: Burns & Oates, 1966.

Dillenberger, John. *God Hidden and Revealed*. Philadelphia: Huhlenberg Press, 1953.

Ebeling, Gerhard. *Dogmatik des christlichen Glaubens*, I. Tübingen: Mohr, ³1987.

Feuerbach, Ludwig. *Das Wesen des Christentums*, critical ed. Ed. R. Quenzel. Reklams Universalbibliothek, 1841.

_____. *Das Wesen der Religion*. Leipzig: Alfred Kröner, 1851.

Gilkey, Langdon. *Reaping the Whirlwind*. Indianapolis: Bobbs Merrill, 1969.

Gloege, G. "Dogmatik." ³RGG, II.

Hall, Roland. "Monism and Pluralism." *The Encyclopedia of Philosophy*, V. Rpt., 1972.

Hanson, Richard P. C. *The Continuity of Christian Doctrine*. New York, Seabury, 1981.

Heppe, Heinrich. *Die Dogmatik der evangelisch-reformierte Kirche: Dargestellt und aus den Quellen belegt*. Neukirchen: E. Bizer, ²1958. ET = *Reformed Dogmatics: Set Out and Illustrated from the Sources*. Tr. G. T. Thomson. London: Allen & Unwin, 1950.

Joest, Wilfried. *Fundamentaltheologie*. Stuttgart: Kohlhammer, 1974.

. *Dogmatik*, I. Göttingen: Vandenhoeck & Ruprecht, ²1987.

Kinder, Ernst. "Dogmatik und Dogma." *Dogma und Denkstrukturen*. Ed. W. Joest & W. Pannenberg. Göttingen: Vandenhoeck & Ruprecht, 1963. 9-28.

Kreck, Walter. *Grundfragen der Dogmatik*. Munich: Kaiser, 1970.

Lanczkowski, G. "Symbolismus: I. Religionsgeschichtlich." ³RGG, VI.

Muller, Richard, ed. *Dictionary of Latin and Greek Theological Terms*. Grand Rapids: Baker, 1985.

Ott, Heinrich. "What is Systematic Theology?" *The Later Heiddegger and Theology*. New Frontiers in Theology, I. Ed. J. M. Robinson & J. B. Cobb. New York: Harper & Row, 1963. 77-111.

Pelikan, Jaroslav. *The Spirit of Eastern Christendom 600-1700*. Chicago: Univ. of Chicago, 1974.

Sauter, G. "Dogmatik I." TRE, IX.

Schleiermacher, Friedrich. *Der christliche Glaube*, II. Ed. Martin Redekker. Berlin: de Gruyter, 1960. ET = *The Christian Faith*. Ed. H. R. Mackintosh & J. S. Stewart. Edinburgh: T. & T. Clark, 1902.

Sykes, S. W. "Systematic Theology." *A New Dictionary of Christian Theology*. Ed. A. Richardson & J. Bowden. London: SCM, 1983.

Tillich, Paul. *Systematic Theology*, I. Chicago: Univ. of Chicago, 1951.

Weber, Otto. *Grundlagen der Dogmatik*, I. Neukirchen: Verlag der Buchhandlung des Erziehungsvereins, 1955. ET = *Foundations of Dogmatics*, I. Grand Rapids: Eerdmans, 1981.

Wiles, Maurice. *The Remaking of Christian Doctrine*. London: SCM, 1974.

INDEX OF NAMES